TIMELESS THEMES

Stories from the Hebrew and Christian Bibles
For Grades 3 and 4

Nannene Gowdy, Mary Ann Moore, and Marjorie Skwire

with Nina Grey, Robert L'H. Miller, and Stephen Washburn

Bible Story Illustrations by Jane Conteh-Morgan

M. Elizabeth Anastos, Editor

A Project of
the Heritages from Judaism and Christianity Curriculum Team

Unitarian Universalist Association

ISBN 1-55896-210-7

Production Editor: Katherine Wolff
Editorial Assistant: Debra Anderson
Designer: Suzanne Morgan

10 9 8 7 6 5 4 3
99 98 97 96 95 94

Acknowledgments

Special thanks to Eugene Navias for his guide to
using the songbook and tape with the curriculum.
Grateful acknowledgment is made to Michael
Gersch for his contributions to the first version of
this program, which he and Nannene Gowdy
created for the children of the South Nassau Uni-
tarian Church, Freeport, NY; Anne Miller, New
Albany, IN, for her description of the open class-
room experience at the First Unitarian Church,
Louisville, KY; and Joyce Hempstead for many of
the drawings within sessions and resources.
    We wish to acknowledge the use of the follow-
ing material: "We Are All Adam," from Word of
Mouth by Religious Education Services, 1982;
Necessary Losses, by Judith Viorst (New York:
Ballantine Books, 1986); *Anger, the Misunderstood
Emotion*, by Carol Tavris (New York: Simon and
Schuster, 1982); chalice lighting in Session 3 by
Satomi Ichikawa, from *Creator of the World*,
translated from the Japanese; *Understanding the Old
Testament*, by Bernhard W. Anderson (Englewood
Cliffs, NJ: Prentice-Hall, 1986). Material for
chalice lighting readings came from the following
sources: Session 32 and Session 18, by Vincent
Silliman, from *Beacon Song and Service Book* (Bos-
ton: UUA, 1951); Session 13, by James Russell
Lowell, "True Freedom," *Hymns for the Celebra-
tion of Life* (Boston: UUA, 1964).

CONTENTS

INTRODUCTION

Timeless Themes: Stories from the Hebrew and Christian Bibles introduces children to religious literature which is central to our culture and to our heritage as Unitarian Universalists. The curriculum consists of a leader guide with 34 session plans—plus an introduction to the biblical literature, a model for using the program in an open-classroom setting, and a bibliography. The songbook *Bible Songs on Timeless Themes* contains 38 songs, spirituals, and hymns to enhance the stories. A cassette tape recording of the songs sung by children and youth is also available. Both the songbook and the cassette tape can be purchased separately.

Why Teach Bible Stories?

Our culture is derived from a predominantly Jewish and Christian ethic. By becoming familiar with the stories which helped to shape those faiths, our children will better understand this heritage. The human issues which inspired these scriptures are ageless. Their settings, social customs, and scientific knowledge may seem outdated, but their vital core of beliefs and values continues to be important. These "timeless themes" include
- the belief in a transcendent power, or God
- the belief that humans are responsible for their actions
- the love of freedom for all people
- the prophetic imperative to speak out against injustice
- the respect for the beliefs of others, and our common humanity
- the love of one's neighbor
- the forgiveness for wrongdoing.

What Should We Call the Scriptures?

This program examines two sets of scriptures: the Hebrew Bible and the Christian Bible, which is composed of the Old Testament and the New Testament. The Hebrew Bible and the Old Testament are essentially the same, except for a variation in the order in which they are arranged. In telling stories from the Hebrew scripture, we have followed the order in which they appear in the Hebrew Bible.

To maintain the integrity of each of the scriptures, we refer specifically to Hebrew scripture or Christian scripture. The term New Testament is occasionally used for that portion of Christian scripture which is unique to Christianity.

Which Stories Should We Tell?

Our primary goal was to select stories commonly told in our culture. A variety of literary forms are included, such as myth, legend, history, and poetry. In many of these stories, several themes are apparent and several approaches might be taken. We have focused on those themes which seem most appropriate for this age level and most relevant to the children's experience. The activities in each session serve to strengthen the relationship among the three basic components of story, theme, and child.

What About Patriarchal Themes?

There is no question of the patriarchal bias of these scriptures. Though contemporary feminist scholars are opening a new area of biblical study, the scriptures reflect a long historical period of patriarchy. We have dealt with this issue by discussing it directly, by using as many stories about women as seems feasible, and by degenderizing language in many sections. Where degenderization does not seem appropriate, we address the issue directly in the "Background" section and in suggested discussion with the children. We were aided in our efforts to use gender-inclusive language by the fortuitous 1989 publication of the New Revised Standard Version of the Christian Bible. The stories told here are taken from that version.

What Name Should We Use for God?

There are a number of names for God in Hebrew and Christian scripture, including Yahweh, Elohim, Jehovah, and Lord. In this program, only "God" is used, although the background material may use other names to help teachers gain a better understanding of the sources of biblical literature.

Sources of Hebrew Literature

The writings in the Pentateuch, or the first five books of the Hebrew Bible, are thought to derive from four basic documents. Each of these documents represents a tradition of oral transmission which eventually came to be written down and combined with other sources. Scholars have devoted years of study to the task of separating the sources and trying to determine the original document for each, but no original written version of any of them has ever come to light. Thus, though scholarly research validates the authenticity of each of the four, we have no intact manuscripts for proof (except, perhaps, in the case of D, which is essentially the Book of Deuteronomy). Briefly, the documents are as follows:

- J, which takes its designation from the word Yahweh (also written Jahveh) for the name of God, is probably the oldest written source of biblical material, dating from approximately 950 B.C.E., in the southern part of Israel (Judah). J includes the second creation story (Genesis 2), the Tower of Babel, Abraham and Sarah, parts of the Noah story, and other legends.
- E takes its name from Elohim, the word it uses for God. E also includes a good bit of legendary material, but from northern traditions. Written down in approximately 750 B.C.E., E soon became blended with J (a combination referred to as JE) to form a more complete legendary history. Among E's stories are Abraham and Isaac and Moses in the Bulrushes.
- D takes its name from Deuteronomy, the fifth book in the Hebrew Bible. It is a book of law and ritual practice specifically composed in 621 B.C.E. to reform temple worship.
- P is the priestly document, composed in approximately 500 B.C.E. to preserve the traditions of the temple after its destruction, and to bring together in a systematic way the rituals and laws of the Jewish religion. Because P comments on and consolidates older traditions, bits of it are found in each of the first five books of the Bible. P is formal, methodical, and often dry as dust! Occasionally, as in the creation story of Genesis 1, it rises to poetic beauty. It is P that introduces the idea of God's divine plan.

Many stories in the Hebrew scriptures are derived from more than one source, edited in one or more generations to suit the political or religious climate. In this curriculum we have sometimes commented on the Pentateuchal sources in the background for teachers, but the children's discussions and activities focus on the elements of story and theme. For example, in the story of Adam and Eve, the two stories of creation are pointed out, and children are encouraged to think of other familiar stories which they know in more than one version. The focus, however, is on the two stories of creation and the theme of loneliness.

Hebrew literature is represented in these sessions by several literary forms, such as poetry, fiction, proverbs, and history. In some cases, we have called the form to the children's attention, but often it is mentioned only in the background material. Some teachers may wish to share bits of this background material, but care should be taken to maintain the focus of story and theme, and not to overwhelm the children with too much information.

Sources of New Testament Literature

All the New Testament stories presented here

come from the first four books, the gospels, and our discussion of New Testament literature is confined to those books.

Although there are four gospels in the New Testament, only three (Matthew, Mark, and Luke) are referred to as "synoptics," taking a common view. Each presents the life and teachings of Jesus, with many parallels to the other two in structure, content, and style. Often the synoptics are placed side by side for easy comparison. Variously referred to as parallels or harmonies, these parallel versions of the synoptics can be very helpful in looking at gospel materials (see the bibliography).

The synoptic gospels share common source material and use one another as sources. Mark is thought to be the earliest gospel, dating from approximately 70 C.E. Matthew and Luke almost certainly used Mark as a source. But they also contain common material not found in Mark, so a hypothetical document, "Q," is used to explain that phenomenon. This "two-source" theory is accepted by most, but not all, New Testament scholars.

Written in approximately 100 C.E., John is the latest of the four gospels. John varies considerably from the three synoptics, and many stories recounted in John's gospel are not included in the others. Though there is evidence that its author was familiar with the common tradition of the synoptics, the gospel of John was shaped by an individual style and theology, and cannot easily be placed in parallel with the other three.

The stories collected here may be derived from one gospel writer or several. A biblical reference at the beginning of each session will tell you where to find the story in the New Testament. If the story can be found in more than one gospel, the chief source of the children's story will be referenced first, followed by the parallels. By locating the specified passage in a gospel parallels reference book, you will be able to read all versions side by side.

Purposes and Methods

Our primary purpose in presenting this curriculum is to introduce eight- and nine-year olds to some of the best-known stories in the biblical literature, stories to which they will hear references throughout their lives. Deriving religious and personal meanings from these writings begins with learning the stories, as does the motivation to engage in further study of the Bible. In retelling the stories we have retained as much of the biblical language as seems appropriate in order to introduce children to its color and cadence.

Many biblical stories are long, containing lengthy descriptive material and, occasionally, stories within stories. Because this can be very confusing for children, in most instances we chose not to tell these stories in their entirety. Leaders are free, of course, to read more of the original story, if they judge their group to be receptive. We have occasionally included a bit of background information in the "Motivating Questions" section of the session plan to place the story in an understandable context.

Our second purpose is to create a connecting link between the writers of the Bibles who lived long ago and contemporary third- and fourth-graders. We chose to do that by focusing on the universal human themes with which the biblical writers struggled. Themes such as jealousy, forgiveness, and healing are as potent today as they were thousands of years ago. We are aware that other themes are also present in many of the stories. These stories have mythlike qualities and, like myths, can have many different meanings. We chose themes we believe will be meaningful to children of this age. Further, we have provided discussion questions and age-appropriate activities to reinforce the children's understanding of the stories and themes, thereby helping them to internalize the metaphors and meanings.

Finally, our third purpose is to promote Unitarian Universalist values. This is not easy, for there are many Unitarian Universalist views of the Hebrew and Christian Bibles, and many of us experience conflict between our Unitarian Universalist values and some of the values expressed in the Bibles. Our method of dealing with this was to ensure that in each session there was at least one discussion question that invites the children to think about issues that either support or challenge Unitarian Universalist principles and purposes. These questions are the "chalice questions," designated by the symbol ⚲.

The Hebrew and Christian Bibles contain a rich and complex body of religious literature. There are several valid methodological approaches that can be used in studying this literature. One common method is to present these writings to support a particular theological viewpoint. Another is to study the scriptures in the light of recent scholarly research. A third method is to examine the sources of the writings and the manner in which they were edited. A fourth way is to search the biblical passages for individual, personal meaning and aesthetic enjoyment. Biblical study often takes more than one of these approaches simultaneously. In choosing an educational method we must set realistic goals in accordance with the abilities, needs, and interests of the target audience.

As these children mature we hope they have the opportunity to relate to the biblical stories in a variety of ways—through academic research, through personal religious meanings, through aesthetic enjoyment. We hope that their experience with this curriculum will lay the groundwork for continuing study and appreciation of this religious literature.

The God of the Hebrew and Christian Bibles

The God presented in the Hebrew and Christian Bibles is likely to be difficult for eight- and nine-year-old children to understand. Helping our Unitarian Universalist children to compare the God of the Hebrews with their own partly formed concepts of God may enable them to achieve a perspective on possible problems the Hebrew God presents. The biblical God is projected as male, promoting patriarchal values; today many people perceive God as both male and female, thus promoting gender equality. The biblical God, in many instances, is warlike and appears to encourage the resolution of conflict by violent means, whereas Unitarian Universalist principles foster peacemaking. And finally, the biblical God often appears to be demanding a narrow and prejudiced kind of allegiance from "his" followers, whereas we encourage tolerance and openness.

There are also many positive attributes of the biblical God with which children can readily identify. One is God the creator, the source of all the wondrous things in the world. Another is God who freed the Hebrews from oppression and slavery. A third positive attribute is the biblical God who demands that people live a life of righteousness—not coveting, stealing, or

killing. Another is God the protector and provider of human well-being. And still another, which most Unitarian Universalists readily embrace, is the God of the Hebrew prophets who demands that God's people promote justice. Finally, this God is also identified with love, forgiveness, and healing.

Human concepts of God serve many purposes. They help us to explain ultimate reality, to symbolize our values, and to point to the mysteries of life beyond which we cannot penetrate. The concept of God presented in the Hebrew and Christian Bibles is as complicated and contradictory as life itself. It reflects views of the cosmos and of human nature which prevailed roughly from 2000 B.C.E. to 100 C.E. It mirrors a patriarchal society. It images societies in which war and violence were acceptable. However, it also models visions of freedom, justice, love, and forgiveness.

If the children are disturbed to hear stories of the punishing, vengeful, and violent God, it may be helpful to hold a discussion on the following concepts.

- Ideas about God are often complicated and difficult to understand.
- Ideas about God always have something about them that is a mystery.
- Ideas about God have characteristics that we humans perceive as both good and bad, because both good and bad things happen in our lives.
- Our ideas of God reflect the time and place in which we live. Those who raise sheep for a living will see their God as a shepherd; those who live in a culture where men are in charge will see God as a male; those who live in a culture which uses punishment and war to solve problems will have a God who is punishing and warlike.
- Despite the fact that many people live amid poverty, oppression, and violence, they can envision a better world and a better way to live—a way of love, justice, and peace; and their God reflects these qualities.
- As Unitarian Universalists, we can make up our own minds about what to think about God. We may also believe that there is no God, if our minds and hearts lead us in that direction.
- Exploring different ideas of God helps us as we try to decide for ourselves what we believe about God.
- Concepts of God change historically in our

culture through the centuries, and they will change for each of us over our lifetime.

Leading This Program

It is important that the director of religious education and the leaders read the introductory sections of the leader guide and the songbook, become familiar with the session format, and hear the songs before beginning the program. This will alert them to things that need to be obtained or done in advance of the sessions. Each session calls for preparation, from studying the background and reviewing the session plan to gathering materials and preparing for each activity.

We strongly recommend co-leaders or a leadership team for this program. Co-leadership provides a richer experience for the children by giving them two or more adults with whom they can develop positive and trusting relationships.

Co-leadership also provides significant benefits for the adult leaders. Co-leaders do not feel isolated from the congregation, because each is working and planning with another member. They can share the responsibilities of preparation and leadership and provide helpful feedback to increase each other's competence and skill. Co-leadership also enables each leader to miss a session or two if necessary, without causing a significant disruption for the children. The co-leaders may even develop a strong friendship!

A leadership team may include one or two team leaders, plus storytellers and art, drama, and music assistants. See *Timeless Themes* in an Open Classroom" for a model of team intraresponsibility.

The Size of Your Group

This program is designed for a group of at least five or six children and preferably no more than twelve to fifteen. Interactions within large groups are more difficult to orchestrate: quiet, shy children find it harder to be fully involved, and each activity takes longer. If you have a large group and dividing it is not feasible, take careful note of the time each portion of a session requires and plan accordingly. (For open classrooms, see section toward the end of this introduction.)

Session Structure

- Gathering: An initial activity related to the story or theme in which to engage the children as they gather for the session. If everyone arrives at the same time from a worship service or prior activity, incorporate the gathering activity into the session where feasible.
- Motivating Questions: The leader poses questions related to the theme to involve the children in a brief discussion of their own experiences around this theme.
- The Story: The leader preferably *tells* the story rather than reading it to the children, keeping closely to the text as written.
- Discussion: A discussion of the story to engage the children in a consideration of the theme, both in the story's historical context and in terms of its relevance to the participants today.
- Activities: Varied activities help to reinforce concepts introduced by the story and its theme.
- Closing: A song, biblical verse, brief summary statement, or other short activity to bring closure to the session. (*Note:* Some groups may want to have an opening exercise in addition to or in place of the closing. We recommend, however, that the closing not be sacrificed, for it provides a needed formal ending to the experience of the morning.)

The Stories

The stories, including dialogue, are told in the biblical language wherever it is understandable by children of this age and are taken from the New Revised Standard Version (1989) of the Christian Bible. Although the program avoids certain images that would be confusing or overly violent, some of the stories necessarily depict violent acts. We cannot shield our children from knowledge of violence perpetrated by human beings, but we can use that knowledge to guide them toward an understanding of nonviolent ways to resolve conflicts.

We urge you to read the story as it is written in this program, for we have chosen to be true to the biblical text, not inserting additional material to make it more entertaining to the children. In some instances, you may want to read the story as it is written here and then again from a Bible storybook, and discuss the differences between the two versions with the children.

We recommend that you review the choices carefully when selecting Bible storybooks. Many Bible-story collections on the market today have extraneous and inaccurate additions to make them more attractive to children. Many have a theological bias incorporated within them. In the bibliography, we have listed a few that we recommend. There are others; research your local bookstores and libraries for those that are free of embellishments.

In the stories, God is consistently referred to as "God" and not "he." We discuss this issue with the children when a very familiar phrase occurs, by saying something like, "You may have heard this phrase with the pronoun, 'he,' but we believe that God is both male and female. When the writers of the scriptures said 'man' or 'men,' they often meant to include women, but it was the custom in those times to write in masculine terms."

Session Length

Each session is planned for approximately 60 to 70 minutes, although it may take longer to complete all of the proposed activities in some sessions. If you have considerably more or less than one hour, you may select from among the additional activities described or use the alternative activities and time-saver ideas suggested at the end of some sessions. You may want to take two Sundays for the sessions that have more complex activities.

Reflection and Planning for the Next Session
We suggest that after each session the leaders set aside time for reflection and apply their observations and insights to planning for the next session. Questions such as the following might be helpful: What went well in this session? What did not go well, or could have been improved? If we were to lead this session again, what would we change? Do any of the children present a problem or indicate a need for some special attention? Can the minister or director of religious education help us by providing some information about this child? What preparation do we need for the next session? Which of us will be responsible for what portion of that session?

This kind of deliberate evaluation of your experience is the best way to recognize your strengths and weaknesses and, working from this recognition, to grow as a teacher.

Your minister, your director of religious education, or the chairperson of your Religious Education Committee may be able to help with information, resources, or concerns about a child. Don't hesitate to ask.

Age Level

Although designed primarily for children aged eight and nine, *Timeless Themes* can be used with seven- to ten-year olds. Some of the themes and activities may be difficult for seven-year olds to understand and do, however, so we do not recommend using it with that age level unless you are grouping second-graders with older children.

Developmental Characteristics of Eight- and Nine-Year Olds

As we developed *Timeless Themes*, the following characteristics of third- and fourth-graders informed our work:
- they want to know about the important stories and people of their heritage
- they are capable of learning about people of a different time and place, and comparing ancient times with their own
- they need opportunities to explore and respond to themes that these stories raise, in an atmosphere that is open and inviting
- they can gain the broadest understanding of the stories and themes through participation in a variety of activities, including discussion, crafts, music, drama, games, and service to others.

Eight- and nine-year olds still seek approval and a warm, friendly relationship with the important adults in their lives, particularly parents and teachers. Parental guidance and support are a major influence on their school achievement and play an important role as the children expand their interests and activities outside the home.

Children at this age are increasingly able and interested in assuming responsibilities. Adult role models give them strong cues about acceptable behavior as they begin to make value judgments about their own behavior, set standards for themselves, and strive toward personal independence.

Eight- and nine-year olds can apply logical thought to situations and they are beginning to understand the relationship between cause and effect. They can perceive similarities between two things that share observable features or abstract attributes. They use language to exchange ideas, often spending much time in talking.

At this stage in their development, however, children may vary greatly in reading ability and language skills. Do not ask a child to read aloud in class unless you are aware of his or her reading ability, for children this age are sensitive about not meeting adult standards and worry about ridicule from their peers.

At this age, children expend a great deal of energy in physical game-playing, mostly in same-sex groups. This is a time when both boys and girls conform strongly to their culturally imposed gender roles, preferring to be with others of their own sex, and forming cliques and clubs. Peer relationships are becoming increasingly important. Antagonism between girls and boys frequently leads to quarrels. Competition, between the sexes and within each sex, becomes more common and is often accompanied by considerable boasting.

Children of this age have a strong need to "belong"—to their families, their school community, and their church if they go to one. In their religious development, they begin to identify with their faith community and take on the stories, beliefs, and practices that symbolize membership in that community. This is therefore an excellent time to introduce them to religious lore and legends, but it is important to be aware that the children will derive from these stories only the meanings that they are developmentally ready to absorb. As we communicate to the children that they will discover further and deeper meanings as they grow older, we must also tell the stories in a way that will not have to be denied later.

Timeless Themes in an Open Classroom

The First Unitarian Church of Louisville, KY, offers an Open Classroom experience for grades two through six during the Adult Religious Education Hour, 10 to 11 a.m. each Sunday. The program is well organized and well attended. The children are familiar with the format and are self-guided and very self-disciplined. *Time-less Themes* is well suited to an open classroom. By field testing it, the First Unitarian Church helped the UUA assess the program's appropriateness for use in small religious education programs that have a wide age range of children in one group.

The Format

On entering, each child receives a checklist of the hour's activities and a paper cutout shape on which to write his or her answer to the day's focus question. These shapes, different each Sunday depending on the theme, are then hung on a tree to provide an attractive reminder of the topic we are addressing that morning. *Timeless Themes* has excellent focus questions. Everyone does this activity and then proceeds to the Storyteller's Corner, where the day's lead-in discussion, story, and follow-up questions are covered. Children then disperse to their choice of several activities: two or three craft projects—individual or group; one or more writing or discussion centers; games and puzzles; songs, sometimes optional, sometimes required; and always a cooking project. A leader is at each table to instruct or assist as needed, and to initiate and conduct an informal discussion.

Leadership in the open classroom consists of the "Questioneer" (coordinator) at the entry, the Storyteller, the Chief Cook (each week four children sign up to cook and the food relates in some way to the day's study); a Song Leader; and several activity leaders. All but the Questioneer and Song Leader are volunteers on a once-a-month rotation schedule. Teacher recruitment on this basis is very easy, with many adults showing up for more than their scheduled stints.

Children like the open classroom format, and newcomers assimilate quickly into the routine. Even the most active youngsters are very self-directed in this setting and, for whatever reason, become so involved in the activities that discipline problems are nonexistent. Second-graders and learning disabled children do well because they hear the story and can reread it if they choose, from an array of Bible storybooks put out for browsing. Visitors are often startled to see 20 to 30 children and adults so busy that the only sound is a low buzz of happy, active people at work.

Usually the story is told three times—once to children who arrive on time, again to those who arrive a bit late, and perhaps again to those whose parents don't attend the adult class or Forum at 10, but who arrive early for the service. This flexible arrival time makes the open classroom format expecially useful. The *Timeless Themes* program proved to be easily adaptable to the open classroom format. The focus question is tailor-made for such use, the story is there, along with excellent lead-in and follow-up questions for discussion, and there's always, at minimum, one good activity, often two or three.

Church schools that choose to use the open classroom method with this curriculum will need to seek out from libraries, bookstores, and church goods stores an assortment of craft ideas, Bible-story games and puzzles, and similar resources. They are easy to find. A feltboard and flannel figures were a hit with the children, who enjoyed arranging scenes from the story they heard—and retelling the story for latecomers or parents. Enlarged copies of puzzles can be made into posters for group solving. If space must be shared with other groups, posterboard and easels enable the open classroom to be portable.

The Cooking Center is always popular. To those who don't have easy access to a kitchen—be reassured. All recipes can be prepared with an electric skillet or saucepan, a toaster oven, or, occasionally, a microwave oven. Many recipes require no appliances. Running water in the room is helpful but not essential. Recipes in this and other UUA curricula are very good, and public libraries have cookbook collections in which one can find interesting and easy Middle Eastern recipes.

Two Session Adaptations
Noah
Begin by having each arrival hang a blue paper raindrop on the tree, after writing on it of a time "when you did something you were ordered to do, even though you didn't know why you had to do it." Everyone hears the story and discusses it based on the follow-up questions. First Unitarian had a large floor puzzle, from a religious bookstore, of a scene of the ark and animals, cartoon-style. After hearing the story, each child was given two puzzle pieces to try to fit into the puzzle. They enjoyed completing it little by little as others arrived. From there, they went to the Song Leader to learn "Who Built the Ark?" You could use an electronic keyboard, easily transported from one area to another, along with reproduced copies of the songs. Because

this session contains so much material, you could cover it over a two-week span. One week's cooking was simple: from several boxes of animal crackers, the cooks found pairs of elephants, lions, bears, and so forth. The children made icing—enjoying mixing lots of colors together to make "animal colors" and produced frosted animal cookie sandwiches. Voila! The animals came "two by two"!

The second week's cooking project used the microwave oven to melt marshmallows and margarine as directed on the Rice Krispies box, stirring the melted mixture into the Rice Krispies, also as directed, and, with buttered hands, molding the warm mixture into the shape of a rainbow. A large piece of cardboard covered with foil makes a good base for this. Divide a batch of white icing into small portions to color with food coloring in rainbow hues, and you have produced an edible rainbow. This is fast and easy. Make enough for two rainbows, one for consumption and one for sharing with the Coffee Hour crowd.

The four activity tables were arranged so the children could choose to make a pair of clay animals, the big paper rainbow, the ark, or clothespin dolls of Noah's family. At First Unitarian, everyone was very busy! The local school-supply store had packages of modeling clay in various "flesh-colored" shades of tans, brown, ocher, peach, and russet, which were used to create humans for the Garden of Eden session. These clay colors were excellent for Noah's family and their animals. A number of versions of the Noah story were available, along with a feltboard and figures. A large poster of Noah cartoons from newspapers and magazines served this session well, with blank paper for children to design their own cartoons. At First Unitarian, these activities kept children completely occupied, but if more activities are needed, pick from assorted flood stories and cuneiform writing from the 1976 UUA program *Focus on Noah*.

For the second week's focus question, use a paper dove and ask the children to write of "a promise (covenant) you wouldn't break." (One child in Kentucky who had spent some time undergoing inpatient counseling for suicide threats wrote, "I promise not to die." Sometimes our leadership roles bring us more than we expect.) As a variation on the story, children could listen to Bill Cosby's recording *Noah*. They'll love the humor, but they may "get it" better if they hear the real story first. At all times during this session, stress the theme of obedience and care in following directions.

The completed rainbow, ark, family, and animals are arranged on a small table and proudly displayed to the congregation after the adult worship service.

Joseph

For the session on "Joseph and His Brothers," the focus question "Tell about a time when you were jealous of somebody, and why" is answered on a green "Imp of Jealousy" shape to hang on the classroom tree. Children then meet with the Storyteller for the lead-in questions, story, and follow-up as outlined in the session plan. At First Unitarian, the cooking group made a cereal snack treat, using the popular Chex recipe with other cereals thrown in, to follow the grain theme. Children went from the Story Corner to the Song Center to learn "Joseph." The Song Leader had played the tune softly on the keyboard during the storytelling time, possibly providing a bit of subliminal input. With this as with other songs, when the leader plays and sings the song as the hour continues, the children pick up on the song, humming or singing it softly while working on activities.

In this session, the children could choose to make a decorated coat, using a brown-paper grocery bag as a base and adding stripes made from many colored crepe-paper streamers. Cut long enough, these come down to the floor, disguising the fact that the bag itself is more vest-length than coat-length. The finished effect can be gorgeous, with colored strips swirling as the children moved about. In Kentucky, the adult leader at that table added the idea of cut-out paper suns, moons, and stars glued to the top of the bag.

Another leader at First Unitarian guided the making of origami "Joseph's coats," which some children glued to drawing paper to make collage pictures of scenes from the story. With plain and fancy origami papers, they made several, for Joseph and his brothers. Also on hand were three or four related word and picture puzzles, a number of storybooks about Joseph, and flannelboard figures to reenact the story.

Special Recipes for Timeless Themes

Among the more popular items by the cooks at First Unitarian were the "Baby in a Basket" treats for "Moses in the Bulrushes" (see recipe); the "Tower of Salad"—a typical six-layered salad found in many cookbooks—for the "Tower of Babel"; "Lot's Cucumber Coins"—sliced cucumber with a spoonful of cottage cheese on top, sprinkled with seasoned salt, served on a wheat thin—for "Sodom and Gomorrah"; a birthday cake built four layers high, alternating light and dark, iced and decorated to look like a wall for "The Walls Came Tumbling Down"; angel-hair pasta with parmesan for Samson; and for Solomon, veggie flowers—toothpick stems, flower parts, and leaves from pieces of carrot, radish, zucchini, summer squash, cucumber, scallions, green pepper, green peas—stuck into big potatoes as bases. They looked like flower gardens, and the Coffee Hour crowd loved picking and eating the flowers!

Baby in a Basket Recipe

Ingredients: bananas, red grapes, soft cream cheese, food coloring, and fruit roll-ups.

- One child cuts each banana in two and slices each half lengthwise, to make four banana "baskets."
- Second child scoops the cream cheese into a little bowl and adds a few drops of food coloring, creaming it with a spoon until the cream cheese is colored. (Let the child choose the color for the baby's bed, which is what the cream cheese is to be.)
- Third child spreads a "bed" of cream cheese on each banana and adds a grape for the baby's head.
- Fourth child puts on a piece of fruit roll-up for a blanket on each "basket." Use a toothpick to fasten the blanket if necessary.
- Arrange all the babies-in-baskets on a platter or tray and pass them to the Open Classroom participants.

Note: You'd better cut the pieces of fruit roll-up for them to use as blankets. The only kind of roll-ups made now have cutout designs on them, and you'll need to use the outside edge strips as blankets. Kids can eat scraps if there are any. Some of the cut-out designs may also make pretty blankets. See how it goes.

Resources and Supplies

Several resources should be kept in your room, available for each session:

- large wall map of Bible lands from the period of the Hebrew Bible through the time of Jesus in the New Testament
- an easy-to-read Bible atlas (see references for this and the wall map in the bibliography)
- the songbook *Bible Songs on Timeless Themes*, the song tape, and a tape player/recorder
- illustrated Bible storybooks
- a chalice or candleholder, candle, and matches
- newsprint and masking tape
- drawing paper, crayons, colored pencils, and markers
- chalk if you use a chalkboard.

Biblical Terms

B.C.E.
Stands for "Before the Common Era," for the years prior to the year A.D. 1 in our present calendar system.

C.E.
Stands for "Common Era," which begins with the year 1 of our present calendar system. Many scholars today regard B.C.E. and C.E. as more universal terms and more inclusive of all religious groups than B.C. (Before Christ) and A.D. (Anno Domini—Year of Our Lord).

Bibles
Hebrew Bible: the 39 books of the scriptures (writings) of Judaism, which are also known to Christians as the "Old Testament." Modern scholars regard the term "Hebrew Bible" to be more accurate.
Christian Bible: the 66 books of the Christian scriptures, which include the 39 books of the Hebrew Bible and the 27 books of the "New Testament" based on the life and teachings of Jesus.

Canaan, Canaanite
The ancient name of a territory and its people that included parts of what is now Israel (with occupied territories) and Lebanon.

Covenant
A formal agreement between two parties (individuals, nations, groups of nations, etc.) in which each assumes some obligation to maintain the agreement.

Essenes
A sect of Judaism from the middle of the second century B.C.E. until the war with Rome in C.E. 66-70. Essenes have been identified with the inhabitants of Qumran who wrote the Dead Sea Scrolls. Although John the Baptist and Jesus have been said to have had some connection with the Essenes, there is no convincing evidence of this.

Exile
Refers to the period in the 6th century B.C.E. in which groups of Judeans were deported to the Mesopotamian city of Babylon, 597 to 582 B.C.E. During this period, the city of Jerusalem fell to the armies of Nebuchadnezzar and the Temple of Solomon was burned.

God
The Christian term "Lord" is not inclusive and is thus avoided. The Hebrew names for God—Yahweh, Elohim, and Adonai—have been avoided in this program as confusing for eight- and nine-year olds. For the Hebrews, God's name was too sacred to be voiced by humans. For that reason, the tetragrammaton YHWH, a form without vowels, is sometimes used in script or print, but not pronounced aloud.

The Land
The land of the Hebrews has had different names. It was Canaan up to the time of Solomon (1250-922 B.C.E.) During the period of the divided monarchy (924-721 B.C.E.), Israel became the name of the Northern Kingdom, and Judah the Southern Kingdom. Following the Return from the Exile (538 B.C.E.), the land as a whole was known as Palestine until the state of Israel was formed in 1948. As a political designation, the nation as a whole is and has always been referred to as Israel. In the scriptures, the people are called "the children of Israel," the collective name given to the twelve tribes descended from Jacob, whose name was also Israel.

Levites
Originally a tribal name given to those who belonged to the tribe of Levi. It evolved into a

name applied to the priests of the temple whose function was to teach and administer the divine law. They became very powerful in the post-exilic period, when the Levitical order came to include all of the temple personnel.

The People
The people of this land were called Hebrews until after the time of Joshua, then Israelites, or the people of Israel, until the return from Babylonian exile. Following the Return, the people were called Jews. "Jew" comes from the Hebrew *yehudi*, meaning a Judahite, or Judean. Rosenberg and Bloom, in *The Book of J*, tell us that "'Hebrews' tends not to be used anymore for the ancient Israelites; 'Hebrew' refers to what is now the language of contemporary Israel, and to what was, in its ancient form, the Old Canaanite language of the Bible" (p. 5).

Pharisees
A group of observant and influential Jews, mainly in Palestine, from the second century B.C.E. to the first century C.E. In the New Testament, they play the role of Jesus' opponents and are almost always cast in a negative light. They were prominent among the people, zealous observers of the law, especially concerned with ritual purity, tithing food according to Mosaic law, and strict observance of the Sabbath.

Philistines
A warlike people who migrated from the Aegean basin to the southern coast of Canaan in the early twelfth century B.C.E. and became one of Israel's principal rivals.

Pre-exilic, Exilic, Post-exilic
Refers to the periods prior, during, and after the Babylonian exile (see "Exile," above). The Exile ended in 538 B.C.E. when the Israelites returned to their land.

Priests
The designated officials who served in the temple performing ritual functions and conducting the sacrificial services. The priesthood was limited to the Levites, members of the family of Levi. According to Deuteronomy, all the Levitical families had a right to the priesthood, for they did not inherit any land as did the other tribes of Israel.

Sadducees
A group in Judaism from the second century B.C.E. through the first century C.E. that retained the older interpretation of the ancient Mosaic law. They rejected the immortality of the soul (resurrection), attributed all human activity to free will and none to fate, and rejected other traditions, especially those of the Pharisees. They were influential with a much smaller group of people than the Pharisees, and like them opposed many of Jesus' teachings. They were active in the temple, associated with the priests and members of the Sanhedrin.

Sanhedrin
A series of councils and courts, spread over several centuries, composed of whoever was powerful and influential at the time and entrusted with various powers. Since religion and politics were so intertwined, the Sanhedrin was always composed of both religious and political leaders.

BIBLIOGRAPHY

Books

Achtemeier, Paul J. et al. *Harper's Bible Dictionary*. San Francisco: Harper & Row, 1985.

Anderson, Bernhard W. *Understanding the Old Testament*. 4th ed. Englewood Cliffs, NJ: Prentice-Hall, 1986.

Brunelli, Roberto. *Macmillan Book of 366 Bible Stories*. New York: Aladdin Books-Macmillan, 1988.

Cohen, Barbara. *I Am Joseph*. New York: Lothrop, Lee and Shephard, 1980.

Cousins, Norman. *Anatomy of an Illness*. New York: Bantam Books, 1981.

Daiches, David. *Moses: The Man and His Vision*. New York: Praeger Publishing, 1975.

Fiorenza, Elisabeth Schussler. *In Memory of Her*. New York: Crossroad Publishing, 1983.

Friedman, Richard Elliott. *Who Wrote the Bible?* New York: Summit Books, 1987.

Furnish, Dorothy. *Living the Bible with Children*. Nashville: Abingdon Press, 1980.

Gobbel, A. Roger, and Gertrude Gobbel. *The Bible: A Child's Playground*. Philadelphia: Fortress Press, 1986.

The Interpreter's Dictionary of the Bible: An Illustrated Encyclopedia. Nashville: Abingdon Press, 1986.

The Jerome Biblical Commentary. Englewood Cliffs, NJ: Prentice-Hall, 1968.

Laymon, Charles M., ed. *Interpreter's One-Volume Commentary on the Bible*. Nashville: Abingdon Press, 1971.

May, Herbert G., ed. *Oxford Bible Atlas*. New York: Oxford University Press, 1987.

Mays, James L. et al. *Harper's Bible Commentary*. San Francisco: Harper & Row, 1988.

Mitchell, Cynthia, ed. *Here a Little Child I Stand: Poems of Prayer and Praise for Children*. New York: Putnam Publishing, 1985.

New English Bible. New York: Oxford University Press, 1970.

New Revised Standard Version Bible. Nashville: Thomas Nelson, 1989.

Perkins, Pheme. *Hearing the Parables of Jesus*. Mahwah, NJ: Paulist Press, 1981.

Rosenberg, David, trans., and Harold Bloom, interpreter. *The Book of J*. New York: Grove Weidenfeld, 1990.

Rossel, Seymour. *A Child's Bible*. 2 vols. West Orange, NJ: Behrman House, 1988. (Recommended for children ages 8 to 10.)

Siegel, Bernie S. *Love, Medicine, and Miracles*. New York: Harper & Row, 1986.

Spier, Peter. *Noah's Ark*. New York: Doubleday, 1981.

Tavris, Carol. *Anger, the Misunderstood Emotion*. New York: Simon and Schuster, 1982.

Throckmorton, Burton H., Jr., ed. *Gospel Parallels*. Nashville: Thomas Nelson, 1979.

Viorst, Judith. *Alexander and the Terrible, Horrible, No Good, Very Bad Day*. New York: Macmillan, 1972.

_____. *I'll Fix Anthony*. New York: Harcourt Brace Jovanovich, 1969.

_____. *Necessary Losses*. New York: Ballantine Books, 1986.

Maps

Aharoni, Yohanan, and Michael Avi-Yonah. *The Macmillan Bible Atlas*. New York: Macmillan, 1977.

The Bible World. 56" x 44" five-in-one wall map of Old and New Testament periods. On solid roller $19.95, on spring roller $28.95 (like a window shade). Abingdon Press, 201 Eighth Avenue S., Nashville, TN 37202, or a local church-goods store.

Student's Atlas of the Bible. American Map Corporation, 46-35 54th Road, Maspeth, NY, 11378; (718) 784-0055 or 1-800-432-6277. Inexpensive, large, clear maps in color.

Newsletter

*Word of Mouth: A Newsletter on Biblical Transla-
tions Using Inclusive Language for Children.*
Religious Education Services, 1824 Catherine,
Bismarck, ND 58501.

USING THE SONGBOOK AND CASSETTE TAPE

In *Timeless Themes* we are informing children's hearts and minds by sharing classic biblical stories from our Jewish and Christian heritages. These stories have inspired faith and hope and acts of justice and compassion for over four thousand years. They have aided the rise and growth of religious movements that have served millions of people the world over. Beyond that, these stories have inspired great artistic expression and creativity in music, poetry, sculpture, dance, drama, architecture, and literature. In the realm of music, the songs based on these stories are particularly accessible to children. Songs, spirituals, rounds, and hymns help children to

- absorb the stories into their minds, hearts, and voices
- sense the deep feelings the stories evoked in those who put them into song
- sing the meanings others have found in these stories and express their own
- experience the bonding that group singing creates and become a community united by song
- have the fun of singing, dancing, and playing songs on musical instruments
- enjoy hearing and making beautiful sounds.

These songs, interwoven into the program, strengthen its spiritual content and depth.

The collection includes at least one song for every story in *Timeless Themes*. As you progress through the program, you can use the songs to

- tell the story
- reinforce the story
- enact the story in musical drama
- probe the meanings in the story
- learn how hymn writers, poets, folk singers, and others experienced the story
- express the feelings the story evokes in us
- celebrate the story at the close of a session or sequence of sessions.

In all of this, you will not only be sharing our religious heritage through music but also be critically reflecting on what it inspires in our minds and spirits. We believe that all of these songs are within the capability of mid- to upper-elementary-age children to learn, sing, and enjoy.

Becoming Familiar with the Songs

In order to use and enjoy the songs within the program, you will need to learn and sing them yourself or find a co-leader or musical person who can. This may be the director of your church choir or junior choir, a choir member, a music educator, or a folk musician with a true voice who can learn, sing, and teach the songs to the children. If you can carry a tune, but don't read music, you can learn the songs from the cassette tape, or have someone musical such as your congregation's music director or organist teach you the songs. What is important is that you use the songs with ingenuity, with the skills you have or can recruit.

Before the first session with the children, read the introduction to the songbook and review all the songs. Know which song goes with which story. Most of the songs are arranged in a sequence paralleling that of the sessions in which they are used. To become familiar with them, listen to the tape and sing along with the songbook in hand. You will notice that the tape introduces a few, not all, of the verses of most songs, enough to demonstrate how the song is sung. Some of the songs will be familiar, but others will be new to you, for they were written for this collection.

Singing the Songs Together

As you plan your sessions, budget time for singing. Will you have time for a song every Sunday, or will you be able to sing only occasionally? It may take the children two or more sessions to learn a song. It's good practice to repeat a song for several Sundays if possible. Repeating a song at the beginning of a session will help the children to recall the story of the previous session and bring last week's absentees on board. As there are several sessions each on Moses, Joseph, and Jesus, one song (or more if you have time) can be enjoyed again and again during those weeks.

If the children are not accustomed to singing together in their religious education groups, begin with a song they already know from this collection or another source. One way to help them become familiar with these Bible songs is to play the "song of the morning" on the tape as they gather.

To teach a song,

- line out the song as did our early American forebears before they had hymnbooks. Sing a line and have the children repeat it immediately. Sing a second line, have the children repeat it, and so on to the end of the song. If the line is long, break it into suitable phrases. The "repeat-after-me" technique can be as gamelike as "Simon Says" and gives the instant reward of singing the song.
- sing the verse and teach the children to sing the chorus.
- play the song on the cassette tape and have the children learn from that, or sing along until they know it well enough to be independent of the tape. Always begin by learning one verse or a chorus well before going on.

Additional Uses of the Songs

Use the songs in programs and presentations about *Timeless Themes* for parents or the congregation, in intergenerational worship, for recreational singing, and with junior choirs. If you have an intergenerational potluck, retreat, or other activity, sing several of the songs, interspersing the familiar with the new. Have a song-fest with other members of your religious education staff. In such a singing-learning session, you can share your experience of how the song goes best with a group of children. If the children are present, ask them how they feel about the songs, how they should be sung and why.

Sing the songs at home, in the car, on a picnic, or around the campfire. They are the kind of songs that families and clans sing. Our family had a great time with "Who Did?" in a four-generation song-fest, from seven-year-old Hugh to ninety-one-year-old Louis.

There are so many potential uses of these songs that we hope you will use them extensively. Of all the arts, music is the most widely used and accessible to us in the liberal church. Of all the forms of music, songs and hymns are the avenue of expression in which we can all most readily participate with heart and voice.

WELCOME

Goals for Participants

- to become acquainted with one another and with their leaders
- to explore some of the reasons for learning Bible stories
- to examine various versions of the Bible
- to reinforce their understanding of fact and fiction
- to experience two basic concepts in biblical literature: oral tradition and the importance of family heritage.

Background

"Hebrew Bible" refers to the scriptures of Judaism, which are also known by Christians as the "Old Testament." Modern scholars regard the term "Hebrew Bible" to be more accurate and less biased. For Judaism, 39 Hebrew books make up the Scriptures. In the Christian Bible, we find the Hebrew Bible plus a "New" Testament of 27 books based on the life and teachings of Jesus.

"Oral tradition" refers to the passage of literary materials (stories, poems, songs, proverbs, etc.) from one generation to the next by word of mouth. In an age when there was no written language, and later when few people could write, all history was learned "by heart" and recited. Gradually the stories and songs were written down, and thus made standard or "official." Many discrepancies in today's bibles can be explained by the fact that stories were passed down in separate oral traditions. Remembering long and intricate passages was a much-admired skill, and the storyteller or singer had a prominent place in the tribal culture of the early Hebrews.

Familiarity with the Bible can help us understand the traditions of the Jewish and Christian religions and the virtually countless allusions to those religions which permeate our culture. But there are other reasons for Unitarian Universalists to look at the Bible. The stories and poetry of biblical literature use everyday experience to demonstrate timeless themes of central importance to the human condition. While there are many things in the Bible which we would probably choose not to teach our young children, there are also many stories that relate significantly to their own life experiences.

When one is teaching the Bible to young children, the best approach is to treat the stories as "living stories," not as prescriptions for living. As the children listen, they can begin to form their own ideas about God, about the relationship between God and people, and about the creative impulse in life. The stories may thus serve as an important building block in a child's personal religion, as well as adding to his or her understanding of the Jewish and Christian roots of Unitarian Universalism.

Teachers with little background in biblical literature and history may find it helpful to have on hand one or two basic reference books. Several are suggested in the bibliography. Your minister, religious educator, or librarian can help you find these or other suitable resources.

Materials

- Pencils, colored markers, and scissors
- 9" x 12" construction paper in varied colors (optional)
- Hole punch and skein of yarn, straight pins, or masking tape
- Stapler or thumbtacks (optional)
- Newsprint (large sheets for display)
- Pictures of family crests, heraldry books
- Handout 1, reproduced on heavy paper or light cardboard (one per child)
- Bibles: several versions, including the King James, Revised Standard, New Revised Stan-

dard (1989), a Hebrew Bible, and a New Testament

- Chalice or candleholder, candle, and matches (to be used each week)

Preparation

- Reflect on your personal feelings toward the Bible, both positive and negative.
- Prepare the bulletin board for the Crest Activity. Prepare a sample crest on a large sheet of newsprint.
- Plan and arrange your meeting space to include areas for art activities, discussion, games, and storage.
- Gather several versions of the Bibles.

Session Plan

Gathering   Varies

As the children arrive, give each a copy of Handout 1. Ask them to cut out their crests, and to write their names across the top. Tell them that they will fill in the four sections of the crest later in the session. Punch two holes, as indicated, and string yarn through the holes, so that the crest nametag may be hung around the child's neck. If you use paper, pins or tape may be used instead. Since you will use the tags for several weeks, heavy paper or light cardboard is best.

Name Game   10 min.

Say, "This year we will be learning many stories from the Bible. Bibles come in many forms, and the stories are told a little differently in each version. When many of these stories were first told, people did not know how to write them. Instead, stories were learned 'by heart' and recited. Storytellers were very important people, for they held the history of the tribe in their minds, so a good memory was much admired. Today we will play a memory game to help us get acquainted. I wonder if we would have been good storytellers.

"When it is your turn, say your first name and a food that begins with the same letter as your name. For example, 'Margie Macaroni,' or 'Bobby Broccoli.' But before you say your own name, try to repeat the names and foods of all those before you. I'll start, and we'll go around the circle. When we get all the way back to me, let's see if I can remember everyone's name."

Encourage the children to help one another whenever someone gets stuck, and offer help yourself. Continue around the circle until it is your turn to repeat all the names. Ask for a few volunteers to try to repeat all of them too.

(It is important, even in large groups, for children and teachers to become familiar with one another's names. If playing the Name Game with the entire group seems unwieldy, divide into as many groups as you have adults to lead. Plan to play the game at the beginning of the next one or two sessions, also.)

Group Rules   15 min.

In many congregations the opening Sunday is often a shorter-than-usual session because of registration or the children's participation in an opening worship service. You will need to decide which activities are most important for your group, and whether some can be incorporated into the next session. Many groups will want to take time during the first week to develop group rules. To relate these to the program's focus, you might say something like, "Among the many kinds of writing we find in the Bible, there are several lists of rules on how people should behave. These are usually called laws or commandments, and we'll learn more about them in a few weeks. Today, we'll be making our own set of rules, to help us get along well as we work and play together this year. Do you have some ideas to help us get started?"

Using newsprint and a marker, list the children's ideas, then allow them to select those that are most important. Be sure to include your own ideas, for you are a member of the group, too. Try to limit the rules to five or fewer, focusing on those that are concrete and inclusive. Make a "good" copy of the rules and post it on the wall or bulletin board for the remainder of the year.

This would be a good time to acquaint the children with the format of each session, and perhaps post a general outline. Tell them that songs are a part of the program, that the songbook that accompanies the program has at least one and sometimes two songs for every Bible story, and that you will be singing songs almost every Sunday. It is especially important to tell them that each session will close with a chalice- or candle-lighting and a few words that highlight the morning's theme.

Crest Nametags   25 min.

With the children seated at tables, tell them to take off their nametags and look at the crest. Ask, "Do you know what this is and what it means?" Show some pictures of family crests from a book of heraldry.

Say, "In the Bible stories we will be hearing this year, families are very important. All through the Bible we are told who 'begat'—gave birth to—whom, or who someone's father, mother, sister, or brother was. Keeping track of families was so important that when these stories came to be written down, some writers put in long lists of 'begats' so that they would be remembered for a long time to come. (Genesis 36 is one example.)

"Crests, like the one you have in front of you, are another way of keeping track of families. Just as each family is different, each family crest is different from those of other families. The pictures, symbols, and words on the crest tell us something about the family.

"Today you are going to make your own personal crests. By looking at them we will be able to see how each of you is a very special person and different from everyone else. In section 1, draw a picture of your favorite food. In section 2, draw a favorite activity—something you really like to do. In section 3, draw something that describes your favorite subject in school, and in section 4, show the members of your family. If you prefer, you may use words rather than pictures."

Display a sample crest with the following words written in each section: 1: food; 2: activity; 3: subject; 4: family.

Allow time for the children to complete their crests. Then gather the group together and invite the children to explain their crests.

Discussion   10-15 min.

You may wish to lead the dicussion informally while the children are at work on their crests. If your group is large, with more than one teacher, an adult can lead a separate discussion at each work table.

Use the questions and information below as a guide to your discussion. It is important to draw out from the children what they already know, and build on it. Too much information can be confusing to the children, so keep it simple.

1. The Hebrew and Christian Bibles—what are they, who wrote them, how old are they?
   The Hebrew and Christian Bibles are collections of stories, many of which were passed by word of mouth for many years before they were written down. Many people believe that the stories came directly from God; others believe they are the result of human attempts to figure out how the world was created and what we are doing here. The stories were collected over a period of thousands of years, and began to be written down about 3,000 years ago. The order of the books varies in the Hebrew and Christian Bibles. The Christian Bible has more books—those in the Hebrew Bible plus a collection of books called the New Testament.

2. Why is it important for us to learn about the Bibles?
   Stories from the Bibles have been used in books, plays, movies, paintings, and sculpture throughout our culture for thousands of years. A person who isn't familiar with these stories is missing much that our world has to offer. The Bibles also hold important truths for many people. These stories talk about some of the most important experiences in the lives of human beings, not just thousands of years ago but also today.

3. To whom are the Bibles important?
   These Bibles are important primarily to Jews, Christians, and Muslims. For many people in these religious groups, including some Unitarian Universalists, these writings are sacred, much more than just ordinary stories.

4. Did these Bible stories really happen?
   Some happened, and some were created to explain why certain events happened. It is important to remember that these Bible stories are not necessarily stories of God's actions, but stories of people trying to understand what they believed to be God's actions.

Closing 5 min.

If extra activities are used, remember to do them before the closing.

Gather the children together. Collect their crest nametags. If possible, mount them on a wall or bulletin board.

Light a chalice or a candle, and say something like, "Stories are a very important part of our lives. They can help us understand ourselves, and how other people have dealt with life's joys and sorrows. The Bible stories which we will hear this year have been told by one generation to the next for thousands of years. Each of us is an important part of that storytelling chain. I hope that you will listen well as we tell and talk about these stories, so that someday you can tell them to your children."

If Your Time Is Limited

- Cut out crests in advance.
- As children arrive, ask them to think of a food that begins with the same letter as their name— this will speed up the Name Game.

If You Have More Time

- Play the Name Game again.
- Ask the children to contribute names of characters they have heard of from the Bible. List these, and say that they will hear about these and many others in the weeks ahead.
- Make a list of "begats" for your own family, or a make-believe family. Be sure to include males and females. For example: Abner and Sophie begat Michael, Michael and Elena begat Josie, Josie and David begat . . .

ADAM AND EVE

Source: Genesis 1-3

Theme: Loneliness

Goals for Participants

- to become familiar with two stories from Genesis which tell of the creation of the first man and the first woman
- to reflect on times in their own lives when they have felt lonely.

Background

In referring to the early Genesis stories, Bernhard Anderson writes: "The stories concerning primeval history . . . are not factual accounts of the sort that the modern historian or scientist demands. These stories are 'historical' only in the sense that they plumb the depth of history's meaning. . . . The manner of presentation is poetic or pictorial, for the narrator is dealing with a subject that eludes the modern historian's investigation—namely, the ultimate source of the human drama in the initiative and purpose of God. . . ."(*Understanding the Old Testament*, p. 167)

In preparing for this session, leaders should reexamine the "background to the biblical literature" in the introduction. In particular, the material on the basic documents of the Hebrew Bible is useful for understanding the two different accounts of creation referred to in this session's story.

Two different stories are found in Genesis because they were transmitted in two separate chains of oral tradition. Genesis 1 recounts the priestly tradition (P) in a formal, ritualistic style. Genesis 2, as told by the J writer, presents the story of the first people in a more "earthy" version. In this telling, we can see Adam and Eve

as real people and identify with their feelings and conflicts, whereas the Genesis 1 version tells us nothing about the personality and emotions of the first man and woman.

The contrast in the two stories should be easy for children to see if you ask, "Which story is more exciting?" or "Which story tells how lonely the first people must have felt?" Feelings of loneliness are probably more common to children today than we suspect. Smaller families, a decrease in "neighborliness," an increase in single-parent families and latchkey children, even the emotional distance of TV sitcoms—all can isolate children and increase their sense of loneliness, so it would be wise to be prepared for their responses.

The Genesis 1 story also explains the Sabbath, the weekly day of rest. It is likely that the Sabbath was observed long before the writing of this story (approximately 6th century B.C.E.), and that the priestly writer(s) arranged and divided the elements of creation to fit the already established seven-day week. Children may like to speculate on what it would be like to have a five-day week, or a ten-day week.

There is considerable evidence (see the UUA program *Cakes for the Queen of Heaven*) that serpents were an important part of cults of the Great Goddess of ancient times. In Canaan the serpent was associated with the worship of Astarte, the consort of Baal. YHWH, the Hebrew God, abhorred anything connected to Baal, so it is not surprising that the serpent acts as the villain of this story. Actually, "agitator" might be a better word than "villain," for it is the serpent who opens the eyes of Adam and Eve to the possibilities of knowledge.

The Hebrew word for earth is *adamah*. Although most familiar versions of the Hebrew Bible have translated the word in the masculine gender, "a man," we have chosen in this story to use the word "earthling" for the being created from the earth by God. Once divided, the earthling takes both masculine and feminine forms. *Word of Mouth*, a newsletter of biblical translations in inclusive language for children, defends the use of "earthling":

We Are All Adam

Unless it is the name of a specific person and is translated as the proper noun Adam, the Hebrew word adam should be translated into English using a generic and non sex-specific word. In *Word of Mouth*, it has been translated as "earthling."

This key biblical word is frequently translated inaccurately into English as "man." However, adam means "earthling"—one created from the earth. Adam is a generic noun which does not tell the sex of the earthling.

The root of adam is *adamah*. *Adamah* means "soil"—the soil from which the food that gives life is created. In ancient Hebrew the word *adam* was assigned the grammatical masculine gender and *adamah* was assigned the grammatical feminine gender. (*Word of Mouth*, Vol. 1, No. 1, Fall 1986)

Materials

- Scissors, glue, and colored markers
- Tape player/recorder, the songbook, and the song tape (to be used each week)
- a blank tape
- Clay, playdough, or plasticine
- Plastic tablecloth or clay mats
- One box, 2' x 2' x 2' or larger, for every four children
- Paints (brown, blue, green) and paintbrushes
- Natural materials (twigs, moss, shells, rocks, etc.)
- Cotton balls
- Small mirror
- Copies of Songs 1 and 2, "Creation" and "The Blessing of the Animals" (optional)

Preparation

- Think through your own answers to the motivating and discussion questions.
- Consider the meaning the Genesis story has for you.
- Listen to the tape and learn the songs.

- Experiment with the materials the children will use. Make an earthling. Begin a diorama. Get a feel for what you will expect the children to accomplish and how long it will take.
- Arrange a table for the diorama. (Cover it with newspapers or a drop cloth to protect it during the work period.)

Session Plan

Gathering   Varies

As children arrive, encourage them to help you prepare the space and gather materials for the diorama. You might ask them what their world would be like if they had the power to create it.

Oral Tradition   15 min.

When everyone has arrived, gather the children on a rug or around a table. Remind them of the name game they played last week and the importance of a good memory in storytelling. Say, "Try to imagine a time before the earth existed. Imagine that we, as a group, have the power to create a world just the way we'd like it to be. It can't be just the way I want it, or just the way you want. It is something we need to do together. I have a tape recorder here, and each of us will have a chance to tell one sentence of our story of creation. We'll go around the circle from person to person, recording the whole story. When we're finished, we'll see if we can remember the whole story correctly. The tape recorder will let us know just how good our memories are! We'll begin with Michael and end up with Jane." (Your group may prefer to add their sentences in random order, rather than working around the circle.)

Large groups may wish to use two tape recorders, so that children need not wait so long for a turn. The two stories could be played for the entire group to hear.

When all have contributed, turn off the tape recorder and ask if anyone can remember the entire story. Perhaps two people would like to retell it, separately or together. Then play the recording. Note the kinds of errors that were made. Did they change the meaning of the story? The order of events? The characters?

Motivating Questions   **5 min.**

Gather the children around a table or on a rug. Ask, "Have you ever been lonely? What did it feel like? What would it be like to be the only human being on earth?" Discuss. Then say, "People in ancient times did not understand how the first man and the first woman were created. There are many myths from around the world that try to explain this. Two of these stories are in the book of Genesis of Hebrew scripture, and we will be hearing them today."

Definitions

create   to make something from the beginning
Genesis the first book of Hebrew scripture and the Christian Bible
myth   a story that is told to explain why things happen as they do
serpent a snake

Read the Story   **5 min.**

Discussion   **10-15 min.**

Note: This is a busy session. If you begin the craft activities at the end of the story, you can use the discussion questions as the children work. Since there are two activities, children may wish to spend all their time on one or the other, or you may choose to assign one group to making earthlings and another to dioramas. While the children are engaged in these activities, play the songs "Creation" and "The Blessing of the Animals" on the tape player.

Lead a discussion of the story guided by the following questions.
1. Were Adam and Eve lonely at the end of the story, or were they homesick for the Garden of Eden? Is being homesick the same as being lonely?
2. If you didn't know why the sun came up in the morning or what made it rain or snow, how would you explain it? How do you think people thousands and thousands of years ago explained what happened in the world around them? Discuss.

3. Today you heard two different stories about the creation of the world. Can you think of another story you have heard told two different ways? (Many fairy tales are told with two or more endings. If the children can't think of examples on their own, try asking what happens at the end of "The Three Little Pigs.")
4. Did Eve and Adam think about what would happen if they listened to the snake? Has anything ever happened to you because you listened to someone who told you to do something you weren't supposed to do?

Note: The more common versions of this story indicate that Eve came from Adam's rib. Current scholarship shows this to be a mistranslation. The earthling was androgynous, and only after an entire side was taken away were there two creatures—a man and a woman.

Making an Earthling   **10 min.**

Gather the children around a table that has been covered with plastic or mats. Give each child a ball of clay or playdough about 2 1/2" in diameter. Tell them to use the clay to form an earthling, as God formed the earthling in the second creation story. Save the earthlings for the next activity. If some children suggest dividing the earthling to form both man and woman, observe how they go about it and refer to the discussion note above if necessary.

Garden of Eden   **20 min.**

Ask the children to imagine what the Garden of Eden might look like. Read the brief description in Genesis 2:5-14 to stimulate their thinking.

Engage the children in making a diorama or models of Eden, about four children to each large box. Use paints or markers to fill in the background; twigs, flowers, leaves, shells, rocks, moss, and so forth to set the scene; cotton for clouds; a mirror for a pond. Use your imaginations!

Once the diorama is completed, ask the children to act out the story of Adam and Eve, using their earthlings. End the drama by singing "Creation" or "The Blessing of the Animals," if time permits.

Closing   **5 min.**

Gather the children in a circle, light a chalice or candle, and close with the following thoughts, in your own words:

"There are many lonely people in our world today. The sense of belonging to a family is not as strong as it has been sometimes in the past. In our congregation there are probably some people who have no close relatives. For them, this church family can be especially important. We need to remember how important our smiles and 'hellos' are to other members of our church family, how much a small kindness can mean when someone feels lonely. Perhaps as you leave here today, you can give someone a cheerful greeting. You may help someone to feel less lonely."

If Your Time Is Limited

- Omit the Oral Tradition activity.
- Omit either earthlings or dioramas activity.
- Instead of dioramas, give the children paper and markers to draw pictures of the Garden of Eden as background for their earthlings.

If You Have More Time

- Sing "Creation" and/or "The Blessing of the Animals."
- Play the Name Game from Session 1 again.

Adam and Eve

In THE BEGINNING, God took three days to create light, separate the sky from the waters, and part the waters from the land. God caused plants to grow on the third day, and then made the sun and the moon on the fourth day. On the fifth day, God created all sea creatures and all birds. On the sixth day, God made all of the land animals, including a man and a woman. Finally, on the seventh day, the Sabbath day, since everything was good, God rested.

The second creation story in Genesis doesn't say how long it took God to create the world. Perhaps it took a day for God to make the earth and the sky, and then cause the rain to fall upon the earth. Perhaps it took much longer. After God created the sea creatures, the birds, and the land animals, the second story says, next, from the dust of the ground, God made an earthling and breathed life into this human. Then God planted a garden in Eden so the earthling could take care of it and receive food. God commanded the earthling, saying, "You may freely eat of every tree of the garden; but of the Tree of the Knowledge of Good and Evil you shall not eat, for in the day that you eat of it you shall die."

The earthling seemed lonely, so God wanted to make a helper. Every beast of the field and every bird of the air was made and brought to the earthling to name. The earthling gave each creature a name, but none of them was just the right helper. Therefore, God caused the earthling to fall into a deep sleep and divided the earthling into a man and a woman.

The man was called Adam, after the Hebrew word for dirt, *adamah*, and the woman was called Eve, after the Hebrew word for living, *chavah*. Adam and Eve lived in the Garden of Eden, free to eat all of the fruit the garden had to offer except the fruit from the Tree of the Knowledge of Good and Evil.

One day a serpent came to Eve and said, "You will not die if you eat the fruit from the Tree of the Knowledge of Good and Evil. God knows that if you eat this fruit you will be like God, knowing good and evil."

Eve, wishing to have more knowledge, ate some of the fruit and also gave some to Adam to eat. Suddenly their new knowledge made them realize they were naked, and they hid from God.

When God found out they had eaten the forbidden fruit, God clothed them and drove them from the Garden of Eden. From that day on, Adam and Eve had to work for their food, clothing, and housing. They felt very alone in the world.

CAIN AND ABEL

Source: Genesis 4

Theme: Jealousy Between Siblings

Goals for Participants

- to become familiar with the story of Cain and Abel, especially as it relates to issues of sibling rivalry
- to explore children's own experiences of feeling anger toward siblings and other rivals.

Background

Because this session focuses on brothers and sisters, special attention must be given to those children who have no siblings. They, too, have much to learn from the dynamics of jealousy between brothers and sisters, and indeed probably have experienced the kind of loving competition that typifies sibling rivalry.

Rivalry is a normal part of family relationships, particularly among siblings. When carried to extremes, as in the story of Cain and Abel, these feelings can be quite destructive, but for most of us, they resolve themselves in more socially acceptable ways. In the words of one writer:

When three-year-old Josh saw his mother hugging his new baby brother he said, as plain as could be, "You can't love us both. And I want you to love only me."

To which his mother responded truthfully, "I love you very much. But...I don't love only you."

And this is a sorrowful fact of life that cannot be denied. We have to divide mother love with our brothers and sisters.

Our parents can help us cope with the loss of our dream of absolute love. But they cannot make us believe that we haven't lost it.

We can, however, learn—if all goes well—that there is sufficient love to go around.

And we also can learn that sisters and brothers offer the possibility of another kind of loving family attachment.

For although sibling rivalry can cause great hardship and suffering, can follow us into adulthood, can become an emotional heritage that is transferred onto all kinds of other relationships, it can also become subordinate to continuing bonds of brotherly/sisterly love. Indeed, in recent years, there have been a growing number of studies on the lifelong involvement of siblings with each other, studies that focus not only on siblings as rivals but as comforters, caretakers, role models, spurs to achievement, faithful allies and best friends. (Judith Viorst, *Necessary Losses* pp. 98-99)

The story of Cain and Abel uses sibling rivalry to illustrate a cultural struggle at the time of its writing between the ancient nomadic Hebrews and the more settled agricultural Canaanites. Which is the better way of life—farming or sheep herding? Which does God prefer?

According to the biblical story, the nomadic offering of a lamb was more pleasing to God, and thus the story served as a sanction for the destruction of the Canaanites. Ironically, in the same period when the ancient Hebrews were bent on destroying the Canaanites, they were also adopting many Canaanite religious and cultural practices.

Sacrifice was the most significant aspect of

worship in ancient Israel and its surroundings. Both animal and vegetable offerings were used, but it was generally supposed that animal offerings carried more power and were more pleasing to YHWH. Smeared on the sacrificial altar, the blood of an animal was visible evidence of the mystery and wonder of life. In addition, blood was thought to have a cleansing effect—an idea that has carried over to 20th-century Christianity in such gospel hymn phrases as "washed in the blood of the Lamb."

Sacrificed animals were eaten within a day's time by the priest and worshipers. (YHWH received only the fragrant odor of cooking!) Animal sacrifices were generally only for the wealthy; the poor generally made vegetable or cereal offerings, in which case only a small amount was actually burnt. The rest was, in effect, payment to the priest (see Mays, *Harper's Bible Commentary*, pp. 1143-44).

So far as it is known, the Land of Nod was mythical. The Hebrew derivation of the word Nod suggests a "homeless" or "restless" place (Mays, p. 710). The most significant aspect of the Land of Nod seems to be that it was not Eden.

Materials

- Newsprint or chalkboard and chalk
- Colored markers, scissors, and masking tape
- Paper plates, two per child
- Tongue depressors, sticks, or rulers (one per child)
- Stapler
- Cassette player and the song tape (to be used for all remaining sessions)
- *I'll Fix Anthony*, by Judith Viorst (optional)
- Copies of Song 3, "Cain"

Preparation

- Think through your own answers to the motivating and discussion questions.
- Familiarize yourself with the art project; make one or two masks and decide which method you will use with your group, or whether you will give the children a choice.
- Plan your space for acting out the story of Cain and Abel, and for displaying the masks.
- Listen to the tape and learn the song "Cain."

Session Plan

Gathering   Varies

As the children arrive, ask them to assist in the preparation of space and materials. Engage them in some conversation about brothers and sisters.

What Makes Me Angry   10-15 min.

Gather everyone together. Write "What Makes Me Angry" at the top of a newsprint sheet, and "What I Can Do About It" at the top of another sheet, and post them side by side where all can see. (If using a chalkboard, divide it vertically with a line and label the two sections as indicated.)

Say, "How many of you have a brother or a sister? If you don't have a brother or sister, do you play with children who do? What are some things that brothers and sisters do to make each other angry? Allow for responses. "What are some things that make you angry?" Refer to your conversations with the children before the session, and remember to include children with no siblings.

List the children's contributions on the appropriate sheet. When everyone has had a chance to contribute, ask "How could you do something about the things that make you angry?" Take one item on the list and ask, for their suggestions about it. Next to that item, on the other sheet of newsprint, list their possible solutions. Your lists might look something like this:

What Makes Me Angry
1) my brother bosses me
2) I have to do my sister's jobs

What I Can Do About It
1) stop playing with him
   ignore him
2) talk to my parents
   make a deal with sister

Be sure to listen carefully to the children's suggestions, and resist the temptation to supply the "correct" adult answer. Be prepared for the fact that some children may suggest rather violent solutions. Ask the entire group, "Is there a better way? Who or what might help you solve this problem?"

Motivating Questions   5-10 min.

Gather the children around a table or on a rug and ask, "Are brothers and sisters always 'enemies'? How do you feel about your brother or sister? Can you think of times when the competition between brothers and sisters might be good? When might it be bad?" Then say, "Many, many plays and stories are about fighting between siblings. The first story about fights between siblings in Hebrew scripture is the story of Cain and Abel, which we will hear today."

Definitions

fugitive a person who runs away
sibling a brother or sister

Read the Story   5 min.

Discussion   10-15 min.

Lead a discussion of the story, guided by the following questions.
1. Why did Cain feel jealous of his brother? Can you remember a time when you felt jealous? How did it feel? What did you do? What are some things we can do when we are feeling jealous of others?
2. Cain thought that he had done something special for God, and that God didn't appreciate it. Have you ever done something special for someone who didn't seem to appreciate it? How did that make you feel?
3. Cain dealt with his jealousy by fighting with Abel and killing him. Certainly this is an unacceptable way of dealing with conflict. Earlier we thought of some better ways of handling our own angry feelings. What might Cain have done?

Mask Making   10 min.

Gather the children at a table. Give each child two paper plates and colored markers. Ask them to make a smiling face on one plate to represent Abel and a frowning face on the other for Cain. Tape a ruler, stick, or tongue depressor to the back of one mask, then staple the two masks together, back to back. The finished product will look like a large lollipop with two faces. When one turns the mask around, the frown changes quickly into a smile. Play the song "Cain" a few times while the children work.

Act Out the Story   10-15 min.

Ask two children to act out the story of Cain and Abel, using their masks. Select another child (or adult) to play God. Because the story involves violence, be sure to set limits such as "no hitting." Then suggest that another pair act out the story, changing the ending so that Cain does not fight with Abel. Ask, "What are some other ways this story could have ended?" Encourage the children to think creatively. If time permits, allow several pairs to play out their endings.

Closing   1 min.

Gather the children together, light a chalice candle, and say, "Cain asks God, 'Am I my brother's keeper?' This very well-known part of the story is seen by many people as a reminder that all human beings are brothers and sisters to one another. These words by a Japanese writer express the same idea:

> Creator of the world
> Help us love one another,
> Help us care for each other
> As sister or brother,
> That friendship may grow
> From nation to nation.
> Bring peace to our world
> O Lord of Creation.
> —Satomi Ichikawa

If Your Time Is Limited

• Omit the Act Out the Story activity.

If You Have More Time

• Sing "Cain."
• Read Judith Viorst's book *I'll Fix Anthony*.

Cain and Abel

CAIN AND ABEL were the sons of Adam and Eve. Cain was the older, and he became a farmer; Abel was the younger, and he raised sheep. When Cain and Abel worshiped God, they brought offerings, because they thought offerings would make God like them better. Cain brought some of what he had grown as an offering, while Abel brought the first born of the sheep.

God seemed to like Abel's offerings better than Cain's. This made Cain very angry, and he frowned deeply. God said to Cain, "Why are you angry, and why are you frowning? If you do well, will you not be accepted? But if you do not do well, evil is waiting for you and your anger will rule you. You must learn to master it."

Cain did not listen to this good advice, but let anger rule him. Cain said to Abel, his brother, "Let us go out to the field."

And when they were in the field, Cain killed Abel.

God called out to Cain, "Where is your brother Abel?"

Cain replied, "I do not know; am I my brother's keeper?"

God said, "What have you done? You have spilled your brother's blood on the ground. Now you are cursed from the ground. When you try to farm the ground, it shall no longer yield to you its strength; you shall be a fugitive and a wanderer on the earth."

Cain cried, "My punishment is greater than I can bear. Today you have driven me away from the ground; and I shall be hidden from your face; I shall be a fugitive and a wanderer on the earth." Then Cain went away from the presence of God and settled in the land of Nod, east of Eden.

SESSION 4

NOAH

Source: Genesis 6-9

Theme: Obedience

Goals for Participants

• to consider what obedience is and how they feel about it
• to become familiar with the story of Noah and the Ark
• to discover other themes in the story, for example, rainy days, floods, how to stop violence, and covenants.

Background

The story of Noah and the flood is found in Genesis 6-9. The writings in this section come from two main sources, J and P (see the introduction). The two versions differ in several respects, such as the numbers of animals and the duration of the flood. The J story is more personal and offers more detail; the P story is more objective and places the story within the larger picture of Israel's history and theology. We have interwoven the two versions in our telling of the story.

In biblical times, people envisioned the world as being located between two bodies of water—the waters above the earth, from which the rains came; and the waters below the earth, which could seep up through the ground. The priestly creation story (Genesis 1:2-7) indicates that in the beginning these waters were one, and that God's second act of creation was to place them on either side of a firmament. In this telling the flood was caused by the loosening of both bodies of water onto the earth: "On the seventeenth day of the month, on that day all the fountains of the great deep burst forth, and the windows of

the heavens were opened" (Genesis 7:11).

People believed that one of the ways God punished their wickedness was by shooting lightning at them with a divine bow and arrow. So when the people saw a rainbow in the sky after a storm, they took it as a sign that they were once again in God's favor.

According to the story, the ark was 450 feet long, 75 feet wide, and 45 feet high. No one seems to know what "gopher wood" actually was.

It is almost universally agreed that this biblical story is derived from the Mesopotamian story of Utnapishtim and the flood, which is described in the Epic of Gilgamesh. While the stories are very much alike, they differ in several respects, most obviously the names of the participants. The divine motivation for sending the flood is also different in the two stories. In the Mesopotamian story, the gods are tired of the noisy people below, but in the Hebrew version, God sends the flood as punishment for corruption and violence. After the flood, Utnapishtim offers a sacrifice and is made immortal; Noah offers a sacrifice and becomes a partner in a covenant with God, who promises never to send such a flood again.

One theme in the flood story is God's punishment of sinful human beings. A second theme is Noah's willingness to trust God and to obey the orders he is given, and a third is the covenant God makes with Noah. With third- and fourth-graders, it seems most appropriate to highlight the theme of trust and obedience, since this is a real issue for children of this age.

In general, third- and fourth-graders are comfortable with obeying those whom they see as older, wiser, and in positions of authority over them. In fact, in these middle elementary years, children feel more secure with clear-cut rules and order in their lives. We live in a complex world, however, and most youngsters of this age are also aware that not all adults have their best interests at heart and that not all the rules of society should be accepted without question. Our task is to guide our children toward the goal of thinking and deciding for themselves about difficult issues. Learning to assess when one should obey authorities and when one should not can be a first step in this process.

Materials

- Scissors, glue, colored markers, and paintbrushes
- Handouts 2 and 3, enough copies for each activity group
- Mural paper for the rainbow, or strips of colored crepe paper (red, orange, yellow, green, blue, purple)
- Masking tape
- Four boxes—small, medium, large, and very large—for the ark (be sure they fit one atop the other), and the largest boxtop for the roof
- Brown paint and clay
- Eight popsicle sticks (or clothespins) for the Noah family
- Scraps of cloth, bits of string, and black pens
- Copies of Songs 4 and 5, "Rise and Shine" and "Who Built the Ark?"

Preparation

- Think through your own answers to the motivating and discussion questions, especially when to obey and when not to.
- Become familiar with the art projects. Make one of the popsicle people, think through the steps for making the ark, and so forth; determine which versions of them can be done in your time frame.
- Cut copies of Handout 3 into three separate sections.
- Learn the songs from the book or tape, or arrange for someone else to teach them.
- Arrange your room for the activities. Set up a display space for the completed ark, preferably against a wall so the rainbow can be mounted above it.

Session Plan

Gathering   Varies

As the children arrive, invite them to draw a rainbow on the mural paper using colored markers, or to help you assemble a crepe-paper rainbow, as described in Handout 3. Attach the rainbow to the wall above the place where the ark will be displayed.

If all the children come at the same time, begin with the next activity and save the rainbow project until the ark-building activity.

Motivating Questions   5 min.

Gather the children onto the rug or around the table and say, "Sometimes your parents or teachers tell you to do something and you don't understand why you have to do it. Often you are told that it is for your own good. Occasionally, doing what you are told means that your friends laugh at you—like the first time they see you in braces or when you are the only one to dress up for a party.

"In the story from Hebrew scripture we're going to hear today, Noah followed the orders God gave him even though others made fun of him. Have you ever had to do something without being given a reason, other than 'because I said so'? Have you ever done things you were ordered to do and others made fun of you?"

Definitions

ark   a large boat
covenant   an agreement between two or more people

Read the Story   5 min.

Discussion   15 min.

Lead a discussion of the story guided by the following questions.

⚜ 1. Do you think Noah should have obeyed God? What would have happened if he hadn't? Should we always obey orders? What if we don't understand the order? What are some situations in which you should not obey orders?

2. Why do you think God flooded the earth? What is violence? Do you think the flood was a good way to stop it? Why do you think God promised not to flood the earth again?

3. How does it feel to be stuck in the house during a few days of rain? How would it feel if it rained for 40 days and 40 nights? What would you do if you were stuck in the house for nearly eight months?

4. The story says that after the waters went down, God made a covenant with Noah saying that he would never flood the earth like that again. Why are covenants important for people to live together peacefully?

Creating an Ark, the Noah Family, and the Animals   25 min.

Tell the children that you will give them directions for making an ark, Noah's family, and the animals. Just as Noah obeyed God and followed God's orders, they also can make an ark by following the directions.

Set out a box or bowl containing copies of the directions for the four activities (Handouts 2 and 3); invite the children to choose a set of directions. Engage them in completing the activities, and display the pieces as they are finished.

Closing   5 min.

Gather the children in a circle on the floor or around a table. Light the chalice. Teach them "Rise and Shine" or "Who Built the Ark?" Sing it all the way through once, and close by saying, "There are times when good things happen when we obey orders and follow directions, such as when we obey safety rules. There are other times when it would be wrong to obey, such as when a stranger orders you to get into a car. Unitarian Universalists believe that we must use our own good judgment to decide when it is good to follow orders and when it is not."

If Your Time Is Limited

• Have the discussion of the story while the children are working on their projects. Wait until all are clear about their tasks before posing the discussion questions.

• Use these time-saving directions for making the ark:
  - Leaders make the ark ahead of time and have the children paint it.
  - Don't paint the ark.
  - Make the ark out of one large and one smaller box, following these directions:
    1. Make a door in the side of a box so the people and the animals can enter. Make two cuts only so the door can open and close.
    2. Turn the smaller box upside down and cut two doors in it. Add windows if you wish. Glue this box in the center of the larger box.
    3. Paint over the whole ark with brown paint, making it as much like wood as you can. When it dries, use a black marker to show where you think the pitch might have been put to make it waterproof.

If You Have More Time

• Teach both songs.

Noah

GOD TOLD NOAH TO BUILD AN ARK, 450 feet long and three stories high, and to cover it with tar so it wouldn't leak. God said, "I am going to bring a flood of waters on the earth, to destroy from under heaven all flesh in which is the breath of life; everything that is on the earth shall die. But I will establish my covenant with you; and you shall come into the ark, you and your family. And of every living thing, of all flesh, you shall bring two of every kind into the ark, to keep them alive with you; they shall be male and female. Of the birds according to their kinds, and of the animals according to their kind, of every creeping thing on the ground according to its kind, two of every kind shall come in to you, to keep them alive. Also take with you every kind of food that is eaten, and store it up; and it shall serve as food for you and for them." Noah did this; he did all that God commanded him.

The story doesn't tell us what Noah's neighbors said when he began to build this huge ark or when he told them that there was going to be a huge flood that would cover all the earth. But Noah believed that what God had told him was true, and he finished the ark.

When the ark was finished, one male and one female of every living thing entered. Noah, his wife, his sons, and their wives also entered the ark. Then it rained for forty days and forty nights, covering the earth with water. Finally, the rain stopped.

The ark floated on the waters for 150 days after the rain stopped. Then a wind blew over the earth, causing the waters to go back, and the ark came to rest on the top of Mount Ararat. At the end of another forty days, Noah opened the window of the ark and sent forth a raven. The raven went to and fro until the waters were dried up from the earth. Then he sent out a dove from him, to see if the waters had subsided from the face of the ground. But the dove found no place to set its foot, for the waters were still on the face of the whole earth, and returned to Noah at the ark. So he put out his hand and took it and brought it into the ark with him.

Noah waited another seven days, and again he sent out the dove from the ark. The dove came back to him in the evening, and there in its beak was a freshly plucked olive leaf; so Noah knew that the waters had subsided from the earth. Then he waited another seven days and sent forth the dove. It did not return. Noah knew it was time to leave the ark, and his family and all the living things came out of the ark onto dry land. They had been in the ark over eight months.

God then said to Noah, "I make my covenant with you, that never again shall all flesh be cut off by the waters of a flood, and never again shall there be a flood to destroy the earth. As a sign of this covenant I will set my bow in the cloud, and it shall be a sign of the covenant between me and the earth." That bow is our beautiful rainbow.

SESSION 5

THE TOWER OF BABEL

Source: Genesis 11

Theme: Communication

Goals for Participants

- to consider how we communicate with one another and how it feels when we can't be understood
- to become familiar with the story of the Tower of Babel.

Background

Authored by the J writers, the story of the Tower of Babel closes the first part of the Hebrew Bible, the Primeval History, by repeating the familiar theme of errant humans and God's judgment of them. This time the sin is the people's desire to "make a name for themselves" or to become renowned. God calls a halt to this by causing the builders of the tower to speak different languages, so that they are unable to communicate with one another. Several scholars believe this story is meant to contrast with the opening of the next section, the Patriarchal History. There, in Genesis 12:2, God promises Abraham, "I will make of you a great nation, and I will bless you, and make your name great, so that you will be a blessing." The inference is that it is wrong for people to make a name for themselves; renown should come only as a gift from God.

This story serves the second purpose of explaining the multiplicity of languages. The story follows the Table of Nations, Genesis 10, which documents in a different way the expanding world of many nations and languages.

The story of the Tower of Babel has roots in ancient Mesopotamian lore, as do many of the writings in the Primeval History. The tower described here was probably similar to Mesopotamian ziggurats. These were large step-towers built by placing squares of decreasing size one on top of the other. Bitumen and bricks, less durable than stone and mortar, were the building materials of the Mesopotamians. The topmost level housed a chapel for a god. The ziggurat called Entemenanki, which was seen and described by 6th- and 7th-century Greeks, might have been similar but could not have been known to the J writers in the 10th century B.C.E. Entemenanki has been described as "a marvel of colored glazed tiles over 295 feet in height."

The phrase "Let us" (instead of "let me") in the utterance ascribed to God, "Come, let us go down, and confuse their language there, so that they will not understand one another's speech" (Genesis 11:7), may be a remnant of an earlier myth referring to a council of gods or a council of advisers to the Heavenly King which was not edited out by the biblical writers.

Materials

- Newsprint and marker, or chalkboard and chalk
- Samples of foreign-language newspapers, books, and/or tapes
- A variety of boxes, in different sizes
- Pieces of styrofoam and cardboard
- Clean tin cans with no sharp edges
- Cylindrical boxes (such as the type oatmeal comes in)
- Other building materials suggested by your imagination, such as Legos, Tinkertoys, or marshmallows and toothpicks
- Scissors, glue, and masking tape
- A bell
- Copies of Song 6, "The Babel Song"

Preparation

- Think through your own answers to the motivating and discussion questions.
- Think through the Tower Building project, and experiment with various materials.
- Become familiar with "The Babel Song" with the help of the tape, or recruit someone else to teach it to the group.
- Arrange and set up your story/discussion, activity, and display areas.
- Collect some books, tapes, or newspapers in foreign languages, and plan your "Gathering" activity. If possible, invite someone who speaks another language to attend the first part of the session.

Session Plan

Gathering   Varies

As the children come in, invite them to sit around the table. Speak to them in a foreign language, have a guest speak to them in a foreign language, or play a portion of a foreign-language tape. (You may decide to do all of these.) Show the group copies of familiar children's stories published in foreign languages, and if you wish, read short sections of one or more. (This activity may be done at this time or just before the Tower Building activity.)

Motivating Questions   5-10 min.

Either stay at the table or move to a rug for the story and questions. Say a few words or sentences to the children in another language or in a made-up language of your own. Involve the children in a discussion based on the following question: How does it feel when you can't understand what someone is trying to tell you, or when you can't make others understand you?

Then say, "People have always wondered why there are so many different languages spoken in the world. Today's story of the Tower of Babel from Hebrew scripture gives one explanation of how this might have happened."

Definitions

asphalt waterproof cement made of oil
mortar cement used to hold building materials together

Read the Story   5 min.

Discussion   10 min.

Lead a discussion of the story guided by the following questions.
1. Why is communication so important? How can we communicate with others without using words?
2. Why were the people building the tower? If they had completed it, what might have happened?
3. How else might God have stopped the construction?
4. What are some of the languages spoken in the world today? (As the children respond to this question list the languages they name on newsprint or chalkboard.)
5. Where do people speak these different languages? Are there languages other than English spoken in your home? (Again, this would be a good time to show a few foreign-language books or newspapers or to play tapes in languages other than English.)
6. Can we get along even though we speak different languages?

Building a Tower Together   20 min.

Divide the children into groups of three, by letting them choose their partners or by assigning them to groups. Tell them that each group is to build a tower. Show them the materials available and encourage them to use their imaginations. Suggest that they take a few minutes to discuss and plan what they might do before they begin constructing the tower, but explain also that they can develop the plan further by talking it over as they go along. Remind them to be sure that everyone has a chance to contribute ideas.

After all the groups have begun their towers, ring a bell to get their attention and ask them to stop and listen for a moment. Then say, "From now until I ring the bell again, you may not speak in English but must speak in a strange language. If you know another language, you may use that, or you may just make up your own "private language." Offer an example of a made-up language. "Continue working together on your towers."

When you determine that they have had enough of speaking in strange tongues, ring the bell again and tell them they are now allowed to speak in English as they finish building their towers.

Invite them to display their completed towers. Those who finish first can look through the foreign language books or listen to the tapes. Allow time for cleaning up.

Closing   10 min.

Gather the children together. Ask them how it felt to work together when they were speaking their private languages and when they were speaking a common language.

Light the chalice candle. Sing "The Babel Song" a few times until they feel comfortable with it. Then close by saying, "For peaceful living, and for accomplishing things together, we need to be able to communicate with each other. We can learn to do this even though the earth's people no longer have one language."

The Tower of Babel

At one time, the whole earth had only one language and the same words. As people came from the east, they found a large flat area of land and settled there. They said to one another, "Come, let us make bricks, and burn them thoroughly." And they had brick for stone and mortar to make the bricks stay together. Then they said, "Come, let us build ourselves a city, and a tower with its top in the heavens, and let us make a name for ourselves, to keep from being scattered abroad upon the face of the whole earth."

And God came down to see the city and the tower, which the people had built. And God said, "Look, they are one people, and they have one language; and this is only the beginning of what they will do; nothing that they propose to do will now be impossible for them." It seemed to God that the people of the city were trying to be as big and important as God. So God said, "Come, let us go down, and confuse their language there, so that they will not understand one another's speech."

After God confused their language, people spoke different languages and couldn't understand one another well enough to continue building. The city, which was now called Babel, and its tower remained unbuilt because no one could understand the directions that were given for building. Arguments broke out because everyone misunderstood everyone else. Neighbor was against neighbor: they could no longer work things out by talking about them. The people, unable to talk to one another and not wanting to continue the fighting, scattered abroad over the face of all the earth.

SODOM AND GOMORRAH

Source: Genesis 18-19

Theme: Punishment

Goals for Participants

- to consider the meaning of wickedness and of punishment
- to become familiar with the story of Sodom and Gomorrah
- to consider other issues related to the story, such as how ancient people explained natural disasters and the value of following directions.

Background

The J writers wove together the story of Sodom and Gomorrah from several traditions. (Only Genesis 19:29 is by P.) The variety of sources contributes to the principal confusion in this story about the number of visitors and who they were. The visitors include three men, God, and two angels; these characters transform themselves back and forth from one to the other, but the pronouns that refer to them are inconsistent. It appears that the editors who transcribed the story simply didn't bother to clean up the inconsistencies among the different sources.

It may also be helpful to know what the Hebrews thought about angels. Angels were thought to be God's messengers, bringing divine messages, rewards, and punishment to earth, and usually appearing in human form. The activities of the "men and angels" in the Bible have precedents in other Near Eastern literature. For example, a Canaanite text explains that angels usually traveled in pairs for fear that one traveling alone would be harmed.

Abraham lived in Mamre, near Hebron. Sodom was considered one of the "cities of the Valley of Siddim," which scholars believe to be under the southern part of the Dead Sea. There are no traces of these cities to be found today, though there is in this area a crystalline salt mountain called Jebel Ustum which has eroded into numerous pinnacles. Any of these pinnacles could easily be imagined to be Lot's wife. This area also contains seepages of bitumen (asphalt) and petroleum, which could have been ignited by an earthquake or lightning, causing a frightening and seemingly inexplicable conflagration.

In biblical times, salt was used in a variety of ways—to enhance the taste of bland food, for medicinal purposes, and in rituals and sacrifices. To eat salt with another implied the existence of a mutual covenant. Thus it became a positive symbol, a symbol of life and life-giving properties. Salt could also have a negative meaning, serving as a reminder of the barrenness and desolation of salty areas.

The names Sodom and Gomorrah have become synonymous with wicked and sinful living. Exactly what kind of wickedness, however, is not totally clear. The story tells us that "the outcry against Sodom and Gomorrah is great and their sin is very grave." There are hints of sexual wrongdoing, with no specific details. The writers of the story probably understood wickedness in terms of a transgression of laws and a lack of concern for the needy.

Hearing this story, eight- and nine-year olds may ask what really happened to the people of Sodom and Gomorrah and to Lot's wife. Children of this age have moved beyond the "belief in magic" stage and want very much to know "what really happened." To hear this story along with modern scientific explanations of what may actually have occurred should further their exploration of these concerns. It is important, however, not to dismiss the story as only a primitive, irrelevant version of what modern science can explain better, since there are other important meanings to be found in the story.

The story of Sodom and Gomorrah speaks about the connection between ultimate powers and morality, and it raises issues of wickedness and punishment. Children of this age are interested in understanding what is right and what is wrong. They feel most comfortable with clear, fair systems of rules and consequences. This story offers them an excellent opportunity to discuss these concerns.

Materials

- Newsprint and colored markers, or a chalkboard and chalk
- Hole punch, string of yarn, and a round or oval paper plate
- A square piece of cloth for each headdress
- Three long strips of cloth for each headdress
- Pieces of cloth for scarves
- Silver and gold foil paper
- Wire coat hangers (one for each angel)
- Aluminum foil
- A belt and a roomy sweater for each angel
- Copies of Song 7, "Sodom and Gomorrah"

Preparation

- Think through your own answers to the motivating and discussion questions.
- Read carefully the instructions for the costumes (at the end of this session plan), decide how much your group can do, given the amount of time you have, and then simplify as necessary. Make a sample of each costume piece.
- Learn the song "Sodom and Gomorrah," or recruit someone else to lead it.
- Think through the steps you will use to guide the children through the role-playing activity.

Session Plan

Gathering   Varies

Engage early arrivals in this activity. Explain to the children that after they hear today's story they will act it out. Describe the costumes that will be needed—headdresses, scarves, wings, and God's mask. Show them the supplies and invite them to begin creating the costumes. (If all the children

arrive at the same time, do this project just before the role-playing activity.)

Motivating Questions   5-10 min.

Gather the children around a table or on a rug and say something like this: "People have always wondered why there are natural disasters like storms, floods, earthquakes, and volcanic eruptions. Long, long ago people thought that such things happened because their god or gods were angry at them and were trying to punish them for being wicked. Often they created a story to explain these natural disasters."

Then engage the children in a discussion of the following questions: "What does it mean to be wicked? What makes one wicked? How does it feel to be punished? Are the wicked always punished? If you have ever been punished for something you didn't do, how did that make you feel? How do you feel when you are punished for something you did do?"

Tell the children, "Today's story from Hebrew scripture may have been created to explain why there are volcanic eruptions, just as the story of Noah may have explained why there are floods."

Definition

pillar   an upright support or column

Read the Story   5 min.

Discussion   15 min.

Lead a discussion of the story guided by the following questions.

1. Long ago people thought that storms, floods, earthquakes, and volcanic eruptions happened because God was angry at them. Do you think a flood or volcanic eruption happens because God is punishing people? Do you think this kind of explanation helped people in ancient times understand the world around them? How would you feel about a God who did these things?
2. Lot's wife did not follow the angels' instructions. Why do you think she didn't? Was she being disobedient, or might she have been caring

about the other people?

3. Salt was very precious in ancient times, because it was necessary for life, yet it was often rare. Why do you think Lot's wife was turned into salt and not stone? Was it better to be turned into salt? Why?

4. Has anything bad ever happened to you as a result of not following directions? Why is it important to follow directions? Are there times when you shouldn't? Why?

Retelling the Story   10 min.

Ask the children to retell the story of the destruction of Sodom and Gomorrah. As they do, write down the key events on newsprint or a chalkboard. Go back over this list and decide with the children what scenes to role-play. They might be the following:

Scene 1: God and the two attendants (angels) come to visit Abraham, and God tells Abraham that Sodom is going to be destroyed.

Scene 2: Abraham asks God whether Sodom could be saved if there are 50 good people living there. 45? 40? 30? 20? 10?

Scene 3: The two attendants (angels) go on to Sodom, meet Lot and his family, determine that they are the only good people, and warn them to leave the city and not to look back.

Scene 4: Lot and his family escape, and the city is destroyed.

Scene 5: Lot's wife looks back and turns into a pillar of salt.

Making Costumes   15 min.

Ask the children to help you make a list of the characters who are needed to role play this story. These might include Abraham, God, Attendant/Angel #1, Attendant/Angel #2, Lot, Lot's wife, Lot's daughter #1, Lot's daughter #2, Wicked townsperson #1, Wicked townsperson #2, and others. Reduce or increase the number of angels, daughters, or townspeople to fit the size of your group.

Tell the children to make the following costume pieces for each character: headdresses for Abraham, Lot, and wicked male townspeople; scarves and jewelry for Lot's wife, daughters, and wicked female townspeople; wings for angels; and a mask for God.

Show your samples of the costume pieces, and explain how they were made. Invite the children to choose which piece each wishes to make.

The Role-Play   15 min.

With the children, determine who will play each part. Invite them to think about the characters they have chosen to play. Ask, "What happened to your character? What kinds of things did she or he do or say? How do you think your character may have felt as these things happened?"

Help children put on the costumes and role-play the scenes.

When the first role-play is over, ask the children to share thoughts they had as they were performing. Stimulate their thinking with questions such as, "How did it feel to be Abraham? The wicked townsperson? Lot? Did you like being your character? Why? Why not? Would some of you have played someone else's character differently?" Pick up on ideas coming out of the children's dialogue, and ask clarifying questions.

Closing   5 min.

Gather the children together and light the chalice candle. Sing "Sodom and Gomorrah" and then say, "In Bible times people believed that natural disasters such as floods or earthquakes were God's way of punishing them for their wickedness. They believed that if they were truly good—or, as they put it, if they kept 'the way of the Lord' by doing righteousness and justice—such things wouldn't happen. Today, we understand that such disasters are part of nature's way. We work to try to predict them, to control them if we can, and to make their effects less damaging. We don't think our goodness or our wickedness can change nature's ways, but we do agree that it's better for people to be good. When people are not good, we try to understand why they aren't, we give them consequences for rules they have broken, and then we help them get back on the right track."

If Your Time Is Limited

- Simplify the costume-making by precutting the circles for jewelry and the eyeholes, punching the holes in the masks, and braiding the strips of cloth yourself (or use only one strip of material to tie on the headdress).
- Have the informal discussion of the story while the children are working on their costumes.

If You Have More Time

- Ask the children to choose different parts and role-play the scenes again.

Making the Costumes

God Mask

Before making this mask, engage the participants in a discussion of what the God of this story (and the other Hebrew Bible stories) is like, and how one might make a mask to stand for that God. Initiate the discussion by saying, "In the Bible there are no actual descriptions of what God looked like, or what people thought God looked like. The Hebrews believed that we could never know what God was really like, and in fact they did not even allow people to make pictures of God. There are, however, many descriptions of what God thought, said, and did. The mask isn't really a picture of the Hebrew God, but it can give us an idea of what that God was like. How would you decorate the mask to look like God?"

One or two children can make the God mask. On a round or oval paper plate, cut out holes for the eyes and punch holes for the ears. Tie a piece of yarn through each earhole. Draw pictures and symbols as designs to depict the God the group has described.

Headdresses

Braid three strips of cloth, tying them together at each end. The braided rope goes over a square piece of cloth placed on the child's head.

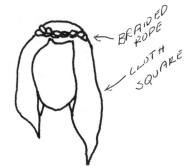

Jewelry

Cut out circles from gold and silver foil. Punch a hole near the top and string the circles onto string or yarn to make necklaces and bracelets.

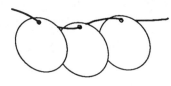

Angel Wings

Fold a coat hanger into the shape of two wings, with the curved hook folded down and hooked onto the lower part. (Illustration) Fold and crush the aluminum foil around each wing. Run a belt through the spaces at the top and attach it around the child wearing the wings.

You might like to say something like the following to the children as they work on the wings:

"In this story it isn't always clear who comes to visit Abraham and Lot. The story begins by saying that God came to visit Abraham, but then when he looks up he sees 'three men.' This makes it seem as if God and two attendants were the visitors. Later, Abraham has his discussion with God about the numbers. That same evening, the story says, two angels came to Lot, so it seems as if the two attendants were the same as the two angels. The Hebrews considered angels to be God's messengers. When you act out the story, whoever plays the attendants or angels can cover up their wings with a sweater in the first part of the story, and then take off the sweater when they go to Lot and become angels."

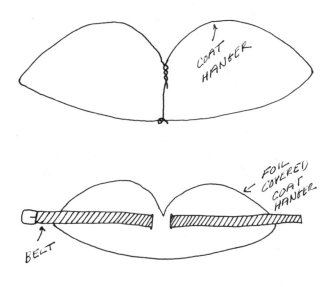

Sodom and Gomorrah

ONE DAY GOD, who was in disguise, and two attendants were traveling toward the cities of Sodom and Gomorrah. On the way they visited Abraham, who is called the father of ancient Israel.

God told Abraham that if Sodom was as wicked as people said, the city would be destroyed. Abraham was concerned because his nephew, Lot, lived in Sodom. Abraham said to God, "Will you indeed sweep away the righteous with the wicked? Suppose there are fifty good people in Sodom? Shall not the judge of all the earth do what is just?"

God said Sodom would be forgiven if there were fifty good people. Abraham pressed God on the point of numbers. He got God to promise not to destroy Sodom if there were forty-five, or forty, or thirty, or twenty, or even ten good people there.

When God's two attendants arrived in Sodom, it was obvious that the only good people in the whole city were Abraham's nephew Lot, Lot's wife, and their two daughters. The attendants, who were angels in disguise, told Lot to take his family and flee from the city before it was destroyed. They warned Lot and his family not to look back for even an instant at the fall of Sodom.

Lot escaped to a small town nearby, before the fire and brimstone—just like a volcanic eruption—came raining down on Sodom and Gomorrah. Lot's wife, who came later as the fire and brimstone were falling, disobeyed the warnings of the angels and looked back at the destruction of Sodom. She turned immediately into a pillar of salt.

Abraham went early in the morning to the place where he had stood before God. He looked down at Sodom and Gomorrah and toward the land of the plain and saw the smoke of the land going up like the smoke of a furnace.

ABRAHAM AND ISAAC

Source: Genesis 21-22

Theme: Change

Goals for Participants

- to become familiar with the story of Abraham and Isaac, and begin to understand why this story was important in the development of the Hebrew religion
- to understand that our ideas can change over time, and that the religious ideas of a whole people also change
- to explore the issue of trust, especially between children and adults.

Background

This is a difficult story for both children and adults, perhaps the most difficult in the Hebrew Bible. We have chosen to include it here because it is so well known that the children will probably hear it, or references to it, in other contexts. This session gives them an opportunity to hear and discuss the story within their own religious community.

People hear stories in very different ways. It is reasonable to assume that in biblical times this story was heard differently from the way we hear it today. Abraham was an established figure in the folk tradition of the Hebrews. People knew certain things about him—that he was good, that he was favored by God, that he was the father of their race. Because they knew these things about Abraham, when they heard the story of Abraham sacrificing his son Isaac, they anticipated the outcome. They knew Abraham to be a hero and were certain that God would treat him justly. As we listen to the same story today, we need to remind ourselves of what

these ancient people knew. Modern children make similar assumptions when they read comics or watch cartoons about superheroes. They know things will turn out all right in the end. They can enjoy the story with all its terror because they are sure that good will prevail.

Why has this story been preserved? What did the teller wish to convey? At first reading one is tempted to say that the message is "Trust God, and God will provide." But the story of Abraham and Isaac has come down to us because it marks a change in the sacrificial patterns of the ancient Hebrews. Until this time, human sacrifice, especially the sacrifice of a male child, was an accepted practice. By providing a ram for the burnt offering, God informs Abraham and his people that human sacrifice is no longer desired. This historic moment marks a transformation in the religion of the Hebrews. The story has been preserved to say, "We can never go back to the old way."

Here is an opportunity to talk about how religious ideas change. In many ancient societies, people not only listened for the voice of God but also believed that they must do whatever God asked of them, regardless of the consequences. Today, however, our ideas have changed: commitment to the will of God no longer includes surrendering our personal responsibility. Today, those who commit acts of violence because they have heard the voice of God instructing them find no solace in either the social or the legal system.

The Used-to-Thinks activity helps children examine how their ideas change over time and think about how unwise it would be to act based on their old ideas.

It seems likely that the story of Abraham and Isaac has itself undergone one or more changes. Scholars suggest that in the original E version, Isaac may actually have been sacrificed. The first ten verses of Genesis 22, leading up to the moment of sacrifice, use the E document's name for God, Elohim. In verse 11, where Abraham's hand is stayed, it is an angel of YHWH (J's name for God) who intervenes. This suggests that an ancient editor, who wished to emphasize the prohibition against human sacrifice, combined two versions of the story to get his point across. Verse 19, interestingly, seems to support the idea of Isaac's sacrifice, for it shows Abraham returning home with his men—with no mention of Isaac!

Abraham's behavior, and Isaac's, reflects the ancient Hebrew acceptance of the idea that God's demands must be obeyed. Isaac dutifully trusts his father, just as Abraham trusts God. Today, the issue of trust, especially trust between adults and children, raises some difficult questions. Our increased awareness of child abuse and abduction has made it necessary to tell our children, "It is possible that someone you trust will try to hurt you." Today's children must know that no one, not even an adult friend or family member, has the right to hurt or endanger them, and that they have the right to say "Stop!" and refuse to comply.

The story of Abraham and Isaac may raise important questions of trust for your group, especially trust between children and adults. If you are uncomfortable about any information shared by a child, be sure to consult with your minister or director of religious education.

Materials

- Scissors, glue, and crayons or colored markers
- Drawing paper
- *Conversations with Children*, by Edith Fisher Hunter, pp. 25-27 (optional)
- A small table or box, and a cloth to cover it
- Flowers for the altar
- Copies of Songs 8 and 9, "Abraham and Isaac" and "Rocka My Soul"

Preparation

- Consider the meaning the story has for you and any difficulties you may have in presenting it to the children.
- Think through your own answers to the motivating and discussion questions.

- Gather magazines and books that have pictures of familiar objects or activities common to the first half of the century—perhaps an old Sears catalog.
- Practice singing the "Abraham and Isaac" and "Rocka My Soul," or recruit someone else to lead them with the children.

Session Plan

Gathering   Varies

Display some magazines and books with pictures showing familiar objects and activities that date from the first half of the century. (Your public library may have a copy of an old Sears catalog.) As the children arrive, involve them in thinking of objects and practices that have changed since their grandparents were children. Suggest changes in clothing, household objects, entertainment, and so forth.

Used-to-Thinks   10 min.

Ask the children to sit in a comfortable position and close their eyes. Say, "We shall take a trip back in memory to a time when we were much younger, but before we do that let's sit quietly for several seconds with our eyes closed and breathe deeply. Take a deep, long breath— breathe in . . . and out. Continue your deep breaths in and out in silence for a moment. Keep your eyes closed." Pause for 30-40 seconds. Then begin speaking slowly, with pauses between phrases. "Now try to remember a time when you were younger. . . . Things looked different to you then. Other people were big, almost giants. . . . Remember how you had to look way up to see their faces? . . . There were lots of things those big people could do that you couldn't, or weren't allowed to do. . . . How did that feel? . . . Sometimes people laughed when you did something they thought was cute or misunderstood something . . . You were embarrassed, felt silly. . . . You didn't know why they thought it was funny. . . . Try to remember what it was that you did or said. . . . Did someone try to explain your mistake? . . . Now feel yourself growing bigger . . . and wiser. . . . You're beginning to understand more things. You're laughing at something you used to do or think. . . . Can you remember? . . . Sit quietly for a moment with your memories." Pause for about 30 seconds. "Now, let's open our eyes, and tell each other about some of what we used to think."

To get the discussion started, be prepared with examples of your own, or if you have a copy of Edith Hunter's *Conversations with Children*, use some of her examples. Three examples are included here. Use the following definitions of "used-to-thinks" to help the children: things we understood one way when we were very small, but understand quite differently now. Examples:

- "I used to think that everybody could swim without having to learn how—so I dived into the ocean just like my dad and got a big mouthful of salt water!"
- "I used to think that when I hid under the covers no one knew I was there."
- "I used to think all mushrooms were poisonous because I read a book about someone dying from a poison mushroom. Now I love mushrooms!"

Conclude by saying, "All of us have learned things as we have grown older. Some of the things we used to be very sure about we later found out were not true at all. In fact, we've just been laughing at a lot of those 'used-to-thinks.' Sometimes whole groups of people can change their ideas over a long period of time. Today we're going to hear a story of how the Hebrews, who lived long ago, changed their minds about the offerings they gave to God. Their ideas will seem strange to us, because religious ideas have changed so much since that long-ago time and are still changing today."

Motivating Questions   5 min.

Ask the children if they remember what the word "sacrifice" means. Remind them of the story about Cain and Abel. Then say, "Sometimes we think that the way society works today is the only way it can be. We don't always realize that society has changed, and is continuing to change. Society has its 'used-to-thinks,' just as people do. For instance, it was once considered acceptable to cut off the hand of a thief, but people today no longer think we should do that.

"Today's story from Hebrew scripture is about how society changed from making human sacrifices to making animal sacrifices. It is the story of Abraham, of whom you've already heard in the story of Sodom and Gomorrah, and his son, Isaac."

Definition

thicket thick shrubs or bushes

Read the Story   5 min.

Discussion   15 min.

Lead a discussion of the story guided by the following questions.

1. In the story, God seems to have a change of mind. At first God asks Abraham to sacrifice Isaac, but later God sends an angel to tell Abraham to stop. Did you ever change your mind right in the middle of doing something? Why? How did it turn out?

2. Is it easy to change your mind? Is it easy to change the way you have been doing things for a long time? What do you think it means when people say, "You can't teach an old dog new tricks?"

3. Why do you think that Abraham obeyed God when he asked him to offer Isaac as a sacrifice? Do you think he trusted that God would change his mind? Does trust always end up with good results?

4. When the ancient Hebrews heard this story, they knew that human sacrifice was no longer acceptable. However, the sacrifice of other animals was acceptable. Would that kind of offering be acceptable today? Does our church take an offering during the worship service? What kind of offering is it? How is it used?

Altar or Alter?   10 min.

Write both words on newsprint or the chalkboard. Say, "Here are two words that sound the same and are very important to this story. *Altar* (with an *a*) means a table or raised place where sacrifices are offered or which serves as the center of worship. *Alter* (with an *e*) means to change something. The story tells us that Abraham built an altar, which probably means he heaped up some stones, upon which he planned to carry out the burnt sacrifice. Many churches have an altar to help focus people's attention during their services. Does our church have an altar? How is it used?"

Drape a small table with an attractive cloth. Invite the children to arrange an altar or worship center from the items you have provided, such as flowers, a chalice, candles, shells, etc. Tell them that you will gather here for your closing.

Circle of Friends   15 min.

This trust game depends on the cooperation of the whole group. It works best with about eight children. The children form a tight circle, shoulder to shoulder. One child stands in the middle, body stiff, arms glued to his or her sides, feet "glued" to floor. Then he or she falls straight backwards to be caught in the outstretched hands of the others. As the group becomes more proficient, they can pass the center person around the circle or back and forth across the middle. Give everyone a chance to be in the center. Be sure to stand close by as the children learn this game, and be careful to explain the need for cooperation in order to make it work.

Closing   5 min.

Ask the children to sit on the floor in front of the altar. Light the chalice or candle and say, "People and ideas change. We've seen that in the story of Abraham and Isaac. Our altar is very different from the altars of the early Hebrews; our ideas and our way of life are different, too. Let's be thankful that we are changing and growing all the time."

If Your Time Is Limited

• Omit the Circle of Friends game.

If You Have More Time

• Sing or listen to "Abraham and Isaac" in the songbook. If your group is not enthusiastic about singing, try this as a choral reading, with the group reading God's part, and a different solo voice responding at the end of each verse as Abraham.

• Learn "Rocka My Soul" from the songbook and sing it as part of the closing, or while you play the Circle of Friends game.

Preparation for Next Session

For the next session, the story of Jacob and Esau, send a letter to the children's parents early in the week. See this sample:

Dear parents of our Timeless Themes members,

Next Sunday we will hear the story of Jacob and Esau from the Hebrew Bible. One of our activities will be to make a "mess of pottage," or stew. We ask that each child bring approximately 1/2 cup of a diced vegetable to contribute to the pot. Potatoes, carrots, spinach, celery, onions— almost any vegetable will do. Please stop by our room after the worship service for a sample of our cooking!

Sincerely,
Leader's Name

If appropriate, add this postscript.
P.S. Since the children will be attending the worship service before the session, please tell them to stop by the room first to add their vegetables to the stew. Thank you.

Abraham and Isaac

ABRAHAM AND HIS WIFE, SARAH, had a son when they were both very old. They named this son Isaac.

When Isaac was still a boy, God tested Abraham's faith. God said to Abraham, "Take your son, your only son Isaac, whom you love, and go to the land of Moriah, and offer him there as a burnt offering on one of the mountains that I shall show you." Abraham did as he was told, taking two servants, wood for the fire for the burnt offering, and Isaac. After three days they arrived at the mountain, and Abraham told the servants to wait while he and Isaac went up on the mountain to worship.

Abraham had Isaac carry the wood for the burnt offering, and Abraham himself took the coals for the fire and the knife. Isaac said, "Father!"

And Abraham said, "Here I am, my son."

Isaac said, "The fire and the wood are here, but where is the lamb for a burnt offering?"

Abraham said, "God will provide the lamb for the burnt offering, my son." So the two of them walked on together.

When they came to the place which God had shown him, Abraham built an altar there, and laid the wood in order. He bound Isaac and laid him on the altar on top of the wood. Then Abraham reached out his hand and took the knife to kill his son. But the angel of God called to him from heaven and said, "Abraham, Abraham!"

And he said, "Here I am."

And the angel said, "Do not lay your hand on the boy or do anything to him; for now I know that you fear God, since you have not withheld your son, your only son, from me."

Abraham looked up and saw a ram, caught in a thicket by its horns. Abraham took the ram and offered it up as a burnt offering instead of his son.

Then the angel said, "I will indeed bless you, and I will make your offspring as numerous as the stars of heaven and as the sand that is on the seashore. And your offspring shall own the towns of their enemies, and by your offspring shall all the nations of the earth gain blessing for themselves, because you have obeyed my voice."

JACOB AND ESAU

Source: Genesis 25-27

Theme: Deception

Goals for Participants

- to become familiar with the story of Jacob and Esau from the Hebrew Bible
- to explore the issue of deception, in the story and in their own experience
- to learn the meaning of the phrase "to sell one's birthright for a mess of pottage."

Background

The theme of deception appears throughout the world's literature, where tricksters appear in all shapes and sizes, from spiders to human beings. Sometimes the trickster becomes the victim of his or her own deception, but just as often he or she appears as the bold initiator of something new. Tricksters are often a means of pointing out human folly, as in the Lakota story of Iktomi the spider, who traps the ducks that stupidly follow his dance directions without thinking for themselves. "Don't be fooled" is the message of this and many other trickster stories.

Perhaps "don't be fooled" is also the intended theme of the Jacob and Esau story. Certainly, the message that has come down through the ages is one of caution lest one "sell one's birthright for a mess of pottage." This story has another obvious theme, however—that of the establishment of the patriarchal line. Abraham, Isaac, and Jacob are a familiar trio in Hebrew literature, and this story tells how the third member of the trio was chosen. There is no doubt what the outcome will be, for while the twins are still in the womb Rebekah is told by YHWH that "the older shall be servant to the younger." The only question is how the drama will unfold.

Being "firstborn" held special meaning for the early Hebrews; family honor and property passed on to the firstborn male of each family. The theme of the firstborn is found throughout the J writer's account of history, and each successive story emphasizes the struggle for rightful inheritance. Cain kills Abel, thus the line descends through him; Shem, the eldest son of Noah, is favored by YHWH and given his father's blessing to carry on the line. Again and again, we are reminded of the importance of both the birth position and a father's blessing.

In the ancient world, blessings and curses were thought to be accurate predictions of the future. Biblical literature records many such examples, and the J writer in particular illustrates the flow of history by a series of blessings and curses. These important pronouncements shaped the nation of Israel. Bernhard Anderson explains that "like an arrow in flight, they could not be retracted. So Jacob, having received his father's blessing, was destined to gain pre-eminence over Esau (Edom), as Israel later did, especially in the time of David" (*Understanding the Old Testament*, p. 176).

What about the moral content of the story? Does it teach children to be dishonest? More likely, the story of Jacob and Esau teaches them that treachery and deception are part of everyday life, and that heroes and heroines are not always what they seem:
"Sunday School versions of this story often try to vindicate Jacob. With slight changes or reinterpretations, they make Jacob the good son and Esau the bad one. But the J writer was more sophisticated than his later interpreters. He told a story in which Jacob was courageous and clever, but also dishonest. He did not make his heroes perfect. . . . His task was rather to compose a story that reflected and explained the political

and social realities of the world that he knew" (Richard Friedman, Who Wrote the Bible?, p. 69).

Children in the early elementary grades have had ample experience with deception, often as victims of older children. The Jacob and Esau story is certainly one they can relate to their own lives. Indeed, the story has special appeal because it is the younger brother who outwits the older, a comforting fantasy for children this age.

Materials

- Pencils, colored markers or crayons, glue, and tape
- Copies of Song 10, "Jacob's Ladder"
- A large pot, cooking utensils, cups or bowls, and spoons
- Ingredients for pottage (see recipe below)
- Light cardboard suitable for cutting, such as cereal boxes or file folders
- Scraps of yarn, leather, fabric, and fake fur
- Sticks about 12" long, one per child

Preparation

- Early in the week, write to the children's parents about the pottage activity (see sample letter at end of previous session plan).
- Think through your own answers to the motivating and discussion questions.
- Depending on the number of children, make 2 or more cardboard puppet patterns (see Resource 1).
- Make a puppet so that you can explain the process clearly to the children.
- Start the pottage (see recipe below).
- Plan how you will fit pottage-cooking into your session time. If necessary, arrange to use the church kitchen.
- Practice singing "Jacob's Ladder," or recruit someone else to lead it.

A Mess of Pottage

Begin this activity at the gathering time or before the session begins. Bring the pottage to a full boil before adding the children's vegetables. If using an electric saucepan, this may take a long time. If you can, bring the mixture to a boil in a regular pan on top of a stove, then transfer it to an electric pan in your room.

The cooking will be easier if you can use an electric saucepan, dutch oven, or large fry pan in your room. Another option, if feasible in your setting, is to have the group meet in the kitchen.

This recipe is for Red Lentil Pottage, which is probably close to what Jacob cooked for Esau. Why red lentil stew? Because the story says that Esau became known after this incident as "Red." The word for red in Hebrew is *edom*. That is, Esau is traditionally regarded as "the father of the Edomites" (Friedman, *Who Wrote the Bible?*, p. 68).

Red Lentil Pottage
2 cups dried lentils
2 1/2 quarts water (10 cups)
1 16-oz. can tomatoes
salt and pepper to taste
4 or 5 cups of diced vegetables, 1 cup of which are onions

The night before, place lentils in pan with water and bring to a boil. Turn off the heat and allow to set overnight. If desired, for more flavor, add canned tomatoes (with green peppers and celery), garlic, and bay leaf with the lentils.

In the morning, bring the lentils to a boil again, then lower the heat and simmer about 1 1/2 hours. When the children arrive, turn up the heat so that the mixture boils. Add diced vegetables, tomatoes (if not cooked with the lentils), and salt and pepper to taste. Lower heat to a simmer and cook about 30 minutes, or until vegetables are tender.

Makes 9-10 cupfuls, enough for a crowd.

Session Plan

Gathering   Varies

As the children arrive, engage them in preparing the pottage. When everyone has arrived and the pottage is simmering, proceed with the next activity. (If the children arrive together from a worship service, you will have asked in your letter that they stop by the room before the service to add their contributions to the pottage.)

Motivating Questions   **5 min.**

Gather at a table or on the rug and briefly discuss the following: Sometimes we want something so much that we think of cheating to get it. Have you ever been cheated? What happened? Have you ever tried to win by being unfair? What happened?

Then say, "Today's story from Hebrew scripture is another about fighting between brothers. Jacob and Esau fought over which one their father, Isaac, liked best."

Definition

pottage stew

Read the Story   **5 min.**

Discussion   **10-15 min.**

Lead a discussion of the story guided by the following questions.
1. In the story, Isaac seemed to like Esau better. Why do you think this was? Was it because he was a hunter? Or because he was older? Or because Isaac may have seen Jacob cheating at things as he was growing up?
2. The story of Cain and Abel was also about the jealousy of two brothers. What is the difference between the way Cain and Abel handled their jealousy and the way Jacob and Esau handled theirs?
⚱ 3. If you are tricked into making a promise, do you think you have to keep that promise?
4. How do you think Esau felt when he found out what Jacob did? How do people feel when they are tricked or deceived? Have you ever played a trick on your parents? Your brother? Your sister?

Making Puppets   **10-15 min.**

Using the cardboard patterns, have each child trace one puppet on cardboard, cut it out, and decorate it to resemble Jacob, Esau, Isaac, or Rebekah. Ask the children if they remember a few distinguishing characteristics of the brothers. (Jacob was smooth-skinned; Esau was hairy.

Esau probably had red hair. Jacob was a shepherd; Esau was a hunter.) Encourage the children to glue yarn scraps and fabric to their figures, as well as decorating with felt markers or crayons. Pieces of fake fur can be glued to Esau's arms to make him hairy.

Tape a stick to the back of each figure to complete the puppet.

Have a music assistant play and sing songs from the songbook, or play the song tape, as the children are making their puppets.

Puppet Conversations   **15 min.**

Ask the children to find a partner who has a different puppet character from theirs. Ask them to think about how these people might feel at the end of the story, having played such a trick or having been fooled. Would Rebekah and Jacob feel guilty about what they had done, or proud of their success? Was Isaac entirely convinced that Esau received his blessing, or did he feel doubtful and uneasy? Was Esau angry? At whom? Once they have thought about the possible feelings of their characters, tell each pair to hold a puppet conversation about their feelings. Here's the beginning of such a conversation between Isaac and Rebekah.

ISAAC: Rebekah, I'm not sure I did the right thing.
REBEKAH: What do you mean, Isaac?
ISAAC: For a moment there I was confused. I love both my boys, and sometimes I have trouble telling them apart. Tell me, did I do it right? Did I really bless Esau?
REBEKAH: You felt his hand, didn't you?

After the children have held their conversations in private, ask if a few will repeat them for the whole group.

Closing   **10 min.**

Serve the pottage. Light a chalice or candle and, when everyone has been served, say a blessing before eating, such as, "We have learned today about the importance of blessings in biblical times. Let us say a short blessing before we begin to eat. Oh God, we are thankful for this food, for good health and good friends."

If Your Time Is Limited

- Use canned lentil soup as a base for the pottage, and bring it to a boil before the children add finely chopped vegetables.
- Have the children begin the puppets during discussion time, adding the finishing touches at the end of the session.
- Assign two or three children to set the table for eating, while others are completing their puppets.

If You Have More Time

- Sing "Jacob's Ladder" from the songbook.
- Remind the children of the "begats" from Session 1. See if they can connect the characters in Sessions 7 and 8, using the biblical term *begat*. Write it down to use in Session 9, "Joseph and His Brothers." For example, Sarah and Abraham begat Isaac, and Rebekah and Isaac begat Jacob and Esau.

Jacob and Esau

JACOB AND ESAU WERE TWINS. Their mother, Rebekah, noticed that even when she was carrying them in her womb, they didn't get along. When they were born, Esau was born first, and Jacob followed, holding onto Esau's heel.

When they grew up, Esau became a hunter and was his father's favorite, for Isaac loved to eat the meat that Esau brought home. Jacob became a shepherd and was the favorite of his mother, Rebekah.

One day Jacob was cooking pottage when Esau came home. Esau asked for some because he was very hungry. Jacob agreed to give him some if Esau would give Jacob the right to be called the firstborn. Esau agreed.

In those days being the firstborn was very important, because the oldest son inherited all of the land, animals and other property left by his parents. Younger sons got nothing. Therefore, Jacob certainly made the better deal by getting Esau to give up his birthright for a bowl of stew!

As Isaac grew older, his eyes grew dim and he could not see. He called for Esau and asked him to go hunting with his bow and arrow for the game Isaac loved to eat. He wanted Esau to prepare the meat and serve it to him, so that he could give Esau his final blessing before he died.

A deathbed blessing was very important to people in ancient times, for they believed that a strong power was released with the blessing which would protect the person to whom it was given. Therefore, Esau was eager to receive this blessing.

Rebekah was listening when Isaac spoke to Esau, and when Esau left to hunt, she told Jacob what had happened. Rebekah commanded, "Go to the flock, and get me two choice baby goats, so that I may prepare from them savory food for your father, such as he likes; and you shall take it to your father to eat, so that he may bless you before he dies."

But Jacob said, "Look, my brother Esau is a hairy man, and I am a man of smooth skin. Perhaps my father will feel me, and I shall seem to be mocking him, and bring a curse on myself and not a blessing." Rebekah told Jacob just to do as she had said and he would receive no curse.

So Jacob brought the goats, and Rebekah prepared the meat the way Isaac loved it. Then she dressed Jacob in Esau's best clothes and put the skins of the goats over Jacob's hands and neck.

Jacob brought the food to his father, saying, "My father."

"Who are you, my son?' Isaac asked.

"I am Esau, your firstborn. I have done as you told me; now sit up and eat of my food, so that you may bless me."

But his father answered, "How is it you have found it so quickly, my son?"

Jacob replied, "Because God, your God, granted me success."

Then Isaac said to Jacob, "Come near, that I may feel you, my son, to know whether you are really my son Esau or not." So Jacob went up to Isaac, who felt him and said, "The voice is Jacob's voice, but the hands are the hands of Esau." Isaac asked him again, "Are you really my son Esau?"

"I am," replied Jacob.

So Isaac ate the food Jacob brought, and drank. Then Isaac said, "Come near and kiss me, my son."

When Jacob came near and kissed his father, Isaac smelled the smell of Esau's clothes. Isaac was convinced and blessed Jacob. So, because of the trick Jacob and his mother played on Esau and Isaac, Jacob not only inherited all of his father's property but also received his deathbed blessing.

Today, when people feel they have been cheated, they say they gave up their birthright for a mess of pottage.

JOSEPH AND HIS BROTHERS

Source: Genesis 37

Theme: Jealousy/Envy

Goals for Participants

- to become familiar with the story of Joseph and his brothers
- to explore their own feelings of jealousy and envy
- to consider the issue of favoritism.

Background

The story of Joseph and his brothers has always appealed to children, for even those with no siblings have felt the strain of competition for their parents', teacher's, or coach's attention. Joseph's fancy coat could be a new catcher's mitt or a special party dress—a symbol of favoritism as seen through the eyes of the less favored.

The coat itself is traditionally called "many-colored," but most translations of the Bible make no reference to color, using such words as "decorated" or "fancy," with "full" or "long" sleeves.

The story of Joseph describes how the nomadic Hebrew people came to live in Egypt, and thus it lays the foundation for the Exodus, the central event in Jewish history. The Joseph story takes the Hebrews from Canaan to Egypt, and the Exodus returns them many generations later to settle on the land. The story concentrates more on the elements of family life than on world events, but it concurs with other historical sources for the 17th century B.C.E.: "The account of the Hebrew descent into Egypt accords well with the circumstances in Egypt. It is quite credible that the pressure of famine forced Jacob's family to settle in 'the land of Goshen,' the

fertile area in the eastern part of the Nile Delta. Semi-nomads in Palestine, a land that depended on seasonal rainfall, would naturally turn their eyes in time of drought toward Egypt, where the periodic overflow of the Nile irrigated the land. We know from Egyptian records that it was the practice for Egyptian officials to allow hunger-stricken people from Palestine and the Sinaitic peninsula to enter the Delta frontier" (Anderson, *Understanding the Old Testament*, p. 47).

The Joseph story was told in the oral traditions of both north (E) and south (J), but there are variations in the tellings. The two writers disagree, for example, on who wished to save Joseph from death. In Genesis 37:21 (E) we have Reuben pleading, "Let us not take his life," while in 37:27 (J) it is Judah who pleads, "Come, let us . . . not lay our hands on him, for he is our brother, our own flesh." Since the J writer recorded the traditions of Judah, the southern kingdom, it is hardly surprising that brother Judah is the hero of his version of the tale. Sometime later, a skilled editor is thought to have blended the two stories to give both brothers credit for saving Joseph's life.

Because this session invites the children to explore their feelings of jealousy and envy, it is important to allow them sufficient time to express the feelings they experience during the Favorite Game activity.

Materials

- Colored markers
- Scissors (one or two pairs that will cut cloth)
- An old sheet or large piece of solid-color fabric (or a hospital gown)
- A scarf or sash
- Newspapers
- Instant camera with flash and film
- Copies of Song 11, "Joseph"

- A recording of "My Favorite Things" from *The Sound of Music* (optional)

Preparation

- Think through your own answers to the motivating and discussion questions.
- Using the pattern and instructions in Resource 2, prepare a large, solid-color coat. An alternative is to obtain a solid-colored hospital gown and allow the children to decorate that.
- Become familiar with the song "Joseph."

Session Plan

Gathering   Varies

As the children arrive, play "My Favorite Things" from *The Sound of Music* if you have it. When everyone has arrived, gather the children into a circle on the rug or at a table.

Motivating Questions   10 min.

Engage the children in a brief discussion based on the following. Have you ever been jealous about gifts someone else received? Did you ever think, "Her present is better than mine?" On someone else's birthday, did you wish you were getting presents too? Has anyone ever been jealous of you?

Then say, "We all have favorite things—our favorite ice cream, movie, TV program, school subject. But when a teacher or a coach has a favorite pupil or player, that seems unfair, and it can cause jealousy. And it's even worse when favoritism happens in a family.

"In biblical stories, being jealous of your brother seems to have been very common. Cain was jealous of Abel because God seemed to like Abel better; and Jacob was jealous of Esau because Isaac liked Esau better. Today's story from Hebrew scripture is about Jacob's twelve sons, and how jealousy caused trouble in their lives."

Definition

sheaf   a bundle of cut stalks of grain tied together in a roll with twine

Read the Story   5 min.

Discussion   10-15 min.

Lead a discussion of the story guided by the following questions.
1. In this story, Joseph's brothers had some very strong feelings. Can you name some of these feelings? Why do you think they felt this way? What are some other ways they might have dealt with their feelings?
2. People in ancient times believed dreams were messages about the future. If you were one of Joseph's brothers, how would you feel about the dreams he reported? Do you think dreams are important?
3. What is a slave? What do you think Joseph might do as a slave?

A Very Special Coat   10 min.

Spread the coat you have prepared on a table covered with newspapers. Encourage the children to make the coat "very special" by decorating it with colored markers.

When the coat has been decorated, select one child to wear it. Put a sash around the waist. Make a big fuss about how great it looks. Take the child's picture wearing the coat. Perhaps one snapshot could be taken alone, and one with the group. Show everyone how nice it looks and tell them how fortunate this child is to be able to wear it.

The Favorite Game   20 min.

With the children seated in a circle, say that you are Jacob, and that the child who is wearing the coat is Joseph, your favorite child. Have "Joseph" sit on your right.

Begin the game by saying, "My favorite food is _____." Going around the circle to your left, ask each child to state his or her favorite food. End with Joseph. When Joseph has completed the sentence, repeat what Joseph said. Begin another round, with your favorite movie, TV program, sport, thing to drink, etc. Again, repeat what Joseph has said before beginning the next round.

For your last round, say "My favorite piece

of clothing is _____." When it is Joseph's turn, have him (her) go to the center of the circle and model the coat, bragging about it a little. Conclude by saying, "Joseph's favorite piece of clothing is this coat that I gave him."

Invite the children to show by their facial expressions and body language how that makes them feel, while you and Joseph pretend not to notice.

Encourage the children to discuss the feelings this game evoked in them. Ask, "How did you feel when I chose _____ to wear the coat? Did you feel better or worse as the game went on? What kind of a game was it when all the attention was on one person? Can you suggest a way we could have played it to make it fairer for everyone? Can you understand how Joseph's brothers felt? How do you think Joseph felt? And Jacob?" Give everyone time to contribute.

Group Photos   10 min.

Tell the children that you'd like to take a few more photos, but that this will require some planning. You want everyone to get inside the coat! They must be very careful so that the coat doesn't rip. Accept their suggestions on how do it, such as adding one child at a time. When all are assembled, take a picture or two. (You might suggest taking one picture of the boys and one of the girls in the coat, since children of this age are often uncomfortable getting physically close to the opposite sex.)

Closing   5 min.

Gather the children in a circle. When all are quiet, light a candle or chalice and read aloud these words adapted from the prayer of St. Francis of Assisi.
"Where hate rules, let us bring love; where sorrow, joy."
"Let us strive more to comfort others than to be comforted, to understand others, than to be understood, to love others more than to be loved."
"For it is in giving that we receive, and in forgiving that we are ourselves forgiven."

Sing "Joseph," verses 1-3. Collect the song sheets to use at the next session. Before the next session, display the coat and photos in your room or on a hallway bulletin board.

If Your Time Is Limited

• Omit the Favorite Game, but be sure to stress the element of favoritism when one child tries on the Very Special Coat for the photography session.

If You Have More Time

• Sing verses 1-3 of "Joseph" two or three times to learn it well.
• Add Joseph to the list of begats you began last week—Rachel and Jacob begat Joseph. (Because Jacob's children had several different mothers, it is probably less confusing to refer only to Joseph. The listing of all twelve brothers is found in Genesis 35:23-26, and their sister, Dinah, in 34:1.)

Joseph and His Brothers

ONE OF JACOB'S SONS was named Joseph. When Joseph was seventeen years old, two of his older brothers did something wrong, and Joseph told their father. This made Joseph's brothers angry. They were also jealous because Jacob gave Joseph a very fine coat with long sleeves. This was a much more luxurious coat than they had, for their coats were sleeveless and short. Now they knew that Jacob loved Joseph more than he loved any of them, and they hated him, and could not speak peaceably to him.

Joseph did nothing to make his brothers like him more. In fact, he made matters worse. He told them about a dream he had in which they were binding sheaves of wheat in a field. He said, "Suddenly, my sheaf rose and stood upright; and your sheaves gathered around it and bowed down to my sheaf." His brothers said, "Are you indeed to rule over us?" So they hated him even more because of his dreams and his words.

Then Joseph went too far. He told of another dream in which the sun, the moon, and eleven stars bowed down to him. His father was upset at this dream, and he scolded Joseph. "What is this dream that you have dreamed? Shall I and your mother and your brothers indeed come to bow ourselves to the ground before you?'

Later, when his brothers were watching the sheep and goats in a far-off field, Jacob sent Joseph to see if all was well with his brothers and the flock. He told Joseph to bring word back to him.

Joseph's brothers saw Joseph coming in the distance. They were still jealous, so they said, "Come now, let us kill him and throw him into one of the pits; then we shall say that a wild animal has devoured him, and we shall see what will become of his dreams."

But Reuben, the oldest, said, "Shed no blood; throw him into this pit here in the wilderness, but lay no hand on him." Reuben was planning to rescue Joseph and return him to their father.

When Joseph arrived they took off his fancy coat and threw him into a dry pit. Then they sat down to eat, and, looking up, they saw a caravan on its way to Egypt. Another brother, Judah, suggested they make a profit by selling Joseph into slavery. All the brothers present agreed, and it was done.

When Reuben returned to the pit to get Joseph out, he found the pit empty. He was very upset, but his brothers did not tell him what they had done. Instead, they took Joseph's coat and poured goat's blood on it and sent it to their father, saying they had found it.

Jacob recognized the coat and said, "It is my son's coat; a wild animal has eaten him; Joseph is without doubt torn to pieces." Jacob mourned for Joseph and refused to be comforted.

Meanwhile, the traders of the caravan sold Joseph in Egypt to Potiphar, the Pharaoh's captain of the guard.

SESSION 10

JOSEPH AND THE DREAMS

Source: Genesis 39-48

Theme: Giving and Forgiving

Goals for Participants

- to think about forgiveness for wrongdoing
- to become familiar with the rest of the story of Joseph
- to discover other themes in the story, such as the meaning of dreams and famines.

Background

The story of Joseph is the final section of the Patriarchal history. It is unusually long and intricate, integrating evenly the J and E sources. It is a dramatic story of universal human appeal, with the theology well in the background. Scholars believe this story to be related to an Egyptian story called "The Tale of Two Brothers." The story of Joseph's seduction by Potiphar's wife may also be related to an Egyptian tale, the myth of Bata and Anubis.

The story's details appear to be authentic. It was common for slaves to be taken from Canaan to Egypt, and many Semitic names are found on Egyptian slave lists. The description of Joseph's position as vizier and the humility he displayed in the exercise of power and in wearing the symbols of his office—fine linen, a gold chain, and a signet ring—reflect what is known of Egyptian customs. To bow before such an official was also the accepted practice.

It is likely that this story takes place during the time the Hyksos ruled Egypt (1730-1570 B.C.E.). The Hyksos, who introduced the horse and chariot to Egypt, were themselves foreigners, and it is thought that they would have been more likely to appoint a foreigner to high office and more likely to be interested in a foreign god.

Dreams were of great importance in ancient times. They were believed to contain messages from the divine and were expected to be shared for their meaning to be properly understood. Dream interpretation was considered a science in Egypt, and certain manuscripts even list the meaning of various symbols for interpretation.

Although the word *forgiveness* is not used in this story, the theme is certainly one of wrongdoing, repentance, forgiveness, and reconciliation. These are familiar themes in the Hebrew Bible, where human relationships are viewed in relation to the covenant between the Hebrews and God. To sin is to stray from God's will, and part of what God expects is that men and women treat one another with justice and kindness. Repentance comes before forgiveness, and in this story Joseph tests his brothers to see if they are truly sorry for what they did.

The story of Joseph raises several appropriate issues for eight- and nine-year olds. They will identify with the issue of sibling rivalry, since jealousy of brothers and sisters and concerns about favoritism are very real for children at this age. As they develop more relationships with friends and adults beyond the family circle, the issue of what it takes to live harmoniously with others also takes on new importance. And, while eight- and nine-year olds are usually outwardly directed, they have an interest in their dreams.

Materials

- Craft or mural paper and colored markers
- Newsprint or chalkboard
- Joseph's special coat
- Light cardboard, and hole punch, and string
- Copies of Song 11, "Joseph"
- Cassette recording of *Joseph and the Amazing Technicolor Dreamcoat* (optional)

Preparation

- Think through your own answers to the motivating and discussion questions.
- Become familiar with verses 4-9 of the song "Joseph," and practice singing them.

Session Plan

Gathering   Varies

Spread the mural or craft paper and markers out on a table. As the children arrive, gather them around the table and invite them to draw something they remember from a dream. Explain to them that they may draw anywhere they wish on the paper and may draw more than one remembrance.

Motivating Questions   5-10 min.

Gather the children on the rug or around the table and engage them in a discussion of the following. "When someone does something hurtful to another, it can be hard to forgive him or her. Can you think of a time when someone had trouble forgiving another person? It may be a real person or someone in a story you read. How do you think the person who did the hurting felt? How did the person who was hurt feel?"

Then say, "Sometimes friends, or even members of our own families, treat us badly. It's hard to forget that they have hurt us, and often we feel like hurting them back. Imagine how hard it would be to give something good to a person who has hurt you.

"In today's story from Hebrew scripture, we will hear how Joseph felt about his brothers after they sold him into slavery."

Definition

prosper to be very successful

Read the Story   5 min.

Discussion   5 min.

Lead a discussion of the story guided by the following questions.
1. Why do you think Joseph forgave his brothers? Would you have? If you were able to forgive your brothers, would you be willing to give them food as Joseph did? Why or why not?
2. Could you have understood what the Pharaoh's dream meant? Have you ever had a dream come true?
3. What is a famine? Are there famines today? Where? Can we help or do anything about famine?

Act Out the Story   25 min.

Explain to the children that they will act out the story of Joseph and his brothers, and with them determine the parts and who will play them. The characters might include Joseph, Pharaoh, Pharaoh's butler, Pharaoh's chief baker, Prison guard, Jacob, Brothers' wives, and Joseph's brothers: Reuben, Gad, Simeon, Asher, Levi, Dan, Judah, Naphtali, Issachar, Benjamin, and Zebulun.

If you have a small group, those who play the Pharaoh, the butler, the baker, and the guard can double as Jacob and the brothers or brothers' wives. Have the children make nametags for the characters they will play. To do this, they will cut a piece of cardboard, write the name on it, punch two holes, cut string long enough to go around the neck, and draw the string through the holes. Those who are playing two parts can write one name on one side and the other name on the other side.

Ask the children to retell the story. Then together decide on the scenes, writing them on newsprint or the chalkboard. For example:

Scene 1: The baker and butler tell Joseph their dreams.
Scene 2: The Pharaoh has a dream; the butler remembers Joseph; Pharaoh summons him, and Joseph interprets the Pharaoh's dream.
Scene 3: Joseph is in charge of everything; his brothers come to him and ask for food; he keeps one and tells the others to bring Benjamin.

Scene 4: Jacob does not want to let Benjamin go; he misses Joseph and worries that he will lose Benjamin too.

Scene 5: The brothers return with Benjamin; Joseph tells them who he is.

Scene 6: The brothers return with Jacob.

Decide where the various scenes will take place. Tell the children to think about how it feels to do something wrong and how it feels to have someone wrong you; how it feels to be forgiven and how it feels to forgive. Have Joseph put on the fancy coat, and the others their nametags.

Engage the children in acting out the story.

Closing   5 min.

Gather together, light the chalice or candle, and sing verses 4-9 of "Joseph." Close by saying, "All of us make mistakes and we sometimes hurt other people. It helps if we say we're sorry and the other person can forgive us, or if we can forgive someone who hurt us, as Joseph did with his brothers."

Preparation for Next Session

Send a letter to parents alerting them to the story you will be telling next week and explaining that adoption will be one of the topics of discussion. See this sample:

Dear parents,

This coming Sunday in our Timeless Themes group we will hear the story "Moses and the Bulrushes." Since the story describes how Moses is given up by his Hebrew mother and adopted by the Egyptian Pharaoh's daughter, there will be some discussion about adoption. We will emphasize the love of the biological mother who, out of fear for his safety, gave her child up, and the love of the adoptive mother who raised him and cared for him.

If these are sensitive issues for your child, either because he or she is adopted or because of a friend or relative who is, we would appreciate a chance to talk with you this coming week. You may wish to mention something about it to your child before the session or be alert to any concerns expressed after the session.

We always appreciate hearing from you.

Sincerely,
Leader's Name

Joseph and the Dreams

After Joseph was bought by Potiphar, Pharaoh's captain of the guard, Joseph became the head of Potiphar's household. Joseph prospered until he was falsely accused of insulting his master's wife and was sent to prison.

While Joseph was in prison, the Pharaoh's chief cupbearer and his chief baker, who were also in prison, had dreams that troubled them. They told their dreams to Joseph, who told them the meaning of their dreams, part of which was that the cupbearer would return to work, but the baker would die.

As Joseph predicted, the cupbearer returned to Pharaoh's service, but the baker was hanged. Yet the chief cupbearer did not remember Joseph. It was not until two years later, when the Pharaoh had a dream that needed interpreting, that the cupbearer remembered Joseph.

The Pharaoh sent for Joseph and said,

"In my dream I was standing on the banks of the Nile; and seven cows, fat and sleek, came up out of the Nile and fed in the reed grass; and seven other cows came up after them, poor, very ugly, and thin. Never had I seen such ugly ones in all the land of Egypt. The thin and ugly cows ate up the first seven fat cows, but when they had eaten them no one would have known that they had done so, for they were still as ugly as before. Then I awoke."

Joseph replied that Pharaoh's dream was a message from God, revealing what was about to happen. He told Pharaoh that the seven fat cows were seven years of good harvests, and the seven lean cows were the seven years of famine that would follow. He warned Pharaoh that he must save one-fifth of the crops for the next seven years, preparing for the famine that would follow.

The Pharaoh was so impressed with Joseph that he made Joseph second-in-command over all Egypt. Everyone in the land, except the Pharaoh, had to obey Joseph.

For seven years Joseph gathered food and stored it, until there was so much he could no longer measure it. Then the famine started. When the people cried to the Pharaoh for food, he told them to go to Joseph and do whatever Joseph told them to do. Gradually people from other countries began coming to Egypt, for none of the other countries had saved food as Egypt had.

Back home, Joseph's family was starving. Joseph's father, Jacob, learned that there was food in Egypt. He sent Joseph's ten older brothers to Egypt to buy food. Joseph recognized his brothers when they bowed down to him, but he pretended not to, and treated them like strangers. He told them he thought they were spies. He kept his brother Simeon in prison, sending the other nine home to their father with instructions to return with Benjamin, their youngest brother.

Jacob did not want Benjamin to go, for he believed he had already lost Joseph and Simeon and was afraid Benjamin would die also. However, hunger forced the brothers to return to Joseph with Benjamin. Joseph then told them who he was. He sent them back to bring Jacob and the rest of their family to live in Egypt, for there were still five years of famine left. Jacob was happy, for his beloved son, Joseph, was alive. Jacob, his family, his cattle, and his goods journeyed from the land of Canaan and came into Egypt, where Jacob's descendants became a great people.

MOSES IN THE BULRUSHES

Source: Exodus 1:1 - 2:10

Theme: Persecution

Goals for Participants

- to consider the meaning of persecution and people's responses to it
- to become familiar with the story of Moses and the bulrushes
- to consider other issues related to the story, such as making hard choices, feeling pity, adoption.

Background

All that is known of Moses comes from the Bible and mostly from the book of Exodus, which tells the story of the "going out" of the Israelites from Egypt, of the covenant made with YHWH, and of the tabernacle. The J authors, 250 years after the likely time of the events depicted in Exodus, offer the earliest account; the E and P writers build on the J document. Originally, the material in Exodus belonged to four separate traditions, but by the J writers' time in the 11th century B.C.E., these separate sources had been woven into a common strand.

The stories about Moses reflect an accurate picture of Egypt in the 13th century B.C.E., though much of the material in Exodus is legendary. The best guess of today's scholars is that the events of Exodus may have taken place from 1290 to 1224 B.C.E., and that the Pharaoh was Ramses II. It would have been customary for nomadic people to be admitted to Egypt in times of famine, and it is known that during this time Ramses II launched vast building projects that needed much slave labor. The number of Egyptian loan-words found in Exodus is another reason to believe in the historicity of the basic story.

Did Moses actually exist? In the oldest section of Exodus, "The Song of Miriam," there is no mention of Moses. On the other hand, it is reasonable to assume that the legends about Moses are based on events in the life of a historic person. Details about him such as his Levite ancestry, his ability to deal with the Egyptians, and the descendants he left support such a belief. Though Exodus 2:10 infers that the name Moses stems from his being drawn out of the water, most scholars believe it is an Egyptian root word for "to be born." It is found in names such as Tutmose, which means "Tut is born."

The nativity story is similar to other such tales in the Near East and elsewhere in which a king is warned that a child who is about to be born will in some way usurp his power. The king then tries to kill the child, who is saved by the deity and eventually does carry out the foreordained plan for his life. Elements in this story are similar, for example, to one about the birth of Sargon I of Agade: ". . . my changeling mother conceived me, in secret she bore me. She set me in a basket of rushes, with bitumen she sealed my lid. She cast me into the river which rose not over me. . . ." (Daiches, *Moses: The Man and His Vision*, p. 32).

The story of a cruel king who tries to kill a child destined for great things, only to be thwarted in the end, has intrinsic psychological appeal. Children identify with the hero who survives persecution and is eventually able to win the battle against such evils. The question of adoption may bring up special concerns. Though most children have concerns about adoption at one time or another, these issues are especially acute for children who are actually adopted. As you pose the discussion question about adoption, be sensitive to the children's worries, and invite them to share their feelings. Reassure the children with thoughts about the biological mother's difficult but loving choice and the adoptive parents' commitment, care, and love.

Materials

- Sheet of mural paper large enough to contain the illustrations of the four parts of the Moses story
- Old newspapers
- Old shirts or other coverups
- Pencils
- Paints, in a variety of colors, and paintbrushes, large and small
- Jars (to hold water for cleaning brushes)
- Rags or paper towels
- Newsprint and marker
- Copies of Song 12, "Little Moses"

Preparation

- Think through your own answers to the motivating and discussion questions.
- Early in the week, send a letter advising parents that you will be discussing adoption (see sample at end of the previous session plan).
- Decide where the mural will be displayed when it is finished.
- Learn the song "Little Moses," or arrange for someone else to teach it, preferably with a guitar or autoharp.

Session Plan

Gathering   Varies

As the children gather, invite them to help you set out the materials for the mural. Have the tape of "Little Moses" playing to help them become familiar with the tune.

Motivating Questions   5-10 min.

Gather the children on a rug or around a table and engage them in a discussion of the following: "Can anyone tell me what the word *persecution* means? What are some examples of persecution?" (Colonists who came to North America, the Jewish Holocaust, Jews in Russia, blacks in the United States.)

"Hebrew scripture tells many stories about people being persecuted because of their religious beliefs. Most of the time, the ancient Israelites were persecuted because they believed in one god instead of the gods their neighbors worshiped. Today's story about Moses is a story of persecution."

Definitions

descendant a person with a long line of ancestors—those who lived before
midwives women who help deliver babies
persecute to bother or harm someone because of his or her beliefs

Read the Story   5 min.

Discussion   15 min.

Lead a discussion of the story guided by the following.
1. When people are being persecuted, they often have to make very hard choices. Moses' mother had to give him up so that he could live. Did she love him even though she gave him up? How do you think his sister, Miriam, felt?
2. Most of the times when the ancient Israelites were persecuted, it was because they believed in one god instead of the gods their neighbors worshiped. Sometimes they were forced to worship the gods of others or die. What are other examples of hard choices people might have to make?
3. Pharaoh's daughter felt pity for Moses. What is pity? What did her feelings of pity cause Pharaoh's daughter to do?
4. Moses was adopted by the Pharaoh's daughter. Do you know anyone who was adopted?

Song   5 min.

Read the words to "Little Moses" with the children, then play the recording of it and invite the children to sing along, or sing to guitar or autoharp accompaniment. Sing it a couple of times.

Making a Mural   20 min.

Lay the mural paper on the table or on the floor. Divide it into four sections and cut them apart. Explain to the children that each week they will use one of the pieces to illustrate the part of the Moses story they have just heard; on the last week they will put it all together. Set aside three pieces, and put the one for this session back on the table or floor. Spread newspaper around it to protect the table from splatters.

Gather around the mural paper. Say, "We have just heard a story about Moses, and for the next three Sundays we will be hearing more stories about him. Today we're going to begin painting a large picture, a mural, showing parts of these stories. Can you tell me some parts of the story we heard today? Which ones would be good to include in our mural?"

Give the children an opportunity to name some of the parts of the story. Suggest others if they leave out something important. List the parts on newsprint, then invite the children to choose the parts they want to draw and paint. Have the children put on old shirts or other coverups.

With pencil, divide the mural paper into four sections. Invite the children in small groups or individually to sketch their part of the story in pencil in one of the sections. As they finish, set out the paints, brushes, and water with which to paint their sketches. Have cloths or paper towels handy for mop-ups.

When the children finish painting, tell them to rinse their brushes and wash their hands.

Closing   5 min.

After cleanup, gather the children, light the chalice or candle, and sing "Little Moses" once more. Then say, "Many of the sad stories we hear are about times when a group of people were persecuted because of their religion, their race, or their way of life. These people face great hardships and often have to make very difficult choices. Unitarian Universalists believe that any kind of persecution is wrong, and we do whatever we can to stop it. We also try to help the victims of persecution make their lives better and their choices easier."

If Your Time Is Limited

- Have the discussion while the children are working on the mural.

If You Have More Time

- Extend closing time by asking whether the children can give examples of people who have helped others escape persecution—abolitionists, those who sheltered Jews during World War II, members of Amnesty International, and the like.

Moses in the Bulrushes

ABOUT 400 YEARS AFTER JOSEPH and his family settled in Egypt, their descendants had become a large number of people. They were such a large number, in fact, that the Pharaoh wanted to decrease the number of Hebrews, as they were called, in his kingdom.

To do this, the Pharaoh told the Hebrew midwives, "When you act as midwife to the Hebrew women, and see them on the birthstool, if it is a boy, kill him; but if it is a girl, she shall live."

But the midwives knew that killing the babies would make God angry, so they did not do as Pharaoh commanded, but let the boys live.

When Pharaoh found out, he called the midwives together and said, "Why have you done this, and allowed the boys to live?"

They answered, "Because the Hebrew women are so healthy they give birth before the midwives come to them."

The Hebrew people continued to multiply and grow strong. Finally Pharaoh commanded all his people, "Every boy that is born to the Hebrews you shall cast into the Nile, but you shall let every girl live."

Soon after this, a Hebrew woman gave birth to a son. She was able to hide him for three months. When she could hide him no longer, she got a basket made of bulrushes, and covered it with tar. She put the child in it and placed it among the reeds on the bank of the river. His sister, Miriam, stood at a distance, to see what would happen to him.

The daughter of Pharaoh came down to bathe at the river, while her maidens walked beside the river. She saw the basket among the reeds and sent her maid to bring it to her. When she opened it she saw the child. He was crying, and she took pity on him. "This must be one of the Hebrews' children," she said.

Miriam approached the Pharaoh's daughter and said, "Shall I go and call you a nurse from the Hebrew women to nurse the child for you?"

Pharaoh's daughter said, "Yes." So Miriam went to get her mother, the mother of the baby.

Pharaoh's daughter said to the mother, "Take this child and nurse it for me, and I will give you your wages." So the mother took the child and nursed it. When the child grew up, she brought him to Pharaoh's daughter, and she took him as her son. She named him Moses, "because," she said, "I drew him out of the water."

MOSES AND THE BURNING BUSH

Source: Exodus 3 - 4:20

Theme: Dedication

Goals for Participants

- to consider what it means to be "called" to serve and to dedicate one's life to that "calling"
- to become familiar with the story of Moses and the burning bush
- to consider other issues related to the story, such as miracles.

Background

This part of the story of Moses reinforces our belief in the historical existence of a Hebrew who was raised in the Egyptian court. Here Moses is shown identifying with a Hebrew who is being beaten and with the other Hebrew workers, even though they resent him when he interferes and confront him angrily: "Who made you a ruler and a judge over us?" He goes into exile because of his actions on the part of the Hebrews, yet the daughters of Reuel/Jethro in Midian mistake him for an Egyptian. And the "miracles" Moses is later empowered to do are those the Egyptian magicians can also produce.

No one is certain where Midian was. There are two possibilities: on the Sinai Peninsula and in the area east of the Gulf of Aqabah.

The two names for Moses' father-in-law, Reuel and Jethro, can be explained by the fact that they appear in different sections, taken from different traditions, and the editors did not feel it was important to harmonize the two versions. In both cases, however, he is depicted as a priest of Midian.

The pharaoh who died is likely to have been Seti I, who died in 1290 B.C.E. The death of a pharaoh would be an auspicious time for the slaves to attempt a rebellion.

It is common in the Near East to take off one's shoes when in the presence of the holy. The angel may have been a messenger from God or an epiphany, and fire—for example, in halos—is often a symbol of God's presence.

In order for Moses to convince the Hebrews of his authority, it was important for him to know God's name. The Hebrew words for God's answer can be translated variously as "I am what I am," "I am who I am," or "I will be what I will be." Albright, a noted biblical scholar, suggests the best meaning is "He causes to be what comes into existence." Some scholars question the likelihood of such an abstract name in those times, but there are examples of other, similar Near Eastern epithets for gods.

Third- and fourth-grade children are beginning to be able to make a commitment and stick to it, even if only for a limited period. In their imagination they can try out the feeling of being "called," and the idea of causes worthy of lifelong dedication, even if they are not quite ready for such dedication themselves. Children this age can identify with the oppression of slaves and their yearning to be free, and imagine an inner commitment to the cause of their freedom.

Another topic of interest will be "what really happened" at the scene of the burning bush and the other miracles. Eight- and nine-year olds are working hard to sort out the facts of things, to understand how things work and what is real. Let them discuss possible explanations, but bring them back to the question of how the miracles relate to commitment and the accomplishment of something so difficult that it might seem a "miracle."

Materials

- The mural paper from the previous session
- Pencils, crayons, colored markers, and colored pencils
- Tissue paper in fiery colors: yellow, orange, red, purple
- Glue
- Copies of Song 13, "Go Down, Moses"
- A large piece of styrofoam and barren branches (optional)

Preparation

- Think through your own answers to the motivating and discussion questions.
- Discuss the meaning of Unitarian Universalist dedication services with your minister, or read the material used in such a service.
- Practice the song "Go Down, Moses," or ask your "music person" to be prepared to lead the children in singing it.

Session Plan

Gathering   Varies

As the participants gather, invite each child to make one or more "flames" by cutting different-sized pieces of colored tissue paper and gluing them together.

Motivating Questions   10 min.

Gather the children on a rug or around a table and engage them in a discussion of the following. What kind of person do you want to be when you grow up? Are there any special interests you have now that you think will be important to you when you've grown up? Do you think there is something special that you are meant to do in your life?

Then say, "There are many stories in Hebrew scripture about people who felt 'called,' people who 'heard' an inner voice urging them to do something. Noah felt called to build an ark. Abraham felt called to sacrifice Isaac. Joseph felt called to interpret dreams. Today's story about Moses is another of these stories in which a

person feels called to dedicate his or her life to a cause."

Definition

bondage slavery

Read the Story   5 min.

Discussion   15 min.

Lead a discussion of the story guided by the following questions.
1. Sometimes people get a feeling that they must do something—that they are "called" to help others. Martin Luther King, Jr., felt called to help black people. Gandhi felt called to help the oppressed of India. Dorothea Dix, a Unitarian, felt called to help the poor, the imprisoned, and the insane. What was Moses "called" to do?
2. Do you think that Moses would have been convinced to go back to Egypt if "miraculous" things had not occurred? Would the Hebrew people have believed him without these "miracles"?
3. Moses, Dix, King, and Gandhi are people who dedicated their lives to serving others. Who are some others who have dedicated their lives to serving others? What did they do? Is there something you feel you should dedicate your life to? What is it?
4. Have you heard about any other people who felt "called" to do something special? Is there something you feel you should dedicate your life to? What is it?

Song   5 min.

Teach the children "Go Down, Moses" and sing two or three verses.

Continuing the Mural   20 min.

Take the second piece of the mural paper and put it on the table or floor. Then say, "Last week we heard a story about baby Moses, and we started our mural with pictures of that story.

Today we have heard about Moses and the burning bush and how Moses felt called to help the Hebrews become free. What parts of this story shall we draw and paint for the next section of our mural?"

Give the children time to think of and mention parts of the story, and list these on newsprint. Suggest others if they omit something important. Then invite the children to choose the parts they want to illustrate. Suggest that they sketch in pencil first, then complete the illustrations with crayons, colored markers, and colored pencils. When the bush is sketched, glue to it all of the tissue-paper flames that were made earlier.

Alternative Activity   10-15 min.

Invite the children to arrange the barren branches in the styrofoam and then decorate them with the tissue paper flames.

Closing   10 min.

Gather together, light the chalice or candle, and sing a verse of "Go Down, Moses." Then invite the children to complete the sentence "Something I could dedicate my life to is_____." Close by saying, "Moses felt 'called' to help his people escape from slavery, and he dedicated his life to this 'calling.' Let us be open to hearing our calls."

Moses and the Burning Bush

ALTHOUGH MOSES WAS RAISED as the grandson of the Pharaoh, he still thought of himself as a Hebrew. Once, when he saw an Egyptian beating a Hebrew slave, Moses tried to stop the Egyptian. In the struggle, the Egyptian was killed. This made the Pharaoh very angry, and Moses had to go into hiding.

While he was in hiding, he married and started to raise a family. Once, while tending his father-in-law's sheep, he saw a bush that burned without being burned down. Moses went closer to look at this amazing bush, up on the side of a mountain. As Moses came closer, God called to him out of the bush, "Moses, Moses!"

Moses answered, "Here I am," and covered his face, because he was afraid to look at God.

God told Moses that the suffering of the Hebrews at the hands of the Egyptians had not gone unnoticed: God had heard the Hebrews' cries. Indeed, God had come to deliver them from the Egyptians and to bring them to a land flowing with milk and honey. Thus God was sending Moses to the Pharaoh to free the Hebrew people from Egypt.

But Moses protested, "Who am I that I should go to Pharaoh and bring the He-brew people out of Egypt? If they ask, 'What is the name of the one who has sent you?' what shall I say?"

God said to Moses, "I am who I am. Say, 'I am has sent me to you. The God of your fathers and mothers, the God of Abraham and Sarah, the God of Isaac and Rebekah, the God of Jacob and Rachel has sent me to you.'"

Moses still protested that people would not believe him. God told Moses to throw the staff he had in his hand on the ground. When Moses did so, the staff turned into a snake, and Moses drew back from it. God told him to grab the snake by the tail, and when Moses did, the snake turned back into a staff.

Then God told Moses to put his hand inside his cloak and then take it out. When Moses did so, his hand developed a very bad disease called leprosy. Then God told Moses to put his hand back inside his cloak and take it out. When Moses did, his hand was restored to health.

God told Moses, "If they will not believe you, or heed the first sign, they may believe the second sign. If they will not believe these two signs or heed you, you shall take some water from the Nile and pour it on the dry ground; and the water that you shall take from the Nile will become blood on the dry ground."

Still Moses protested. He reminded God that he stuttered and wouldn't be able to speak well. God assured Moses that his speech would be taken care of. Moses still begged God to send someone else.

Finally God got angry and told Moses that Moses' brother, Aaron, would be there to speak for him, but that Moses must go. And so Moses and his family went to Egypt. Four times he had tried to get out of going. But he believed it was God who was calling him, so he went.

LET MY PEOPLE GO

Source: Exodus 7–15

Theme: Freedom from Oppression

Goals for Participants

- to become familiar with the story of Moses' leading the Hebrew people out of Egypt
- to reflect on the idea of oppression and on times when they have felt oppressed.

Background

Children at this age have probably learned about slavery in the early days of the United States. Because of this they may associate the word slave with African Americans. This story provides an opportunity to broaden their understanding of oppression and slavery, to help them avoid stereotypical thinking. The motivating questions ask them to think about times when they felt oppressed. This may be difficult for them to do, but if you can relate a short personal story, you may elicit some personal stories from the children.

Beginning with the definition of slavery as "the total subjection of one person to another" (Mays, *Harper's Bible Commentary*, p. 959), children can see that slavery is not necessarily related to color, race, gender, or religion, although all of those categories have been used to define classes of slaves. The Hebrews held different religious beliefs from the Egyptians. They were easy to identify by their patterns of worship, their dress, their daily life—and they had become numerous enough to threaten the ruling class. Thus, though they had been welcomed as settlers by earlier generations of Egyptians, by Moses' time they had become an oppressed class of people, subject to the cruel taskmasters of the Pharaoh.

The Hebrews worked on the tombs, temples, and obelisks designed by Egyptian architects. (The famed pyramids had been built approximately a thousand years earlier.) Because they were called lazy workers—a charge commonly leveled against oppressed classes—the Hebrews were forced to make their bricks without straw. Strawless bricks do not hold together well, yet the Hebrews were required to make their usual quota. It was either no straw, or take extra time to glean the stubble from the fields. Either way, the task was nearly hopeless, and the punishment was a beating. For Moses, the lack of straw was the "last straw." It was time to try the magic that YHWH had shown him.

Popularly known as the ten plagues, the calamities inflicted on Egypt were familiar threats to the well-being of the nation. The power of the Exodus story is that they occur one right after the other. Written down many centuries after it occurred, and drawn from three traditions (J, E, and P), the story as recorded in Exodus is full of repetition and confusion. The plagues were natural occurrences in an unnatural time frame—folk history in its most dramatic form.

The story of the plagues and the crossing of the Reed Sea is the basis for the Jewish celebration of Passover. At the Passover meal the story of the Exodus is recounted through words, symbols, and songs. One seder ritual has to do with the plagues. Before drinking the first cup of wine, one removes a drop for each plague visited upon the Egyptians, diminishing one's own pleasure because of the suffering of the oppressor. The theme of the Passover seder is that our joy in freedom is possible only if we remember our own suffering and the suffering of others.

In the telling of this story, we have referred to the Reed Sea. There is on modern maps a sea called the Red Sea, but the Hebrew term used in Exodus is *yam suph* or Sea of Reeds. Great confusion exists among biblical scholars about the route of the Exodus—in fact, three routes have been suggested, each with respected literary and geographical credentials. The source of confusion seems to be the Greek translation of the Hebrew Scriptures, the Septuagint, dating back perhaps to the third century B.C.E. *Reed* was translated *Red*, and on the basis of that error it was long assumed that the Red Sea was the site of the crossing.

Materials

- Dry cellulose sponges, (approximately 2" x 3") or pieces of foam carpet padding
- Scissors
- Tempera paints in flat dishes
- Sponge-stamp patterns
- Mural paper and newspaper
- Pencils and colored markers or crayons
- Copies of Song 13, "Go Down, Moses" (optional)

Preparation

- Think through your own answers to the motivating and discussion questions.
- Draw the sponge-stamp shapes on newsprint or the chalkboard (see Resource 3).
- Make a sample sponge-stamp, and practice with it; reproduce copies of the sponge-stamp patterns if necessary.
- Mix the paints and cut the sponges to size.
- Print out the words of James Russell Lowell on a sheet of newsprint (see Closing).

Session Plan

Gathering   Varies

As the children arrive, invite them to complete any unfinished parts of the mural from the previous sessions. When everyone has arrived, gather the group together.

Motivating Questions   10 min.

Ask the children, "Has someone bigger or more powerful than you ever made you do something you didn't want to do? What was it? How did it make you feel? Was the other person being fair or cruel?"

After a brief discussion, say, "When people have power and use it in a cruel way, we call that oppression. Last week you heard the story from Hebrew scripture of Moses, called to lead the opressed Hebrew people out of Egypt into the Promised Land. Today's story tells how he actually did it."

Definitions

boils   big sores on the skin
multitude many, many people

Read the Story   10 min.

Discussion   15 min.

Lead a discussion of the story guided by the following questions.

1. What would you have done if you were Pharaoh? Why did Pharaoh want the Hebrews to stay? What do you think the Egyptians thought of the "miracles" Moses performed?
2. How did the Hebrews feel about Moses at the beginning of the story? Do you think the miracles convinced them? How would you feel about leaving your home to wander in the wilderness?
3. The story of the Exodus of the Hebrew people from Egypt has become an important symbol for freedom fighters around the world, and a symbol of how freedom can be gained even when it seems impossible. What are some other examples of people being oppressed? Who? Where? When? By whom?
4. What is a plague? Do you think the plagues in the story were too harsh? Were they all necessary?

The Moses Mural Continued   30 min.

Making Sponge-Stamps
Gather the children in your work area. Assign one plague to each child to depict on the mural: water to blood; frogs; gnats; flies; cattle disease;

boils; hail; locusts; darkness; and death of the firstborn child. Each is to make a sponge-stamp to represent his or her plague. Show them the samples and patterns. Ordinary cellulose sponge cuts fairly easily; foam carpet padding is even easier.

In addition to the plagues, you will need a wave stamp and a person stamp to illustrate the crossing of the Reed Sea. If you have fewer children than stamps, some may wish to make two, or you may eliminate one or more plagues. If your group is very large, you may wish to make more than one mural. This may be a session in which to have extra assistants.

Planning the Mural
When the children have finished cutting their sponge-stamps, lay out the mural paper. In the upper-left-hand corner of the mural section, draw a large circle in pencil. In this circle, have one or more children draw a picture of Pharaoh. Draw ten ray-like sections emanating from the circle, and ask each child to fill one ray with an all-over design stamped with his or her sponge stamp. Each section should overlap the Pharaoh's portrait slightly—for example, a frog jumping into the circle, a swirl of blood crossing the border. The idea is to "annoy" Pharaoh.

In the lower-right-hand corner, use the wave stamp and the person stamp to show the crossing of the Reed Sea. Add Moses' words "Let my people go!" in an appropriate place.

(See an illustration of the mural at the end of Resource 3.)

Sponge Painting
This can be a messy activity. Take time to experiment yourself, so that you may speak from experience. Give the children clear instructions. A bucket of soapy water and a towel nearby will save on cleanup time. Think ahead.

The trick is to use very little paint. Begin by moistening the sponge-stamp and squeezing out all the water. Blot the stamp on newspaper or scrap paper until it is nearly dry. Place a tablespoon of tempera paint in a flat dish. Use the spoon to spread the paint out a little. Dip the bottom edge of the stamp gently into the paint. Print once or twice on newsprint to remove any excess paint, then print as desired on the mural. Sponge painting is most effective when some of the texture of the sponge shows as part of the design.

Allow ample time for cleanup.

Closing   10 min.

Light a chalice or candle, and ask the children to think about these words from a poem by James Russell Lowell:

If there breathe on earth a slave,
Are ye truly free and brave?

Display the words in your classroom for all to see and think about in the weeks to come.

If Your Time Is Limited

- Discuss the story while working on the mural.
- Cut out the sponge-stamps in advance. Or cut stamp shapes from styrofoam trays and affix them to blocks of scrap wood with a quickly drying or tacky glue. Once the glue is set, use stamp pads of various colors. Have shapes, blocks, and stamp pads ready before your group arrives.

If You Have More Time

- Tell the children how the plagues are remembered at the Passover Seder (pronounced say´-der), or ceremonial meal. As each plague is named, participants dip their little fingers into their wineglasses to remove a drop of wine. This drop is flicked off for each remaining plague. The ritual is a reminder that the joy of freedom bears a cost, that the happiness of this holiday is diminished by the suffering of the Egyptians who experienced the plagues. You might have your group re-enact the ritual with cups of water or juice, as you read aloud the list of plagues found in the sponge-stamp directions.
- Sing "Go Down, Moses" from the songbook. Explain that this is an African American spiritual, and help the children to connect slavery of black Americans to the slavery of the ancient Hebrews.
- Another song for this session is Song 14, "One Morning," about the plague of frogs.

Let My People Go

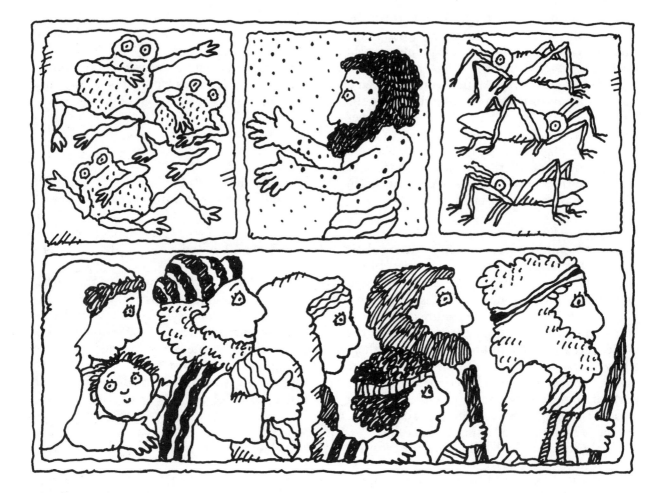

MOSES WAS RELUCTANT TO BE THE ONE to free his people, and the job was by no means an easy one. When Moses first went to the Pharaoh to ask him to let the Hebrews go, the Pharaoh responded by telling his overseers to make the Hebrews work harder. This made the Hebrews angry at Moses. It looked as if they were never going to escape the hardships in Egypt. But God was persistent and didn't let Moses give up.

Moses and his brother, Aaron, went back to the Pharaoh. Aaron threw down his staff before the Pharaoh, and it turned into a snake. The Pharaoh summoned his magicians, who threw down their staffs, which also became snakes. And the Pharaoh still would not listen.

Because of the Pharaoh's hardheartedness, ten plagues were inflicted on the Egyptians. In the first plague, Moses and Aaron went to the Pharaoh again, as he was going to bathe in the Nile. Moses said, "God sent me to say, 'By this you shall know that I am the Lord. See, with the staff that is in my hand I will strike the water that is in the Nile, and it shall be turned to blood. The fish in the river shall die, the river itself shall stink, and the Egyptians shall be unable to drink water from the Nile.'"

When the staff struck the water, all the water in Egypt turned to blood. But the Pharaoh's magicians did the same, so the Pharaoh's heart remained hardened.

Seven days later, Moses again went to the Pharaoh. "Let my people go," he said. "If you refuse to let them go, I will plague your whole country with frogs; the river shall swarm with frogs; they shall come up into your palace, and into the houses of your servants and of your people, and into your ovens and your kneading bowls; the frogs shall come up on you and your people and on all your officials."

The Pharaoh refused to listen, so Moses let loose the plague of frogs. The Pharaoh's magicians did the same, and the Pharaoh did not know what to do with all these frogs; so he promised to let the Hebrews go if Moses would get rid of the frogs. Moses promised the frogs would all die the next day. After the frogs were dead, they were gathered into huge piles, and the land stank.

Once the frogs were dead, the Pharaoh went back on his promise, so in the third plague Moses caused gnats to swarm over all of Egypt, on both the people and the animals. The Pharaoh's magicians told him that this was beyond their magic, but still the Pharaoh would not listen.

As a fourth plague, Moses caused great swarms of flies to cover the Egyptians, but the Hebrew people were not affected. The Pharaoh begged Moses to pray to God to make the flies go away. Moses said he would if the Pharaoh would let them go and not trick them this time. The Pharaoh promised, but as soon as the flies were gone he changed his mind again.

The fifth plague caused all of the Egyptian cattle, horses, sheep, and camels to die, but not one of the cattle of the Hebrews died. Still the heart of the Pharaoh was hardened, and he did not let the people go.

For the sixth plague, before the Pharaoh, Moses threw soot from the ovens up in the air, which caused boils to break out on people and animals. Even the Pharaoh's magicians were afflicted with the boils; but still Pharaoh would not listen.

The seventh plague was hail, which ruined most of the crops. Next came the eighth plague, locusts, which ate the remaining crops. The ninth plague brought darkness over the land for three days. But still the Pharaoh was not willing to let the Hebrew people leave Egypt with their flocks and herds.

Then God announced the tenth and final plague, and Moses reported to his people, "Thus says the Lord: about midnight I will go out through Egypt; every firstborn in the land of Egypt shall die, from the firstborn of the Pharaoh who sits upon his throne to the firstborn of the female slave who is behind the handmill, and all the firstborn of the livestock." So that the plague would not affect the Hebrews, they sacrificed a lamb and spread its blood on their doorposts. In this way, God would know to pass over that household and let the Hebrew firstborn live.

Finally, all the Egyptians rose up and cried out to the Pharaoh to let the Hebrews go. He agreed, and about 600,000 men, women, and children and all of their livestock set out. But once more the Pharaoh changed his mind. When he saw that all of his Hebrew slaves were gone, he and his army set out after them in chariots.

As the Hebrew people were camped by the Reed Sea, they saw the Egyptians coming, and they were very much afraid. Moses told them not to be afraid, and he stretched out his hand, with his staff, and divided the sea on dry ground. Once Moses and his people were across, Moses again stretched out his hand, and the sea closed in upon the horses, chariots, and chariot drivers who were pursuing them.

Moses and his people were now free from the Egyptians, but they had many years of wandering in the wilderness yet before them. Eventually, however, they found Canaan, the land that had been promised to them.

THE TEN COMMANDMENTS

Source: Exodus 19-20, 31:18-34:9

Theme: Rules and Responsibilities

Goals for Participants

- to become familiar with the story of Moses and the Ten Commandments
- to examine the rules and responsibilities they experience in their own lives: those that protect them from danger, those that protect others, those that define relationships among people, and those that seek to connect us to God, or to universal truth.

Background

The first five books of the Hebrew Bible include many laws and ordinances, often freely mixed with narrative passages that give the context or reason for the particular law. The Decalogue, or Ten Commandments, probably existed as an independent document before the E writer placed it in his story of Moses. Another almost identical version can be found in Deuteronomy 5, although in Deuteronomy the Sabbath is observed as a reminder of Israel's bondage in Egypt, that the slaves of the Israelites "may rest as you do," whereas in Exodus the Sabbath is observed because God rested after six days of the labor of creation.

The form of the Ten Commandments used here is common to most Protestant churches. Unitarian Universalists from other religious traditions may be more familiar with other forms.

The first four commandments refer to the relationship of the Israelites with their god, YHWH. The next six refer to relationships among people. Breaking any of the commandments was a breach in the covenant relationship—the two-way agreement that bound YHWH and Israel to-

gether—but the Israelites were told, "If you listen to these laws and are careful to observe them, then the Lord your God will observe the sworn covenant he made with your forefathers and will keep faith with you. He will love you, bless you and cause you to increase" (Deuteronomy 7:12-13a).

The golden calf mentioned in the story is believed by many to have been the central focus of Canaanite worship of this period. An excavation in Israel in the summer of 1990 uncovered the first "golden calf" archaeologists have ever found. Much smaller than the calf described in the story of Moses, it is slightly larger than four inches tall and weighs about a pound. Made of several metals and burnished to provide a golden sheen, the calf is thought to date from about 1550 B.C.E. (*Cleveland Plain Dealer*, July 25, 1990).

Materials

- Scissors and glue
- Twelve clean, used styrofoam meat trays, approximately 4" x 6"
- Dull pencils, one per child
- Black paste shoe polish (markers may be used, but they are more difficult; be sure to experiment in advance)
- Copies of Handout 4 for each child
- Copies of Song 15, "Daiyenu," and Song 16, "The Ten Commandments" (optional)
- Mural from previous sessions
- Cardboard or construction paper
- Gold paper (may use the backs of old Christmas cards)
- Cotton or fiberfill for cloud
- Paint and brushes, if desired
- Chenille pipe cleaners
- Scraps of felt, yarn, and cloth

Preparation

- Think through your own answers to the motivating and discussion questions.
- Print directions for making the stone tablets on newsprint or a chalkboard; make one to familiarize yourself with the process.
- Learn the song "The Ten Commandments," or give it to your music assistant to practice. The song "Daiyenu" is an alternative.

Session Plan

Gathering   Varies

Have supplies laid out for making of "stone tablets." Have your sample tablet on display, along with copies of Handout 4 for all participants. As the children arrive, ask them to choose a commandment and write their name next to it on the list. Remind them to ask if they don't know the meaning of any of the words.

Engage the children in making their own tablets. With scissors, trim the edges off a styrofoam tray and cut it in the shape of a tablet. With a dull pencil, print the commandment on the tablet, with the Hebrew number at the top, the words underneath. Cover the tablet with black paste shoe polish to make it look like stone and make the writing show up. (Tell the children that the letters of the Hebrew alphabet are used as numbers, too. Therefore, the first ten letters of the alphabet are used to "number" the commandments.)

Make an extra set of tablets (two) to place in the ark that will be made in next week's lesson. Use only numbers on these, the first five on one and the second five on the other. Perhaps a child who has finished early would like to make these.

When most of the children have completed their tablets, draw the group together on a rug or around a table. Explain that there will be time later in the session to finish the tablets.

Motivating Questions   10 min.

Ask the children, "What is the difference between a rule and a responsibility?" Through discussion, help to clarify for the children that rules are generally intended to protect us and others, whereas a responsibility is something we feel we ought to do (or not do) because it is right (or wrong). Rules or laws generally come from our sense of responsibility to one another. For example, the rule might be "Don't walk on the grass," but the responsibility it came from would be "Respect your neighbor's property" or "Do unto others as you would have others do unto you."

Close the discussion by saying, "Commandments are very important rules. In today's story from Hebrew scripture, the Ten Commandments describe to the Hebrew people their responsibilities to themselves, to others, and to God."

Definition

repent to be sorry for something you've done

Read the Story   5 min.

Discussion   10 min.

Lead a discussion of the story guided by the following questions.
1. Which commandment do you think is most important? Why?
2. Some rules are easy to understand, like "Don't run out in front of a car." Others aren't as obvious, like "Always say thank you when someone gives you something." If you were starving, do you think you should have to follow the commandment "You shall not steal"? Why?
3. If you could make up a new commandment for everybody, what would it be? (List the children's answers on newsprint or chalkboard. Post it for them to see in weeks to come. Can they suggest a title for the list?)

Mural: Adding the Ten Commandments   25 min.

Gather the children at your work space. On the final section of the continuous mural, pencil in the sketch shown at the end of this session plan. Talk briefly about the sketch with the children.

Guide the children step by step in making "pipe-cleaner people." Each figure requires two long chenille pipe cleaners. Bend one in half, forming a circle for the head by twisting at the neck. Bend feet up (1). Bend the other pipe cleaner in half. Place the bend around the "hips," and wind both ends around the torso, working up to the neck. The ends will become the arms. Form hands on the ends (2). Make a shoulder by bending each arm about half an inch from the neck. Scraps of cloth, felt, yarn, etc., can be used as clothing. The children may clothe the figures while you lead the discussion. See illustration provided here.

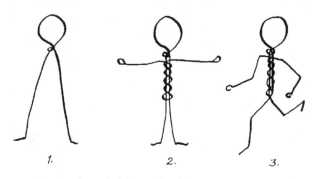

1.   2.   3.

Have the children finish their stone tablets and make the mountain, idol, and broken tablets. Glue all the elements to the mural paper, and take a few minutes to observe and talk about the entire mural.

Closing   5 min.

Gather the children in a circle. Light a chalice or candle and say, "We all need rules to live by. Today's story told us how the Ten Commandments were given to Moses and the Israelites by God. The commandments are still important reminders of our responsibility to one another. On the first Sunday we met we made a list of rules for our group. Let's read them aloud together and see if we think they are still good reminders of our responsibility to each other." (If your group did not not make a list of class rules, read aloud together the Ten Commandments.)

If Your Time Is Limited

- Omit the chenille pipe-cleaner people. Draw stick figures with markers instead.
- Discuss the story while working on the mural.

If You Have More Time

- Sing "The Ten Commandments" or "Daiyenu." The former can also be read as a poem.
- Take your completed four-part mural to a hallway or bulletin board to display it for all to see. Check in advance with your director of religious education or minister for an appropriate place to display it.

The Ten Commandments

AFTER THE HEBREWS LEFT EGYPT, they traveled in the wilderness. It was a very hard trip, and they were hungry and discouraged by the time they camped, three months later, at the foot of Mount Sinai. Mountains were considered holy places then. So Moses went up on Mount Sinai to talk to God. God told Moses that the children of Israel would become a holy nation. When Moses reported to the people what God said, they replied, "Everything that the Lord has spoken we will do."

The next time Moses went up on the mountain, God told him to have the people devote themselves to goodness for two days. On the third day Moses was to come back on the mountain and God would appear.

On the third day there were thunder and lightning and a thick cloud on the mountain. God had come down to the mountaintop in fire and smoke, and the mountain shook violently. God called Moses to come to the top of the mountain, saying, "Come up to me on the mountain, and wait there; and I will give you the tablets of stone, with the law and the commandments, which I have written for their instruction." Moses set out with his assistant, Joshua, while the people waited at the foot of the mountain.

Moses was on the cloud-covered mountain for six days before he heard from God. Moses remained with God for another forty days and forty nights. When God finished speaking with Moses on Mount Sinai, God gave him the two tablets of commandments, two tablets of stone, written with the finger of God.

While Moses was away, the people complained that they didn't know what had happened to him. They wanted Aaron, Moses' brother, to make a god they could worship. Aaron took all the gold in the camp and made a statue of a golden calf. When Moses returned, after forty-seven days, with the two stone tablets, he found the people dancing and worshiping the golden calf. Moses was so angry he threw the stone tablets from his hand and broke them at the foot of the mountain. This broke the covenant between the people and God. Then Moses took the calf they had made, burnt it with fire, ground it to powder, scattered it on the water, and made the people drink it.

Some time later, after the people had shown that they repented, God forgave them. God said to Moses, "Cut two tablets of stone like the former ones, and I will write on the tablets the words that were on the former tablets, which you broke." God was willing to renew the covenant because the people were now willing to follow God's commandments.

This is what the ten commandments said:

1. I am the Lord your God. You shall have no other gods before me.
2. You shall not make for yourself an idol to worship.
3. You shall not make wrongful use of the name of God.
4. Remember the Sabbath day, to keep it holy.
5. Honor your father and mother.
6. You shall not kill.
7. You shall not commit adultery.
8. You shall not steal.
9. You shall not bear false witness against your neighbor.
10. You shall not covet anything that is your neighbor's.

SESSION 15

AND THE WALLS CAME TUMBLING DOWN

Source: Joshua 6

Theme: Personal Identity

Goals for Participants

- to become familiar with the story of Joshua and the battle of Jericho
- to explore their own feelings related to following in another's footsteps.

Background

The book of Joshua fulfills YHWH's promise to the Israelites of a land where they could live in special relationship to their God. Though the story of Jericho probably dates from ancient times, the version in Joshua 6 is shaped by the convictions of 7th-century B.C.E. historians concerned with a law-abiding Israel. At numerous points in the story, instructions and admonitions emphasize the importance of adhering to YHWH's law—the rule of life. These D writers wanted no one to doubt that YHWH was directing the battle, Joshua's career, and the destiny of the Israelites.

After bringing YHWH's law to the Israelites, Moses led his people as far as the eastern bank of the Jordan River. Canaan, the "promised land," and the walled city of Jericho lay just to the west of the river. Because of his advanced age and approaching death, Moses prepared to turn over leadership to Joshua—the transfer of power being accomplished by several ritual acts:

- a meeting of Moses, YHWH, and Joshua in the special tent that housed the Ark of the Covenant (Deuteronomy 31:14-15)
- YHWH's commissioning of Joshua: "Be strong and bold, for you shall bring the Israelites into the land that I promised them; I will be with you" (Deuteronomy 31:23)
- Moses' teaching the Israelites the law that was to be their rule of life, writing it down so that it would remain with them after his death (Deuteronomy 31:22-29)
- the laying of hands on Joshua by Moses (Deuteronomy 34:9).

Joshua bore a heavy burden of leadership. After all, who could possibly fill the shoes of Moses? The D writer says clearly, "There has never yet risen in Israel a prophet like Moses, whom YHWH knew face to face" (Deuteronomy 34:10). Joshua was destined to live out his days in Moses' shadow, his many bloody victories validating his inherited power, but never equaling the accomplishments of his predecessor.

The book of Joshua is a violent military history, but we have chosen not to emphasize the violent nature of the text. Adult readers might wish to explore many of the book's more dominant themes, including issues of nationalism and territorial claims. With the children we will focus on the transfer of power to Joshua and identity issues related to filling another's shoes.

The story of the battle of Jericho is no exception to the violence of the rest of the book, but the narrative also suggests a ritual celebration of a remembered event from Israel's tribal history. So many necessary ritual ingredients are there—the army, followed by seven priests blowing seven ceremonial ram's horns, followed by the Ark of the Covenant, followed by the rear guard, all circling the city according to an exactly prescribed pattern. In many ways the story of Jericho describes a "dance" more than a battle!

"Throughout most of the biblical period, cities were surrounded by a system of fortifications that consisted of walls, towers and gates; populations that lived in unwalled settlements were exposed to great risks. City walls had to be high enough and thick enough and be constructed on such solid foundations that the fortifications and their defenders could deter enemy attacks. There was, in fact, a constant effort made by attackers and defenders to surpass the ingenuity of their opponents; siege warfare was the outgrowth of the competitive effort." (Achtemeier, *Harper's Bible Dictionary*, pp. 1116-7). What happened at the historic site of Jericho, and when, is still a mystery to biblical scholars. Archaeological digs have uncovered remnants of several cities at the ancient site, but the evidence is inconclusive as to whether any of them existed at the time of Joshua's conquest, circa 1200 B.C.E. There is archaeological evidence of much earlier mud-brick walls which appear to have collapsed several centuries before the time of Joshua. For now, the historicity of the book remains a fascinating mystery.

Children in the middle elementary years will recognize the issues of self-identity in this session. It is difficult to be overshadowed by an older brother or sister, or to be expected to be good at sports or academic subjects just because a parent or sibling has excelled in that area. The urge to assert one's own identity, to make a name for oneself, is strong in all of us. In some families, expectations are never made explicit, but children grow up feeling as if they always fall short of the implicit expectations. The motivating questions and the discussion of the story encourage children to draw on their own experiences as they explore this aspect of personal identity.

Materials

- Brown craft paper, approximately 6-8'
- Black or brown markers
- Seven sheets of 12" x 18" construction paper of any color
- Masking tape
- Small box, such as a shoe box
- Shiny wrapping paper—enough to cover box
- Two yardsticks
- Copies of Song 17, "Joshua Fit the Battle of Jericho"
- Two pairs of adult shoes

Preparation

- Think through your own answers to the motivating and discussion questions.
- Think through the role-play; review carefully the directions for the props.
- Learn and practice the song "Joshua Fit the

Battle of Jericho" or describe the role-play setting to the person who will be leading it.
- Reserve space, if necessary, for the Big Shoes Relay.

Session Plan

Gathering   Varies

As the children arrive, invite them to sit around the table and consider the question "Who are you?" When all children are present, say, "Each one of us is a very important person, but we are important in different ways. Think for a moment of all the things that you do in your life. Perhaps you are a Little League ballplayer, perhaps you take ballet lessons and are a dancer. I'm going to ask the same question over and over of you. See if you can give me a different answer each time I ask you." Go around the group asking, "Who are you?" of each child—at least three times. Ask all the adults present, including yourself, to participate. You may need to help children come up with ideas; this is a new way of thinking for them. Remark affirmatively on the number of different responses the group gives.

Motivating Questions   10 min.

Remain at the table or on a rug and briefly discuss these questions with the children: "We've just been talking about the things that are special about us, that tell who we are. Have you ever been identified because you are related to someone else? Such as, 'Oh, you are George's sister.' How did it make you feel? Do you know what it means to follow in someone's footsteps, or to fill someone's shoes?"

Then say, "It's always hard to follow someone who has been well known. In Hebrew scripture, the stories about Moses are the best known. Moses freed the people from slavery in Egypt, brought them God's commandments, and led them to the promised land. When Moses was dying, he chose his assistant, Joshua, to follow him as the leader of the Hebrews. Still, it was hard for Joshua to follow in Moses' footsteps."

Read the Story   5 min.

Discussion   **10 min.**

Lead a discussion of the story guided by the following questions.

1. How do you think Joshua felt following in Moses' footsteps? How would you feel if you were Joshua?
2. Have you ever had to "follow in someone's footsteps" as suggested in the story? Was it easy or difficult?
3. The story suggests that when Jericho fell it was a sign that God had chosen Joshua to be the leader of the Israelites. Do you think that winning a battle means the person would be a good leader for a country?
⚶ 4. Sometimes sports teams or armies pray for God to be on their side. Does winning mean that God is on their side?

Role-Play: Joshua Fit the Battle of Jericho   **20 min.**

Divide the children into groups to make the following items.

The Wall of Jericho
Lay a large sheet of craft paper or newspapers taped together on the floor. Use markers to sketch large stone blocks on it, so that it resembles a wall. (During the role-play, two or three children can hold up the wall, pulling it loosely around them in a circle; the other children will march around them. See illustration at the end of this session plan.)

Trumpets (Ram's Horns)
Roll sheets of construction paper into cones and fasten them with tape—one for each "priest."

Ark of the Covenant
The Ark of the Covenant was a sacred box that represented God's presence among the Israelites. Within it were kept sacred objects, the most important of which (according to tradition) were the tablets of commandments. The Ark was carried on poles and accompanied the nomadic people on their journeys. Once the temple in Jerusalem was built, the Ark had a permanent home. In synagogues today, the Ark is enshrined in the Holy of Holies and is the repository for the Torah scrolls (the first five books of the Hebrew Bible).

To make an ark, place the two stone tablets prepared last week inside a small box and cover the box with shiny paper. Fasten two yardsticks to the bottom with tape. (See illustration at the end of this session plan.)

Learning the Song
Practice singing "Joshua Fit the Battle of Jericho" until the children know it well enough to march at the same time.

Role-Play
With the children's help, assign roles and assemble the procession in the following order: Joshua, the army, (seven) priests blowing horns, the Ark, and the rear guard. Remember, you need two or three children to hold up the wall. (If your group is very small, perhaps you can ask another group to join you.)

Sing the song and march around the wall seven times. After the seventh circuit, make a loud shout and cause the walls to "tumble down." If the children are responsive, play out the story/song once or twice more, changing roles.

Big Shoes Relay   **10 min.**

Gather the children in a long, open area—a hallway will do nicely. Say, "When Joshua followed Moses as the leader of the Israelites, he had very big shoes to fill. This is a game to see how good you are at filling someone else's shoes!"

Tell the children to remove their shoes. Form two lines two to three feet apart. In front of the first child in each line place a pair of adult shoes. Make sure the two pairs are of similar size and difficulty to put on. Each child, in turn, puts on the shoes, runs to a line about 20 feet away, returns, removes the shoes, and goes to the end of the line. The game proceeds until all children have taken a turn. It will probably dissolve in silliness before a winner can be declared!

Closing   **5 min.**

Gather the children together and light your chalice or candle. Take a moment to quiet down together after the game, then say, "There are times when all of us are called upon to be leaders. Sometimes we don't feel strong enough or brave enough. YHWH gave Joshua some advice, saying, 'Be strong and courageous; do not be frightened or dismayed, for

the Lord your God is with you wherever you go.'
Maybe you'll be asked to do something this week
that you're not sure you can do. May you, also, be
strong and courageous."

If Your Time Is Limited

- Use a tape or record of the song for marching
  and don't worry about teaching it to the children.
- Omit decorating the wall.
- Discuss the story while preparing the items for
  the role-play.

If You Have More Time

- Reenact the role-play for parents at the end of
  the session.
- Discuss one or both of these proverbs with your
  group:
  - Those who follow in another's footsteps leave
    no footprints of their own.
  - One who sits down cannot make footprints in
    the sands of time.

And the Walls Came Tumbling Down

GOD TOLD JOSHUA, "Every place that the sole of your foot will tread upon I have given to you, as I promised to Moses. As I was with Moses, so I will be with you."

Joshua wanted the people to admire him as much as they admired Moses, so he did something Moses never did. Joshua captured the city of Jericho. God said to Joshua, "See, I have handed Jericho over to you, along with its king and soldiers. You shall march around the city, all the warriors circling the city once. This shall you do for six days, with seven priests bearing seven trumpets of rams' horns before the ark. On the seventh day you shall march around the city seven times, the priests blowing the trumpets. When they make a long blast with the ram's horn, as soon as you hear the sound of the trumpet, then all the people shall shout with a great shout; and the wall of the city will fall down flat, and all the people shall charge straight ahead."

So Joshua, the son of Nun, summoned the priests and said to them, "Take up the Ark of the Covenant, and have seven priests carry seven trumpets of rams' horns in front of the Ark of God."

To the people he said, "Go forward and march around the city; have the armed men pass on before the Ark of God." Joshua also commanded the people, "You shall not shout or let your voice be heard, nor shall you utter a word, until the day I tell you to shout. Then you shall shout." So the Ark of God went around the city, circling it once; and they came into the camp and spent the night.

Then Joshua rose early in the morning, and the priests took up the Ark of God. The seven priests carrying the seven trumpets of rams' horns before the Ark of God passed on, blowing the trumpets continually. The armed men went before them, and the rear guard came after the Ark of God, while the trumpets blew continually. They marched around the city once, and returned to the camp. They did this for six days.

On the seventh day, they marched around the city seven times. At the seventh time, the priests blew the trumpets and Joshua said to the people, "Shout! For God has given you the city."

As soon as the people heard the sound of the trumpet, they raised a great shout, and the wall fell down flat; so the people charged straight ahead into the city and captured it.

This was a sign to the Hebrew people that God had chosen Joshua as their leader. And Joshua is still best known for this battle. As a well-known spiritual says, "Joshua fit (fought) the battle of Jericho, and the walls came tumblin' down."

SAMSON AND DELILAH

Source: Judges 13-16

Theme: The Use of Strength

Goals for Participants

• to think about what makes us strong and how to use our strength
• to become familiar with the story of Samson and Delilah
• to discover other themes in the story—for example, superheroes, "getting even," betrayal of secrets.

Background

The story of Samson and Delilah is found in the book of Judges. The events described in this book take place after the conquest of Canaan and before Saul is anointed as king (approximately 1200-1040 B.C.E.).

According to the scriptures, during this time the people of Israel departed continually from the ways of YHWH, often to worship the Canaanite god Baal. This break in their covenant with God led to their subjection by other peoples in the area.

Eventually, however, the Israelites mended their ways, and God sent leaders—"judges"—to free them from their oppression. The Hebrew word that has been translated as "judge" really indicates more of a "deliverer" than an administrator of justice. The people whose lives and actions are described in the book of Judges were charismatic leaders, full of the spirit of God, who delivered the Israelites from their pagan oppressors, often through military action.

Samson was one of these twelve "judges," as were Deborah, Barak, Gideon, Abimelech, and Jephthah.

At birth Samson was dedicated to serve God,

and as such he was required to leave his hair uncut. As the story points out, his uncut hair, a sign of God's presence, was the source of his great strength. Most of the other deliverers led troops against the enemy, but Samson was more of a one-man army. When his hair was cut, God's presence departed from him, and he was left vulnerable.

The story of Samson is derived from several folktales. The name Samson itself may be a derivative of a word meaning "sun," and it is possible that the tales about him are related to stories about a sun god.

The Philistines were a migrating sea people from the Aegean and Crete. They were repulsed from Egypt after 1200 B.C.E. by Ramses III, and they then settled on the southern coastal plane of Palestine (named for them), which the Israelites also claimed. Samson had amorous relationships with three Philistine women, two of whom then betrayed him to their countrymen. *Delilah* may mean "traitoress" and therefore may be a descriptive term rather than a personal name.

Those who believe that the Israelites were God's chosen people, destined to live in Palestine, may see Samson as a hero who delivers his people from their oppressors. For us, however, this story raises the broader issue of how one's strength can and should be used.

We all gain a sense of security from a feeling of strength, and third- and fourth-grade children are certainly concerned about being strong and about relating to those who are either stronger or weaker than they. It is important, therefore, to help them see that there are kinds of strength other than pure physical strength. How to use their strength to help rather than harm those who are weaker is also an important topic. Probably the most potent issue for children this age, however, is how to deal with those who use their superior strength to bully them. This story offers an opportunity to reflect on how they feel about this problem and how they may begin to solve it.

Materials

- Construction-paper barbells

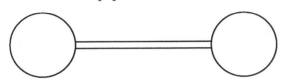

- Light-colored drawing paper, 9" x 12" or 12" x 18"
- Lined paper
- Pencils and slim felt-tip markers or colored pencils
- Copies of Song 18, "Samson and Delilah"

Preparation

- Think through your own answers to the motivating and discussion questions.
- Prepare the sample "story line"; make a sample cartoon and/or write a short story about SuperHero.
- Rule a line through the center of each paper barbell for the children's statements (see Gathering).
- Listen to and learn the song "Samson and Delilah," or ask someone else to learn it and lead the children in singing it.

Session Plan

Gathering   Varies

Set out the construction-paper barbells and pencils. As the children arrive, invite each to take one and write on it an ending to the following sentence: "A time when I was really strong was . . . " Remember to encourage the children to think of strength as including courage and mental ability, as well as physical strength. After all have written their responses, ask for volunteers to share theirs with the group. Then post the barbells on the bulletin board or other display area.

Motivating Questions   10 min.

Continue the discussion by saying, "Tell me about the cartoon people on TV or in the comics who are especially strong. In what ways are they extra-strong? What other ways to be strong are there besides physical stength?

"How do these characters use their strength? To fight against evil? To accomplish good things? Other ways?"

Definition

Philistines a seafaring people of the Aegean area, and a traditional enemy of the ancient Israelites

Read the Story   5 min.

Discussion   10 min.

Lead a discussion guided by the following questions.
1. Samson had a very strong body. What were some of the things he could do that most people couldn't do?
2. When the Philistines tricked him or did something mean to him, Samson used his strength to get even with them. What do you think about that? Should we use our strength to get even with other people?
3. What are some ways we could use our strength to help people?
4. Delilah betrayed Samson. Have you ever told someone a secret and then found out that the person betrayed you by telling the secret to others? How did it feel when the person you trusted did this? How do you think Samson felt when Delilah betrayed him by telling his secret?
5. Have you ever not kept a secret that someone told you? Why or why not?

Song   5 min.

Teach the children "Samson and Delilah" and sing it through twice.

SuperHero in Cartoon and Story   20 min.

Tell the children that they have a choice of drawing a cartoon or writing a short story about SuperHero, "the strongest person in the world." Point out the supply of writing and drawing paper, markers, and colored pencils. If you have drawn a cartoon or written a short story of a SuperHero, show it to the group as an example. Remind them that cartoons use both pictures and words; the words are usually placed in "balloons." A "story line" may help to give them a framework for the task. Post it on the wall or bulletin board and read it aloud, saying that this is one guide to writing the story or creating the cartoon, but they are free to devise their own outline.

Story Line
In a cartoon or story, show
1. SuperHero, the Strongest Person in the World!
2. A person, or a group of people, in need of help
3. SuperHero comes to the rescue!

Tell the cartoonists that they may draw a one- or two-block cartoon or a strip cartoon of three or four blocks. Tell those who want to draw a strip cartoon first to take a sheet of drawing paper, cut it in half lengthwise, and then fold or mark the strips into two, three, or four blocks to resemble a cartoon strip.

When the children have finished, invite them to share their cartoons and stories with one another.

Closing   5 min.

Gather the children back onto the rug or around the table, and light your chalice or candle. Then say, "There are many ways of being strong: physical strength, courage, using our minds in a mighty way. All of us want to be strong. Let us remember to use our strength for good and not for harm."

If Your Time Is Limited

- Omit the barbells and sentence completions. Incorporate the sharing of "a time when you felt really strong" into the motivating questions.
- Hold an informal discussion of the story and its themes while the children are creating their cartoons.

If You Have More Time

- Continue a discussion of different kinds of strength and how to use it.
- Sing a few of the other songs the group has learned. What are their favorites?

Samson and Delilah

SAMSON, THE STRONGEST MAN in Hebrew scripture, was a superhero. Samson's birth was announced by an angel of God, who told Samson's mother that his hair must never be cut. She and Samson obeyed this command because they believed that not cutting one's hair was a sign of being dedicated to God.

When Samson grew to be a man, he saw a Philistine woman whom he wanted to marry. He asked his parents to arrange the marriage, which they did reluctantly. On his way to his bride, a young lion roared at Samson. Samson had no weapons, so he killed the lion with his bare hands. Shortly after his marriage, Samson was tricked by his bride and her family. To get even, he burned down fields belonging to the Philistines. The Philistines got even by burning Samson's bride and her father. Samson avenged himself by "striking them down hip and thigh with great slaughter."

The Philistines, being mightier than the Israelites, went to fight Samson's people. The Israelites decided to tie up Samson and turn him over to the Philistines so that the Israelites would not be destroyed. Samson agreed to the plan. But when he was delivered into the hands of the Philistines, he easily broke the ropes that bound him, and, picking up the jawbone of a donkey, he killed a thousand men.

The Philistines again tried to capture Samson by trapping him in the city of Gaza. However, at midnight Samson rose up, took hold of the doors of the city gate and the two posts, pulled them up, bar and all, put them on his shoulders, and carried them to the top of the hill.

After this, Samson fell in love with another Philistine woman, Delilah. She was offered 1,100 pieces of silver by each of the Philistine lords if she could persuade Samson to tell her the source of his tremendous strength. Three times he told her stories that were untrue, and three times the Philistines who came to capture him were unable to lay a hand upon him. Finally Samson told Delilah the truth: "A razor has never come upon my head; for I have been consecrated to God from my mother's womb. If my head were shaved, then my strength would leave me; I would become weak, and be like anyone else."

Delilah had Samson fall asleep upon her lap; then she called in a man to shave off the seven locks on Samson's head. Delilah taunted Samson by waking him and calling, "The Philistines are upon you, Samson."

Samson awoke and ran out to fight the Philistines. But his strength had left him, and the Philistines seized him, gouged out his eyes, and put him in prison in Gaza.

After Samson had been prison for a while, the Philistines had a big festival. They brought Samson out of prison so he could entertain them. Samson, being blind, asked to lean against the pillars of the building. What the Philistines didn't realize was that Samson's hair had begun to grow out while he was in prison, and some of his strength had returned.

All the lords and ladies of the Philistines had gathered to make fun of Samson. Samson leaned against the two main pillars of the building, causing it to collapse on everyone there, including himself. In getting even, Samson killed more than those he had killed during his entire life.

SESSION 17

DAVID AND GOLIATH

Source: I Samuel 17

Theme: Someone Small Can Accomplish Something Big

Goals for Participants

- to become familiar with the story of David and Goliath
- to explore their experiences of being small and wanting to accomplish big things
- to consider the issue of violence, and alternate ways of solving problems.

Background

David is an important person in the history of Israel. He is mentioned 800 times in the Hebrew Bible and 60 in the Christian scriptures. David was the youngest son of the Bethlehemite Jesse. He became the king of Judah in the south and then king of the united kingdom of Judah and Israel, establishing its capital at Jerusalem. David may have had eight wives and as many as 19 children.

The information about David comes from several sources (I and II Samuel and Chronicles), and these sources sometimes disagree. There are stories that say that it was not David but someone named Elhanan who killed Goliath.

Even so, the stories about David are among the most historical in the scriptures. Variously called "The Court History of David," "The Narrative of Succession," and "The Succession Document," II Samuel 9-20 is considered a truly historical document. Believed to have been written by a contemporary of David, it deals with the issues of who should succeed David as king of Israel.

The story of David and Goliath, however, is ascribed more to legend than to history. It is one of two legends that explain how David came to serve King Saul, the other having to do with Saul's need for David's skills as a musician.

The Philistines are believed to have been descendants of the "peoples of the sea" who came from Crete (called Caphtor in the Bible) and Cyprus. They invaded Egypt and Israel, occupying territory along the coastal plain and living in five major cities: Gaza, Ashkelon, Ashdod, Ekron, and Gath. Gath was long considered to have been the home of giants. During David's time, the Philistines had begun to encroach on the land of the Hebrews.

The Philistines subjugated the indigenous Canaanite population. They were a warrior overlord class, possessed of iron, chariots, and superior military organization. Goliath's military armor as described in scripture is reminiscent of that of Homeric heroes.

Goliath's height is described as six cubits and a span. A cubit is a unit of measurement based on the length from the elbow to the tip of the middle finger, approximately 18 inches. A span is the distance between the ends of an extended thumb and the little finger, or about eight inches. This would make Goliath about 10 feet tall. Recently discovered manuscripts, however, describe him as closer to six and one-half feet.

The setting for this battle between the Israelites and the Philistines was in a valley, with each side occupying opposing hill country.

Children will readily identify with this tale of the youngest being able to overcome the mighty Goliath when all others were afraid to do so. The story invites them into a world of their imagination where they, who are small and equipped with only simple weapons, manage to overcome someone who is huge, powerful, and mightily outfitted. For children living in a world controlled by powerful others, to hear and talk about such stories can bring about a kind of catharsis that enhances their own sense of power and wholeness.

In the story, however, David becomes powerful by the use of violence. This is not something we wish to promote with children, and thus it is important to discuss the use of violence and alternatives to violence. The latter can also promote feelings of power and wholeness.

Materials

- Two large sheets of brown craft paper or other heavy paper
- Pencils, scissors, and crayons or colored markers
- Colored construction paper
- Aluminum foil
- Stapler and masking tape
- Stepstool
- 3" x 5" slips of paper
- Copies of Song 19, "Little David"

Preparation

- Think through your own answers to the motivating and discussion questions.
- Review the steps involved in making the figures.
- Measure and cut the sheets of craft paper for the figures, one to be the size of a child in the group and one to be the size of someone over six feet.
- Invite someone who is over six feet tall to come to the session to be the model for the Goliath figure.
- Learn the song "Little David," or arrange for someone else to teach it.

Session Plan

Gathering   Varies

As the children arrive, engage them in making paper figures of David and Goliath. Place a doubled sheet of heavy craft paper, the size of a tall adult, on the floor. Have your six-foot volunteer lie down on the paper, and tell the children to trace around him or her in pencil or crayon.

Then put down another doubled sheet of craft paper, this time the size of a child. Invite one of the children to lie down and the others to trace around him or her. Help the children cut out the two figures.

If everyone arrives at the same time, save this activity until later in the session.

Motivating Questions   10 min.

Gather the children on a rug or around a table and engage them in a discussion of the following questions. Have you ever wanted to do something important but were told you were too little or too young? What was it you wanted to do? Who told you you were too small? How did you feel?

Was there ever a time when you did something others thought you were too small or too young to do? What was it? How did it feel?

Then say, "If you have an older brother or sister, you know what it's like to always be too young to do what they are doing. You know that someday you will be old enough to do the things they are doing now. But by then you will be older, too, and they will be doing things you are still too young to do.

"Today's story from Hebrew scripture tells about a boy everyone thought was too young to do anything important."

Read the Story   5 min.

Discussion   15 min.

Lead a discussion of the story guided by the following questions.
1. What do you think of the way David was able to defeat Goliath? Can you think of any other way he could have won? How do you think he felt when he saw Goliath?
2. It has been said that David used his brain to defeat Goliath. What do you think that means?
3. Goliath was like a bully. Have you had any experiences with bullies? David stopped Goliath's bullying by killing him. How could we deal with bullies without having to use violence?
4. How do you think the people of Israel felt when David was able to kill the frightening

Goliath? How do you think his brothers felt, especially Eliab who had told him to go home?

Song   10 min.

Close the discussion by teaching and singing the well-known spiritual "Little David."

Making David and Goliath   15-25 min.

Tell the children what David and Goliath may have looked like. Read I Samuel 17:4-7 and I Samuel 17:40-42, or paraphase the passages in your own words.

Have a few children draw facial features on the figures of David and Goliath. Hang the figures on the wall. Then invite the children to create accessories out of construction paper and foil (for metallic armor). These can be a helmet, sword, armor, and boots for Goliath; and slingshot, shepherd's staff, and clothing for David. Tape them to the figures. Provide a stepstool for attaching items to Goliath; this will emphasize the size difference.

Clothing David   10 min.

When the figures are finished, set out pencils, markers, and slips of paper, and invite the children to write or draw descriptions of times they, who were little or young, accomplished something big. Tape these slips onto the figure of David. Encourage the children to put up as many as they can remember.

Closing   5 min.

Gather the group together and light the chalice or candle. Admire the figures you have made, and close by saying. "Sometimes it is hard to be the youngest or the smallest, but a person who is small can also accomplish great things."

If Your Time Is Limited

• Discuss the story and its themes while the children are adding accessories to the figures.

• Draw the outlines of the tall person and a child in advance.

If You Have More Time

• Sing "Little David" again.

David and Goliath

DAVID, THE SON OF JESSE, was the youngest of eight brothers. His three oldest brothers went off to fight the Philistines, the enemies of Israel. The other four were needed to help tend the sheep and make the cheese. David only got to be the errand boy, taking food to his brothers who were fighting.

While David was delivering food at the battlefield, he heard Goliath, a Philistine, say, "Today I defy the ranks of Israel! Give me a man that we may fight together." David saw all the men of Israel flee from this giant of a man. David asked everyone what would be given to the person who killed Goliath. The soldiers told him that the king would give that person many riches and the king's own daughter to marry. David's brother, Eliab, got angry at David for asking these questions and told him to go back to tending sheep.

King Saul heard that David was asking about the reward for killing Goliath, so he sent for the young man. David told Saul about the lion and the bear he had killed as they were trying to take his father's sheep. He said, "God who saved me from the paw of the lion and the paw of the bear will save me from the hand of this Philistine."

This convinced Saul, for he said, "Go, and may God be with you." Then Saul put armor, a bronze helmet, a coat of mail, and a sword on David. But these things were so heavy David couldn't move. So David took them all off, picked up his shepherd's staff, selected five smooth stones for his slingshot, and drew near the Philistine.

When Goliath saw the handsome youth before him, he said, "Am I a dog, that you come to me with sticks? Come to me and I will give your flesh to the birds of the air and the wild animals of the field."

David replied that God would save him, but not with the sword and spear. At this the Philistine drew nearer to meet David. David ran quickly toward the battle line to meet Goliath. David put his hand in his bag, took out a stone, slung it from his slingshot, and struck Goliath on the forehead. The stone sank into his forehead, and Goliath fell face down on the ground.

After that day David went to live with King Saul and married the king's daughter, Michal. No longer was he the little brother who was not able to do what his older brothers could do. When he grew older, David became the most famous king Israel ever had.

SESSION 18

WISE KING SOLOMON

Source: I Kings 3:16-28

Theme: Using Wisdom

Goals for Participants

- to become familiar with the story of Solomon's judgment
- to develop an understanding of the value of wisdom
- to learn the meaning of the word *proverb*.

Background

It is hard to know 3,000 years after Solomon lived whether he was as wise as the Bible story makes him out to be. It was common in biblical times to attribute wisdom to a "good" king. Perhaps some people thought, "Solomon did so many wonderful things and built such a glorious temple that he must have been very wise."

The biblical writer (D) made a particular effort to prove that Solomon's wisdom was genuine. Before giving examples of his wisdom, D tells of a dream in which YHWH grants Solomon's wish for a wise and understanding heart (I Kings 3:4-15). Whether Solomon gained his reputation by his deeds, by his virtue, or as a gift from YHWH, it is undeniable that through the centuries Solomon's name has become synonymous with wisdom.

The story of Solomon's judgment touches upon a universal theme. At least 22 examples from world folklore have been identified as bearing a close resemblance to this tale of a disputed child (Mays, *Harper's Bible Commentary*, p. 309). In recent years the news media have publicized many struggles over the custody of a child. The ethical issues raised by modern science have added to the complexity of the problem,

but many of the human concerns remain the same. If a child-custody case is currently in the news, it may be appropriate to relate the news story to the biblical story. Leaders will want, however, to take account of the age and maturity of their participants and the complexities of the case before deciding whether to introduce it.

Many parts of the Hebrew Bible are attributed to Solomon because of his reputation as a wise man: the Song of Songs, Ecclesiastes, and sections of Proverbs. Several proverbs are included in this session.

Children of middle elementary years may have difficulty understanding the concept of a proverb because of the metaphors or analogies employed. For adults it is enough to say that a proverb is a short saying that communicates a familiar truth or observation about life. With children, the literal meaning of the proverb may need to be explained or discussed before its application can be understood. Consider the saying "A stitch in time saves nine." Children can easily understand that a quick repair of a small rip in a shirt will prevent a much larger rip requiring many stitches, and be led to apply that analogy to situations in life.

Proverbs are usually derived from folk sayings, and it is not unusual to find contradictory proverbs in the same cultural setting. This discovery may lead children to a tentative understanding of the nature of true wisdom. For example, does a soft answer always dispel anger?

Materials

- Strips of paper about 24" long and 3" inches wide for the crowns (one for each child)
- Several staplers
- Odds and ends of decorative materials
- A fast-drying glue, tape, and crayons or markers

- Large chair or "throne"
- Baby doll
- Copies of Solomon's proverbs (see Resource 4) cut into slips
- Newsprint, markers, and tape (or chalkboard and chalk)
- Copies of Songs 20 and 21, "Pass the Crown" and "The Little Ants"

Preparation

- If you have been personally involved in a dispute over custody of a child, it would be well to think through your possible emotional involvement in issues that may arise and discuss this with your teaching partner, religious educator, or minister prior to the session.
- Become familiar with the slightly different flow of this session.
- Think through your own answers to the motivating and discussion questions.
- Rehearse the song/chant "Pass the Crown" and/or "The Little Ants."

Session Plan

Gathering   Varies

As the children arrive, invite each one to make a crown for a king or a judge. Encourage them to use their imaginations, making full use of the materials available to create distinctive crowns. Tape, staple, or glue the ends together, and help them to fit the crowns on their heads.

Read the Story   20 min.

If possible, ask two adults to act the roles of the mothers claiming the living baby. Have them renew and elaborate their arguments for each new judge.

Discussion   10-15 min.

Lead a discussion of the story guided by the following questions.

1. Compare our solutions to that of Solomon. Why do you think Solomon's decision was a wise one? What "wise" decisions did we make?

2. Are people born wise, or do they acquire wisdom over a lifetime?

3. Have you ever had a fight over something— perhaps a toy, or the TV? How was the fight solved? Did you need a "wise" person? Who was it?

✦4. How would our world be different if we all were wise in settling disputes?

Proverbs   15 min.

Gather the children at a table and say, "Solomon's wisdom is found in other places in the Bible. The book of Proverbs contains many wise sayings, many of which are said to have come from Solomon. I will ask each of you to pick a saying and draw a picture about it. Many of these sayings are commonly used in our culture, so some of them may sound familiar. Perhaps you have been given the same advice! All of these proverbs have been attributed to Solomon."

Place the proverbs face down on a table, and ask each child to pick one. Read the proverbs aloud, and discuss them to be sure each child understands her or his proverb.

Ask the children to think about how they can illustrate their proverb and do a quick drawing using paper and markers or crayons. Tell them to tape or glue the proverb to the drawing, and post the completed drawings on the wall or bulletin board. Read the proverbs again so that all can see how they were interpreted.

Pass the Crown Game   15 min.

Ask if someone will volunteer to give her or his crown for the game.

Version One (Competitive)
With everyone sitting in a circle on the floor, one child places the crown on his or her head. Together the group chants or sings the following words, keeping a steady rhythm:

Pass the *crown* from me to *you*, to *you*;
Just *pass* the *crown* and *do* just as I *do*.

On each accented word the crown is passed to the head of the next child to the left. When the chant is finished, the child wearing the crown is "out." He or she stands up and places the crown on the head of the next child to begin another round. Eliminated players step back from the circle but continue to chant with the group as additional rounds are played. The game ends when only one player remains.

Version Two (Cooperative)
Re-form the circle, with everyone wearing a crown. The play proceeds as before, but this time all crowns are passed on the accented beats. This will call for group coordination, but becomes easier the second or third time. There is no elimination or winner in this version of the game, but most groups like to see if they can increase the speed of the chant and still keep the hats on their heads. The attempt should produce a good many laughs.

When you have played both versions of the game, ask which one the group liked better, and why. If no one else mentions it, point out that the second version requires more cooperation and that no one is left out for even a short time. Say, "Wise decisions often require us to look at a problem in a new way. When we played this game one way, not everyone could stay in the game, and we could use only one of our crowns. By taking a new look at the game, we were all able to use our crowns and stay in the game. When you find yourself in an argument over a game, you might put your mind to work to see if you can come up with new way of playing. You and your friends might invent a whole new game!"

Closing   2 min.

Place a candle or chalice in the center of the circle. Say, "Being wise is more than saying wise words. Being wise means using our minds to think and our hearts to understand." Ask the children to repeat after you:
> May we have eyes that see,
> Hearts that love,
> And hands that are ready to serve.

If Your Time Is Limited

- Omit the Pass the Crown game.

If You Have More Time

- Play Pass the Crown again.
- Learn and sing "The Little Ants" if you haven't already.

Wise King Solomon

KING SOLOMON, THE SON OF DAVID, who killed Goliath, is famous for his wisdom. There is a story in Hebrew scripture that is often told to show how wise he was.

Two women came to King Solomon, each claiming to be the mother of the same baby. The two women lived together in the same house. The first woman had a baby, and three days later the other woman had a baby. There were only the two women and their babies in the house. On the night the second baby was born, one of the babies died. Each woman claimed to be the mother of the living baby.

Stop the story and ask, "How would you decide to whom the baby belongs?" Allow each child a turn at being the king, sitting on the king's throne and wearing a crown, to give his or her solution to the dilemma. Record their *answers in brief form on newsprint or chalkboard. Then continue reading the story.*

When King Solomon was asked by the two women to make the decision about the baby, he said, "Bring me a sword." A sword was brought. Then he said, "Divide the living child in two; then give half to one, and half to the other."

The woman whose child was alive said, "Please, my lord, give her the living child; certainly do not kill it!"

But the other woman said, "It shall be neither mine or yours; divide it."

Solomon said, "Give the living child to the first woman; do not kill it; she is its mother." King Solomon was wise enough to know that the true mother would give the child up rather than allow it to be killed.

JONAH AND THE LARGE FISH

Source: The Book of Jonah

Theme: Running Away from Responsibilities

Goals for Participants

- to examine their experiences of running away from responsibilities
- to become familiar with the story of Jonah
- to discover other themes in the story such as making up excuses and repentance.

Background

The small book of Jonah is considered to be among the twelve Minor Prophets, though it is very different in style from the others. Rather than the writings of a prophet, it is a story similar to an allegory or a parable about a recalcitrant prophet. The author is unknown, although the book is believed to be the work of one person. It is thought to have been written between 400 and 200 B.C.E., after the Exile.

This book used to be considered historical or semihistorical because Jonah, the son of Amittai, seemed to be the same historical personage who is mentioned in II Kings 14:25. Today, however, it is thought that the author used the name of that little-known prophet as a symbol for Israel, or for a prophet who typified the narrow exclusivity of post-exilic times.

Nineveh, located on the east side of the Tigris River, was the capital of Assyria. This kingdom in upper Mesopotamia existed from about 900 to 612 B.C.E., when it was conquered by a combined force of Babylonians and Medes. Tarshish might have been the Greek Tartessos, but at any rate, it was used in the book to represent a place far away.

Most interpreters believe that the story of Jonah was written to counter post-exilic attitudes of narrow nationalism and religious exclusivity. The first section of the story contrasts Jonah's unwillingness to preach to the Ninevites to a God who cares about saving these non-Jewish neighbors and to mariners who are open to help from any of the gods. The second section contrasts Jonah's anger at the repentance of the Ninevites with their openness to salvation from a foreign god.

Most of us know this story as "Jonah and the Whale," but the scripture says only "a large fish." Although whales are not technically fish, they are probably the only sea animal large enough to swallow a human whole.

Children often want to flee from a task that seems hard or wrong to them, so they should easily identify with Jonah's desire to sail in the opposite direction, as far away as possible from where he was told to go. They will enjoy thinking up excuses for not doing something they ought to be doing. Children this age will also have had experiences of excluding others, and with being excluded themselves. The story provides a useful opportunity to discuss this sensitive issue.

Materials

- 3" x 5" index cards
- Pencils
- Markham poem printed on newsprint (see "Circle Poem and Ritual")
- Two pieces of chalk, or a long cord
- Copies of Song 22, "Who Did Swallow Jonah?"

Preparation

- Think through your own answers to the motivating and discussion questions.

- Review the steps for the Excuse Game.
- Become familiar with the directions for the Circle Ritual; determine which of the alternatives you will do and where you will do it.
- Become familiar with the song "Who Did Swallow Jonah?" or arrange for someone else to lead it.
- Post the words to the Markham poem.

Session Plan

Gathering   Varies

As the children arrive, ask them to think about things they wish they didn't have to do and to write these down on index cards. (Children of this age vary in their ability to write down their ideas. Be sensitive to this and offer to help any who would rather have you or another adult write for them.) After everyone has arrived and had a chance to write down one or more ideas, place the cards to one side.

Motivating Questions   10-15 min.

Gather the children on a rug or around a table. Engage them in a discussion based on the following questions: When there is something we must do that we don't want to do, we often feel like running away. Have you ever had that feeling? What was it you didn't want to do? How did you try to run away from it? Where did you think you could go? What happened? Did you have to do it anyway?

Then say, "All of us have been told at some time or other to do something that we don't want to do. It's amazing, isn't it, how many excuses we can find for not doing what we're told? Today's story from Hebrew scripture is about Jonah, who didn't want to do what God told him to do."

Definitions

heretic   a person who doesn't believe what a church tells her or him to believe

rebel   a person who goes against the usual way of doing things

a thing to flout something or someone to make fun of or ignore

Read the Story   5 min.

Discussion   15 min.

Lead a discussion of the story guided by the following questions.
1. When Jonah ran away from what God wanted him to do, he ended up in the belly of a large fish. What would it feel like to be in the belly of a large fish for three days and three nights?
2. In the end, Jonah had to do the thing he didn't want to do. How do you think he felt about this? Would it have been easier if he had just done as he was told the first time? Is it always easier to do what you're supposed to do? Why is it so hard to do sometimes?
3. Jonah was being asked to help bring wicked people into the circle of good people, to include them. How would you feel if you were told you had to include people you didn't want to? What does it feel like when you are left out?
4. In the end, the Ninevites begged God to forgive them for their wickedness. Is it hard for people to admit they have been doing wrong? Why? Even if it is hard, how do you think they feel afterward?

The Excuse Game   10-15 min.

Gather the children in a circle. Make a small circle of cord, or draw one with chalk in the center of the children's circle. Then ask the first child to draw one of the "things I wish I didn't have to do" cards. Invite the children to jump into the small circle one at a time and offer excuses for not doing "the thing I wish I didn't have to do." Allow four or five excuses for each card, and then go on to the next, until everyone has had a chance to draw at least one.

Some examples of excuses to the demand, "Do your homework!"

I can't, I left it at school.
I can't, my right hand is broken.
I can't, I'm going on the space shuttle tomorrow.

Song   15 min.

Teach, or have a music assistant teach, "Who Did Swallow Jonah?" After the group knows the whole song, divide them into two groups. Have one group sing the first "Who did?"; then the other group echoes the second "Who did?," repeating this twice. Then have the first group sing "Who did swallow Jonah?" with the second group echoing the second "Jonah?" Repeat this pattern two more times, then have the first group sing "Who did swallow Jonah?," with the second group echoing it, and then everyone coming together for the last word, a robust "whole?," at the end.

Circle Poem and Ritual   5 min.

Remind the children that, in the story, God asked Jonah to go tell the people of Nineveh to repent of their wickedness and to become good people. Jonah was being asked to bring people he didn't like into a circle of goodness. Point to the posted poem (see below) and read it in unison with the children. Explain that it was written by Edwin Markham, a Unitarian, and is often quoted by Unitarian Universalists because it states what we believe. Help the children understand the meaning of the poem by defining words they do not know.

> They drew a circle which kept me out,
> A heretic, a rebel, a thing to flout.
> But love and I had the wit to win.
> We drew a circle which drew them in.
> —Edwin Markham (adapted)

Ask the children to stand in a circle close to one another. Give the chalk (or cord) to one of the children to draw or make a circle on the floor around the group. Tell them to repeat the poem. You, the leader(s), look longingly at the circle as the first two lines are said, then when the children begin the third line, take a piece of chalk and draw a bigger circle (or extend the cord to make a larger circle) to include you and them. This ritual would be fun to do outdoors if the weather is feasible.

Closing   5 min.

Light the chalice or candle and say the poem in unison one more time. Then say, "It's usual to want to run away from things we wish we didn't have to do. It's usual to think up excuses. In the meantime, though, the task is still there waiting for us, and sometimes it can feel like we are lost in the belly of a whale while we're trying to get out of doing what we must do. In the end, it may be better just to do it and get it over with quickly."

If Your Time Is Limited

- Choose to do either the Excuse Game or the song.
- Omit the Circle Ritual, and read the Markham poem at the Closing.

If You Have More Time

- Do all the activities.
- Set out drawing paper and markers and invite the children to try to imagine what it would be like to be inside a large fish and then to draw a picture of it.

Preparation for Session 23

Invite someone who has been a refugee to come to Session 23, and giving him or her one-half hour before the session closing. Explain that you are inviting her or him to share some of her or his experiences with the children, and that there will be refreshments afterward. Suggestions for finding such a person:
- Ask someone you know.
- Ask your minister or religious educator for suggestions.
- Check with the other clergy in your community.
- Check with ethnic organizations in your community.

Jonah and the Large Fish

GOD SAID TO JONAH, "Go at once to the great city of Nineveh and cry out against it; for their wickedness has come up before me." Jonah knew that if he gave the people of Nineveh God's warning, they would beg for forgiveness. Jonah was also sure that they would be forgiven, since God was a merciful God. Jonah didn't like the Ninevites and didn't want them to be forgiven, so he took a ship to Tarshish, a town in the opposite direction from Nineveh, and the one farthest away.

While that ship was sailing to Tarshish, a terrible storm came up. The sailors were very afraid, and they threw all their cargo into the sea to lighten the ship in the water. Jonah, meanwhile, was fast asleep below deck.

The captain woke Jonah and begged him to call upon his God to keep them from dying. Then the sailors questioned him. "Where do you come from? Why are you here?" When they found out that he was running away from his God, they cried, "What is this you have done? What shall we do to you, that the sea may quiet down for us?"

Jonah answered, "Pick me up and throw me into the sea; then the sea will quiet down for you; for I know it is because of me that this great storm has come upon you."

Still they tried to get back to land, but the storm got worse. Finally, they realized that they would have to throw Jonah into the sea if the rest of them were to be saved. So they picked Jonah up and threw him into the sea. The sea stopped its raging, and the sailors were certain that God had caused the storm.

God then provided a large fish to swallow Jonah; and Jonah was in the belly of the fish for three nights and three days. Then Jonah prayed to God for deliverance; God spoke to the fish, and it spewed Jonah out upon the dry land.

Again, God told Jonah to go to Nineveh, and this time Jonah went. The people of Nineveh listened to Jonah, and they begged God to forgive them. God heard their cries and was full of mercy for the Ninevites, just as Jonah knew God would be. Therefore they were forgiven. This made Jonah angry, but God finally convinced him that the people of Nineveh were worth saving.

SESSION 20

JOB

Source: Job 1-2, 42:7-17

Theme: Coping with Life's Ups and Downs

Goals for Participants

- to become familiar with the story of Job
- to explore the question of why bad things happen.

Background

It is in the story of Job that Satan is encountered for the first time in these sessions. Later Jewish and Christian traditions portray Satan as the archenemy of God, but it is more likely that when Job was written (circa 600 B.C.E.) the Hebrew name Satan referred to one of many angels—one whose special job was to keep track of things on earth. (See Anderson, *Understanding the Old Testament*, p. 589.) So instead of seeking to destroy God's work, the Satan of this story is testing one person's faith in God.

The book of Job is composed of two prose sections—a prologue and an epilogue—and a long poetic midsection. The prose tells the basic story and has all the characteristics of a good folktale, including "living happily ever after" at the end. It pictures Job as blameless and upright, a man whom ancient hearers would expect to be restored to good fortune. Readers today may "hear" this story differently, and may need to remind themselves that the folktale focuses on Job's devotion to God. As in the story of Abraham in Session 7, we are led to believe that if Job keeps faith with YHWH, he will prosper. And indeed he does—twice over. Children may wish to argue that Job's dead children and servants could not possibly be restored. Remind them that this is, and has always been, a story. Help

them to see in it the strong affirmation of the goodness of life through times of good and evil.

The folktale provides a concrete setting for the poetic reflections of the midsection. This poetry speaks eloquently of the human condition in such a way that each reader recognizes the struggles as his or her own. Though the book is long, leaders will want to sample some of the poetry. Interestingly, the prose and poetry sections were written separately, by different authors, in different places, at different times, and using different names for God. (YHWH is used throughout the prologue and epilogue, whereas more general terms for God are found in the poems.)

Children may be interested in the story's account of the customs surrounding mourning. When things got bad, Job ripped his clothing, shaved his head, and sat in ashes. His friends who sat with him for seven days also tore their robes and sprinkled dust on their heads. All of these were common biblical ways of mourning death as well as other tragedies of life. The custom of "sitting shiv'ah," where family members gather at home, sit on low stools, and receive visitors for a week following a burial, continues in Jewish families to this day.

Materials

- Drawing paper and markers or crayons
- *Alexander and the Terrible, Horrible, No Good, Very Bad Day,* by Judith Viorst
- Copies of Song 23, "Job's Round" (optional)
- Acetate transparencies, markers designed for transparencies, and overhead projector (you may be able to borrow or rent one from a local school or library)

OR

Felt scraps, sharp scissors, and flannelboard (cardboard covered with solid-color flannel)

Preparation

• Think through your own answers to the motivating and discussion questions.
• Decide which art activity you will use for the "Illustrating the Story" section.
• Practice singing the song "Job's Round," or recruit someone to lead it.

Session Plan

Gathering   Varies

As the children arrive, invite them to draw a picture of themselves having "a really bad day." Display the pictures where everyone can see them.

Motivating Questions   10 min.

Gather the children together and ask, "What is 'good luck'? What is 'bad luck'? What are some of the reasons bad things happen to people?" You may want to list their responses on newsprint.

Then say, "Everyone has times when nothing seems to go right. Usually these periods don't last very long, and we simply say we've had a bad day. But for some people these periods last for years. After a while, these people begin to believe that it is more than just bad luck, that some magical force must be out to get them. Today's story from Hebrew scripture is about Job, a man famous throughout history for having extremely bad luck."

Definition

curse   to swear at God

Read the Story   5 min.

Discussion   15 min.

Lead a discussion of the story guided by the following questions.
1. This story is really very much like a fairy tale.

We could easily add the words "And Job lived happily ever after" at the end of it. Do you think this story could have happened in real life? Why, or why not?
2. Satan bets that Job can be pressured into cursing God. God bets that Job will be faithful enough not to utter such a curse. Many terrible things happen to Job because God decides to test his faith. Do you think that is right or fair? Why?
3. Think about a bad day you've had—perhaps the one you drew a picture of earlier. How did you manage to get through it? What or who helped make things better?

Illustrating the Story   25 min.

Two activities are described. Choose the one that best suits the materials and equipment you have available. If your group is large, you might choose to divide the group and do both activities.

Overhead Projector Presentation
Although this activity is suggested for use with an overhead projector, transparencies may be made and taped together in a book, with a white cover to serve as a background.

Review the characters in the story with the children. Say, "We'll need to list all of the people and animals in the story so that we can do this activity. But we don't need to have thousands of cattle and sheep—one or two will do! God and Satan appear in the story, but since they are not 'people or animals' we'll need to think of some way to represent them."

List the characters, animals, and possessions as the children suggest them, and ask each child to illustrate one, or one group. Your list might look like this: Job, Job's wife, Job's children (10), three friends, cattle, sheep, donkeys, camels, God, and Satan.

Plan the transparencies with the children so that when they are stacked one on top of the other they make a complete picture of Job before (and after) his ill fortune. It may take some trial and error to make the completed picture without too much overlap. The easiest plan is to have Job in the center, the friends in front of him, his wife and children beside and behind him, and the animals around the edges. Adjust the number of transparencies to the size of your group.

Retell the story, beginning with all the transparencies on the projector. As the story progresses, remove the items indicated, one at a time. When Job's fortunes are restored, replace all transparencies.

(Before this activity, the leader should mark a copy of the story in the following manner: underline each item that is taken away from Job, and place a number in the margin to indicate the order of removal. While the children are working on their transparencies, move among them and tell them the appropriate number to write in the corner of their drawing. Before retelling the story, stack the transparencies in order, with #1 on top.)

Flannelboard Presentation
Create the list of characters as described above. Invite each child to use felt scraps to create one item from the list. Keep the design simple and in appropriate scale, if possible. Place the figures on a flannelboard, removing and replacing them to tell the story of Job.

A Modern Story   10 min.

Gather the children and tell them that you'd like to read a story of a boy about their own age who had a particularly bad day. Read *Alexander and the Terrible, Horrible, No Good, Very Bad Day.*

Closing   5 min.

Gather the children, light the chalice or candle, and say, "When something bad happens to us, we need friends who will help us through the bad time. Job's friends wanted to help him, but they spent more time blaming Job than comforting him. Job tells them what would be the best help of all when he says, 'Listen carefully to my words, and let this be your consolation.'"

If Your Time Is Limited

- Choose the flannelboard alternative to illustrate the story.
- Omit *Alexander and the Terrible, Horrible, No Good, Very Bad Day.*

If You Have More Time

- Learn to sing "Job's Round."
- Invite an "audience" for the retelling of your story with illustrations.

Preparation for Next Session

Send a letter to parents before the next session. See this sample:

Dear parents,
    Next week, in our Timeless Themes group, we will be hearing and discussing the story of Ruth. We will discuss themes in the story such as kindness to people from other countries, ways of feeding the poor, and changing religions.
    Many Unitarian Universalists have had the experience of changing their religion. For most of us, this was a decision we wanted to make and therefore we felt positive about it. Still there may be things about our former religious affiliation that we have missed. If children have changed their religious community as part of their parents' decision, they may have some mixed feelings about the change.
We hope you will find an opportunity to discuss your family's religious background with your child, sharing with each other feelings about the changes that may have been made. They will have a chance to discuss these issues with others in our group at next week's session. Thank you for your help.

Sincerely,
Leader's Name

Job

JOB HAD TEN CHILDREN and many, many sheep, camels, oxen, donkeys, and servants. He was also a good man, who took care of his household. God was pleased with Job and bragged about him to Satan, one of God's angels. Satan replied, "Why shouldn't Job be good? Haven't you protected him and all that he has? But if you make things hard for him, he will curse you to your face!"

God didn't believe that Job would stop being good, so God told Satan, "All that he has is in your power; only Job himself you must not harm."

Satan caused Job's oxen and donkeys to be taken by enemies, who killed all of the servants. A fire burned up all of his sheep. The camels were taken by another enemy. A wind knocked down the house of Job's oldest son, and all of Job's children were killed.

Job went into mourning by ripping his robe and shaving his head, but he did not curse God. So God told Satan, "Job still persists in his integrity, although you incited me against him, to destroy him for no reason."

Satan replied, "All that people have they will give to save their lives. But touch his bone and his flesh, and he will curse you to your face."

God said, "He is in your power; only spare his life."

Job was then afflicted with terrible sores from head to foot. He went to sit in the ashes and scrape his sores, but still he did not curse God.

Three of Job's friends came and sat with him for seven days and seven nights. After sitting in silence all that time, they started to give him advice, but none of it helped. In fact, some of it was just plain bad advice, because they thought Job must have done something bad to deserve all this bad luck.

Job cursed the fact that he was ever born. He complained loudly about the bitterness of his soul. But he never cursed God.

Job rejected the advice of his friends, and this pleased God. God said to one of Job's friends, "My anger is on fire against you and against your two friends; for you have not spoken of me what is right, as my servant Job has. When Job prays for you, I will accept his prayer not to punish you."

After Job prayed for his three friends, God restored all of Job's fortunes and gave him twice as much as he had before.

SESSION 21

THE RELIGION OF RUTH

Source: The Book of Ruth

Theme: Kindness to People from Another Country

Goals for Participants

- to become familiar with the story of Ruth
- to consider the theme of kindness to people from another country
- to discover other themes in the story, such as feeding hungry people and how religions evolve.

Background

The book of Ruth consists of the beautifully told story of the foreign woman who became the great-grandmother of David. It is in the form of a short story or a novella, one of the few examples of this form in the Hebrew Bible. The author is not known, and opinions differ as to when it was written. Scholars now lean toward sometime between 950 B.C.E. and 850 B.C.E., which is also the time of the J writers and the court history of David. The book is written in literate, courtly language, although the characters are more rustic.

The last part of the story, which tells how Ruth became David's ancestor, is a later addition, so the story probably existed earlier in some form unrelated to David. Traditionally, David was believed to be the son of Jesse (the son of Obed, the son of Boaz). The source for this is I Chronicles 2:11-13 and I Samuel 16:6-13. The setting of this story is the time of the Judges, roughly one or two hundred years earlier.

Moab, Ruth's home, was in the land immediately east of the Dead Sea, a grain-growing, sheep-raising tableland, 3,000 feet above sea level and 4,300 feet above the Dead Sea. Strangers were allowed to come to Moab during times of famine, but they were not granted all the rights of the Moabites. The major god of the Moabites was Chemosh, a "martial fertility" god, and there were numerous other fertility gods and goddesses.

The Hebrew social structure of those times was that of the clan. The clan was the major source of one's identity. If one clan member was wronged, all were wronged, and it was required that some clan member avenge that wrong. It was important for the clan's property to remain within the clan, so if one member was forced to sell, another member would buy. It was also believed that immortality was assured through the next generation, so if a clan member died without children, his brother, brother-in-law, or other clan members could provide heirs for him by marrying his widow (a custom called a levirite marriage). Elimelech and his sons left no heirs so, in the story of Ruth, the responsibility came to Boaz to marry Ruth as a way of providing heirs and keeping the family property in the clan.

Wheat was a major source of food, planted in the fall when the winter rains had started and harvested in May and June. Sickles were used for reaping, and the grain was obtained by threshing with a stick, dragging an instrument over the stalks, or having cattle trample them. The wheat was winnowed in the late afternoon and evening, when the winds blew in the right direction to carry away the chaff. It was put through a sieve to get rid of foreign matter and finally was roasted or made into flat rounds of bread.

In this story there are several examples of kindness to those from another country: the Moabites allowed Elimezlech's family to settle in their land during a famine; Orpah and Ruth, Moabites, were loyal and loving to their Hebrew mother-in-law; and Boaz was especially kind to

Ruth, who was now herself a stranger.

When Ruth chose to follow her mother-in-law, she was also choosing to change her religion, to become a Hebrew. Because of this, the story of Ruth is part of Jewish conversion ceremonies. Many of our Unitarian Universalist children will be familiar with the experience of changing religions, and this will be a topic of interest for them.

As our world becomes smaller and smaller, our children will have more and more contact with people from other countries. They may already have had such experiences, either here or while traveling abroad. Here again, the story of Ruth will be of interest. Similarly, feeding the hungry and poor is today an all-too-common problem, as it was in biblical times. Children this age are quick to relate to this issue, whether they encounter it in the news media or in a story such as this one.

Materials

- Copies of Songs 24 and 25, "One Man Shall Mow My Meadow" and "Song of Ruth" (optional)
- 9" x 12" white construction paper (one per child), colored markers, and large envelope or envelopes (for optional activity)
- muffin pans, paper baking cups, and two large mixing bowls
- mixing spoons and measuring spoons and cups

For each 1 dozen regular-sized muffins:
- 2 cups all-purpose flour
- 1 teaspoon salt
- 1/3 cup sugar (can be brown sugar)
- 3 teaspoons baking powder
- 1 egg
- 1/2 cup vegetable oil
- 3/4 cup milk
- Options: add 1 cup fresh or frozen blueberries or 1 cup raisins or 1 cup mashed bananas, along with 1/2 teaspoon nutmeg and 1/4 teaspoon cinnamon. If you use bananas, use only 1/3 cup milk.

Preparation

- Send home a letter inviting the children to discuss their religous background with their parents (see sample letter at end of previous session plan).
- Think through your own answers to the motivating and discussion questions.
- Listen to and learn "Song of Ruth" and/or "One Man Shall Mow My Meadow," or ask another person to teach them (if you will have time for the song activity).
- Determine how many muffins the children will be making. If you are making muffins for a guest, you will probably want to make one dozen to give to the guest and enough more for your group. If you are sending muffins to a group, you will probably want to make two or three dozen, plus the amount needed for your group. If you are having a bake sale, you will want to make as many as your supplies and the cooking space will allow. Arrange to use the church kitchen.
- If you choose to hold a bake sale and donate the proceeds to an organization that provides services to people from other countries, you will need to make arrangements for the time and place of your bake sale; decide on a price for the muffins; and prepare a notice for the newsletter, the order of service, or church bulletin board. You might also invite a representative of the recipient organization to attend.

Session Plan

Gathering   Varies

If you have invited guests, welcome them and introduce them to the children, after the group has assembled. Then proceed with the next activity. In some cases, it may be better for the guests to arrive a little later (during discussion time or when the muffins are almost done).

Making Muffins   20 min.

Now explain to the children that together you will be making muffins today. When all the children have arrived, go to the church kitchen or move to your work area and prepare the muffins.
1. Preheat the oven to 400°.
2. Invite one group of children to measure out

and mix in one bowl the following ingredients: flour, salt, sugar, and baking powder.
3. Have a second group measure and mix in another bowl: eggs, oil, and milk.
4. Have a third group place the paper baking cups in muffin pans
5. Combine all ingredients, mix gently, and fill paper cups half full.
6. Bake at 400° for 20-25 minutes. Set a timer where you can hear it.
7. Clean up.

Motivating Questions   10-15 min.

While the muffins are baking, gather the children on a rug or around a table. (If you have invited a guest from another country, invite him or her to share thoughts about the questions, or you may want the children to use these questions to interview the visitor.) Engage the children in a discussion of the following questions: Do you know people who are from another country? What country are they from? How have other people treated them?

Have you ever traveled in another country? Where? How did it feel to be living in a strange land? How were you treated? Are some things especially hard when you're in a foreign country?

Then say, "People don't always remain in the country or the religion in which they were born and brought up. Actually, most adult Unitarian Universalists have come out of another religion. Many times in Hebrew scripture the Hebrews expressed the fear that some of their people would be tempted to follow the religions of neighboring countries, and to worship the golden calf of Ba'al. Today's story about Ruth is a celebration of a woman from Moab who changed her religion to become a Hebrew."

Definitions

glean to gather up grain left after a field is harvested
thresh to separate seed by repeated beating

Read the Story   5 min.

Taking Muffins Out of the Oven   2 min.

Whenever the baking time is up, check to see if the muffins are done. (Insert a toothpick; if it comes out clean, they're done.) Remove the muffins from the oven and set to cool.

Discussion   15 min.

Lead a discussion of the story guided by the following questions.
1. What do you think would have been hard for Naomi and her family when they were strangers in Moab? What was hard for Ruth when she came to Bethlehem as a newcomer?
2. What kindnesses were shown to these people from other countries? What kindnesses would help anyone who was in a strange land?
3. People don't always remain in the religion in which they were born and brought up. Most Unitarian Universalist adults have come out of another religion. When Ruth left her homeland of Moab and came to live with the Hebrews, she also changed her religion. Have any of you changed your religion? What religion did you practice before? Have your parents changed their religion? What religion did they practice before? How do you think it feels to change your religion?
⚜ 4. Naomi's family was allowed to move to another country when her country suffered from a famine, and Ruth was allowed to glean the fields because she was poor. How do we help hungry people today? What more could we do?

Distribution of Muffins   5-10 min.

If you have a guest with you, present the muffins to him or her at this time, and invite your guest to join you in your Closing. If you are sending muffins to a group, prepare them for delivery.

If you chose to hold a bake sale, you can either hold your Closing and then prepare for the sale or save the Closing until after the sale.

Closing   5 min.

Gather the children, light the chalice or candle, and say, "It is hard for someone to leave the country they were born in and grew up in. It can be hard to change one's religion. Besides being lonely for friends and familiar sights, people who make these changes must often learn a new language and new ways of doing things. If we were strangers in another country we would want people there to help us and to treat us kindly. Let us remember to show kindness to people we meet who are from other countries."

If Your Time Is Limited

- Leaders mix muffin ingredients ahead of time, or use a muffin mix.

If You Have More Time

- Lead the group in singing "Song of Ruth" and/or "One Man Shall Mow My Meadow."
- Invite the children to make Welcome Cards for the people to whom you are giving the muffins, or for any other people from other countries whom you or they know. Show the children how to fold a 9" x 12" piece of construction paper into fourths, similar to other greeting cards. Then invite them to decorate their cards with welcoming greetings and pictures or designs. Go around the group and let each share his or her card with the others. Then place them in envelopes for delivery.

The Religion of Ruth

THOUSANDS OF YEARS AGO there was a famine in Israel. Elimelech, his wife, Naomi, and their two sons traveled from Bethlehem to the neighboring country of Moab, looking for a better place to live. But Elimelech died, and Naomi was left with her two sons. The boys grew up and married Moabite women. Ten years later, the two sons died also. Naomi was left in a strange land with two daughters-in-law and no grandchildren.

In those days women were unable to work to support themselves, and so they needed the help of their families. Therefore, Naomi decided to return to her family in the land of Judah. She told her daughters-in-law that they were free to return to their families. One daughter-in-law returned to her mother's house, but Ruth clung to Naomi. Naomi tried again to persuade Ruth to leave her. But Ruth replied, "Do not press me to leave you or to turn back from following you! Where you go, I will go; where you live, I will live; your people shall be my people, and your God my God."

Naomi returned to Bethlehem, taking Ruth with her. They were very poor and had trouble finding enough to eat. There was a law in Israel that the poor were allowed to glean the fields. Every day, then, Ruth went to glean the fields so that they would have something to eat. Naomi told Ruth to glean in the fields of her wealthy relative, Boaz.

Boaz noticed Ruth, and when he found out she was the Moabite who had been so good to his relative Naomi, he gave her special protection. Ruth was allowed to drink water provided for the field workers, and the young men were ordered not to bother her. Boaz also told his workers to leave extra grain for Ruth to glean.

After the harvest was over, the grain needed to be threshed. During the threshing, Boaz and Ruth had a chance to get to know one another better, and they decided to marry. In this way Ruth and Naomi were provided for, and Ruth, a foreign woman raised in another religion, became the great-grandmother of David, the most famous king in Israel.

FIERY FURNACES AND ROARING LIONS

Source: Daniel 3 and 6

Theme: Miracles

Goals for Participants

- to become familiar with two stories of Daniel which involve miracles
- to explore the idea of "miracle."

Background

The story of Daniel is set in the sixth century B.C.E., when the royalty, craftspeople, military officers, and other leaders of Judah were deported to Babylon. Since the Exile spanned approximately 50 years, those who were exiled needed to find ways of living as strangers in a strange land.

Very few of the original exiles ever returned home. Psalm 137 offers a moving lament and a pledge to remember Jerusalem. The stories in today's session demonstrate how difficult it was for the exiles to practice their religion faithfully when surrounded by foreign gods and forced to obey a foreign king. The stories portray Daniel as an example of courageous faith.

Though the story of Daniel is set during the Exile, it was actually written during a much later period of Hebrew history, and with a hidden purpose. Dating from the second century B.C.E., the book is part of a body of apocalyptic literature which was prevalent up through the days of the early Christian church.

An apocalypse deals with mysteries, often revealed by angels in a miraculous manner. The focus of apocalyptic writings is on the end of the world—usually depicted as a sudden cataclysm. A battle or natural disaster may bring about a cosmic transformation. Some kind of judgment will take place, followed by restoration or salvation. The language is obscure, the author anonymous. The object is to hide the meaning of the text from the enemy, but inform true believers of what they must fear and encourage them to hope for the new world order that will follow.

In the apocalyptic tradition, the author of Daniel predicts a time of terrible trouble, but ends with a promise of everlasting life for all whose names are inscribed in the book of life. The end, predicted to arrive in three and a half years, did not arrive on schedule, but the hope of everlasting life became a key part of Christian theology.

In the Hebrew Bible the book of Daniel is included in the section of Writings, but the Christian Bible places it among the Prophets. Daniel is one of the few books in either Bible which can be dated with reasonable accuracy—based largely on the scholarly premise that prophecy is accurate only when the events have already happened, while predictions about future events are less reliable. The references in the text to the desecration of the temple in Jerusalem, which scholars have firmly dated at 167 B.C.E., demonstrate that the author knew of this event. On the other hand, the author shows considerable confusion about events surrounding the end of the reign of Antiochus, which occurred late in 164 B.C.E. Thus, on the assumption that the references to 167 are based on historical fact, while the references to 164 are predictions of the future, biblical scholars date the book of Daniel early in the year 164 B.C.E.

The two stories in this session describe miracles, traditionally understood as special interventions by God in people's lives. A better definition for children might be something like "amazing happenings for which we have no complete explanation." It is important to allow children enough time to discuss their own ideas about miracles, and perhaps come up with a working definition based on their reading and experience.

If the children get stuck in debating the truth or nontruth of miracles, you might ask them to consider things that "seem like miracles." Even if we disavow miracles, the phrase, "It seems like a miracle" carries meaning for most people.

Materials

- List of names and pronunciations (see Gathering)
- Drawing paper
- Pencils and markers or crayons
- Masking tape or duct tape and several staplers
- Yellow ribbon or yarn (optional)
- Newsprint, or chalkboard and chalk
- Copies of Songs 22 and 26, "Who Did Swallow Jonah?" and "Wonder Where Is Good Old Daniel"
- Paper plates, plain white or yellow (one per child)
- 9" x 12" sheets of yellow construction paper (one per child), cut into strips 1" x 9"
- sticks about 12" long (such as rulers, paint stirrers, or cardboard tubes from wire hangers), one per child

Preparation

- Think through your own answers to the motivating and discussion questions.
- Make a mask, so that you understand the process.
- Learn the words to "Who Did Swallow Jonah?" and "Wonder Where Is Good Old Daniel," or find someone to teach them to the group.

Session Plan

Gathering   Varies

As the children arrive, explain that some of the names in today's stories are tricky to say. Have Babylon (bab' uh-lahn), Darius (dah´-ri-uhs), Shadrach (shad' rak), Meshach (mee' shak), Abednego (ah-bed' nay-goh), and Nebuchadnezzar (neb'-uh-ked-nez´ er) written on newsprint or the chalkboard, and engage the children in learning the correct pronunciations.

Motivating Questions   10 min.

When all the children have arrived, gather them together around a table or on a rug. Say, "Miracle stories—stories in which people are able to do things that they ordinarily wouldn't be able to do—are probably the most popular kind of story told. Leaping tall buildings in a single bound, making time stand still, and being invisible are all popular ingredients for miracle stories. What do you think a miracle is? Can you think of some examples of miracles that you know about?" Allow enough time for a variety of ideas to emerge.

Then say, "Today we will be hearing two well-known miracle stories from the book of Daniel in the Hebrew scripture. In both stories a miracle happened because the God of Israel protected the people who were in danger."

Read the Story   5 min.

Discussion   15 min.

Lead a discussion of the story guided by the following questions.
1. What were the two miracles? Why do you think Shadrach, Meshach, Abednego, and Daniel were chosen for the miracles?
2. Can you think of any logical or scientific reasons for the miracles?
3. Once a tornado tore through a house, destroying it. In the house was a baby in a cradle. The baby, cradle and all, was lifted into a nearby tree, and found unharmed and still asleep. Some people think this is a miracle. If you could be part of a miracle, or perform one, what would it be? (Give each child a chance to "create a miracle.")

Musical Kneeling   10 min.

Version One (Competitive)
Gather the children in an open, carpeted area of the room, and say, "In the story, the king ordered that every time the people heard music, they were supposed to fall to their knees. We're going to play a game that's a little bit like Musical Chairs, except that each time the music starts, kneel down. When the music stops, stand up and walk around. The last one to kneel when the music starts will be

'thrown in the fiery furnace.'" (Indicate where.)

Play until only one child is left. Allow that child to start and stop the music for the next round. Play several rounds if there is time. The music tape that accompanies this program will work well for this activity.

Version Two (Cooperative)
Play the game again, but explain that this time the object is to keep everyone out of the fiery furnace. Each time the music starts, the players must look around at the others. No one is to kneel until all can do it at the same time. If one person is trapped, everyone ends up in the furnace. To make the game more interesting, keep time to see how long they can stay free. Play several times, if necessary, to see if they can improve their "free time." Discuss the "miracle" of cooperation: by sticking together a whole group can be saved.

Making Lion Masks   10 min.

Gather in your work space and engage the children in making lion masks. On each paper plate draw the eyes, nose, whiskers, and mouth of a lion. Wrap a strip of yellow construction paper tightly around a pencil to make a curl. Staple one end of the curl to the edge of the paper plate. Repeat until the yellow curls surround the lion's face. Tape a ruler or similar stick to the back of the mask. You may wish to give the children the option of using yarn or ribbon for the mane. If so, be sure to gather or request these items.

Learning and Dramatizing a Song   20 min.

Teach the children these words to the music for "Who Did Swallow Jonah"?

Daniel, Daniel, Daniel, Daniel
Daniel in the li-li-li-li;
Daniel, Daniel, Daniel, Daniel,
Daniel in the li-li-li-li;
Daniel in the lions',
Daniel in the lions',
Daniel in the lions' den.

Ask the children to think of a way to dramatize the song, using their masks. For example, the lions sit in a circle waving their masks during the first four lines while "Daniel" paces. During the last three lines, they threaten him ferociously, perhaps ending the song with their masks practically touching him. Let the children decide how to play this verse of the song, and try it out a few times. Then suggest that they could make up another verse—so that Daniel can get out! Remind them of the sequence of events in the story. Then record their words on newsprint or a chalkboard, revising the lyrics as the group comes to a consensus. Decide how to act out this verse, and then sing the two verses together.

Closing   2 min.

Light a candle or chalice, and say, "In the book of Daniel we find a prayer that Daniel used to praise his God. Let's close our morning with Daniel's words: 'To you, O God of my ancestors, I give thanks and praise, for you have given me wisdom and power'" (Daniel 2:23).

If Your Time Is Limited

- Omit the song dramatization.
- Play only one version of the Musical Kneeling activity.

If You Have More Time

- Sing "Wonder Where Is Good Old Daniel."
- Ask the children to make a drawing of their "miracles."

Preparation for Next Session

This coming session is the time you will have guests who have at some time been refugees. This may be a person or persons from your congregation or from the community. If arrangements have not as yet been made for this visit, invite someone you know who has been a refugee, or obtain suggestions from your religious educator or minister; from other clergy in the community, or from an organization that brings together people of a specific national origin, such as persons from Asia, Central or South America, or Eastern Europe.

Tell the prospective guests of the story and focus of the session, and ask them to speak of their experience in being a refugee. See this sample letter:

Dear parents,

This Sunday in our Timeless Themes group, we will meet some members of our congregation [or some people from our community] who are familiar with the difficult experience of being a refugee. If your family has had a similar experience, or if you know someone who has, you may wish to talk about this with your child.

At the close of our session, we will share refreshments with our guests. If your child would like to contribute to this "party," cookies, crackers, or some other such snack would be most welcome. Thank you!

Sincerely,
Leader's Name

Fiery Furnaces and Roaring Lions

NEBUCHADNEZZAR, the king of Babylon, invaded Israel with his army and captured members of the royal family, whom he took back to Babylon. These captives made Nebuchadnezzar angry because they refused to worship the Babylonian gods, preferring to worship their god, the God of Israel. The king gave an order that every time the people heard music, they were supposed to fall down on their knees and worship the golden statue that the king had set up. The king declared, "Whoever does not fall down and worship shall immediately be thrown into a furnace of blazing fire."

Several men reported to the king that the Jews Shadrach, Meshach, and Abednego were not following his order to fall on their knees and worship the golden statue when they heard music. They were called before the king, but they told him they could not do as he ordered. The king was so filled with rage that his face was distorted. He ordered the furnace to be heated seven times hotter than it usually was.

Shadrach, Meschach, and Abednego were tied up (still dressed) and thrown into the furnace of blazing fire. The flames were so hot that the men who threw Shadrach, Meshach, and Abednego into the fire were killed by the heat.

But Shadrach, Meshach and Abednego walked out of the furnace untouched. Their hair was not even singed, nor their clothes harmed. Nebuchadnezzar said, "Blessed be the God of Shadrach, Meshach and Abednego, who has sent an angel and delivered God's servants who trust in God." The king then ordered that no one was to speak against this God.

Years later, the lessons of the fiery furnace were forgotten, and Darius, the new king of Babylon, decreed that no one was to pray to any god or human, but only to King Darius, for thirty days. Anyone who did not do so was to be cast into the lion's den.

Daniel was a favorite of King Darius, so there were men in the kingdom who wanted to get Daniel into trouble. These men spied on Daniel and saw him praying to the God of the Jews. They immediately ran and told the king.

This troubled Darius very much. He tried to excuse Daniel, but the men reminded him that once a king commanded a law, the law could not be changed.

When Daniel was cast into the lion's den, King Darius said, "May your God, whom you faithfully serve, deliver you." Then the entrance was sealed with a stone. The king went to his palace, but he was unable to eat, and sleep fled from him.

At the break of day, King Darius hurried to the den. He cried out to Daniel, and Daniel replied, "My God sent an angel and shut the lions' mouths so that they would not hurt me, because I was found blameless before God; and also before you, O King, I have done one no wrong." The king was exceedingly glad. He ordered Daniel be taken out of the lions' den, and the spies were cast into the den. The lions no longer had their mouths closed.

SESSION 23

THE FLIGHT TO EGYPT

Source: Matthew 2

Theme: Refugees

Goals for Participants

- to be introduced to the New Testament of the Christian Bible
- to consider the experience of leaving one's home to avoid danger
- to become familiar with the story in Matthew of Jesus' birth and the flight to Egypt
- to discover other themes in the story—for example, dreams and angels as messengers from God.

Background

The first half of this story, told by the gospel writer Matthew, is very familiar, as it is one of the two infancy narratives read by most of us at Christmastime. The second half, describing the trip to and from Egypt, may not be as well known. The other nativity story (Luke 2:1-20) tells of the manger, shepherds, and angels. The two nativity stories and that of the flight to Egypt were written independently of one another, created by early Christians to enhance their developing theology.

The book of Matthew is one of the four gospels, with Mark, Luke, and John. Matthew, Mark, and Luke are called synoptic gospels, because they share much common material. Mark is believed to be the earliest. Matthew and Luke use material from Mark, material from an assumed source of sayings of Jesus (Q), plus material that is unique to each of them.

This nativity story is unique to Matthew. Though all the gospel writers aim to tell the story of Jesus' life, teachings, and passion, each writer has his own special interests. One of Matthew's concerns was to demonstrate to Jewish Christians that Jesus was the Messiah who had been prophesied in the Hebrew Bible, and he uses numerous quotations for that purpose. Several parallels are drawn between Moses and Jesus: both were rescued from a massacre of young children; both came out of Egypt.

Matthew was also interested, however, in laying the groundwork for the idea that Gentiles, as well as Jews, would be included in this new era. Thus he shows the Jew Herod rejecting Jesus and the Gentile wise men worshiping him. Matthew was not written by the apostle Matthew; the author is believed to have been someone associated with a rabbinical school in Syria. Matthew was probably written between 80 and 100 C.E.

The King Herod in this story was Herod the Great, who was appointed by the Romans to rule in Palestine (see "The Land" in the "Biblical Terms" section). Herod ruled from 37 to 4 B.C.E., which suggests that the date of Jesus' birth was more likely to have been 4 B.C.E. Herod was known to have been a cruel and violent person, even murdering members of his own family, but none of the historical accounts mentions a massacre of young children. His son, Herod Antipas, was the one who ordered the execution of John the Baptist.

Dreams were of great importance in the ancient Near East. They were believed to contain messages from God, sometimes in clear language and sometimes in symbols that needed to be interpreted. Manuscripts have been found that list rules for interpretation and the meanings of various symbols. Angels were also considered to be messengers from God. Appearing usually in human form, they brought God's messages to earth, announced special events, protected the good and righteous, and conveyed God's displeasure to the sinful. In this story,

118   •   *Timeless Themes*

dreams serve as the vehicles for God's messages and protection, though in one case an angel appears in a dream.

The theme of "a child who is destined for great things having to escape from a powerful person who wishes her or him evil" is familiar to children from fairy tales, myths, and other stories. You may wish to remind the children of the story of the infant Moses, who was also rescued from a massacre of children. The idea that an adult would wish children ill is frightening to children, but it is important for them to have the opportunity to discuss their fears.

Many of our children will themselves have moved, and they may wish to share those experiences and their feelings about them. Some may also have heard of or even met people who have had to move because of a threatening situation. Children of this age can empathize with such situations and will benefit from having an opportunity to offer friendship to people who have suffered in such a way.

Materials

- A map showing Egypt and Palestine, and a map showing the homeland of your invited guest(s) and North America
- Refreshments
- Napkins, place mats, and paper cups and plates
- Objects connected with the refugee's country, for decorations
- Music from the refugee's country—tapes or records (and record player, if needed)
- Copies of Songs 27, 28, and 29, "The Coventry Carol," "Mary Had a Baby," and "Amen."

Preparation

- Think through your own answers to the motivating and discussion questions.
- Send home a letter inviting the children to bring in contributions for refreshments (see sample letter at end of previous session plan).
- This is the session to which you have invited someone who has been a refugee. You have asked this person or persons to share some of their experiences with the children. Let them know at what time you'd like them to arrive, and mention that the children will be serving refreshments.

- Learn one or more of these songs—"Mary Had a Baby," "The Coventry Carol," or "Amen," verses 1 and 2—or arrange for someone else to teach them.
- Display the maps close to your discussion area.
- Prepare the area for the party: set up record or cassette player and music; obtain and arrange decorative objects from the guest's country; set out napkins, paper plates, and the like.
- Print the list of stories in the Hebrew Bible and the Christian New Testament on newsprint, and post on a wall or bulletin board (see end of session plan). Display this chart for the remainder of the program.

Session Plan

Gathering   Varies

As the children arrive, have the music playing. Ask the children to place the refreshments they have brought in the area where the party will be. Invite them to help you set the tables and display the objects from your guest's country.

Introduction to the New Testament   10 min.

When all the children have arrived, gather around a table or on the rug and say, "The stories we have heard up to now are stories that were written in Hebrew, and are found both in Hebrew scripture, which Jews use, and in Christian scripture, where they are called the Old Testament. The stories we will be hearing from now on are from the New Testament of the Christian Bible, stories that are sacred to Christians but not to Jews. These stories were written in Greek."

Refer to the chart of the story listing you have posted, and point out that the stories in Hebrew scripture and in the Old Testament of the Christian Bible are the same, though they appear in a slightly different order. Then explain that the stories in the New Testament are the ones about Jesus, who was a Jew and very familiar with the stories in the Hebrew Bible.

Explain that we count the years on our calendars—1991, 1992, and so on—from the year of Jesus' birth. (Scholars today, however, believe that his birth was more likely to have been in 4-6 B.C.E.) Explain that A.D. means "anno domini," or "the year of our Lord," and that B.C. means "before Christ." Both refer to Jesus, who is often called "Lord" or "Christ." Tell them that it is becoming common to use C.E. and B.C.E., which stand for the "common era" and "before the common era."

Motivating Questions   5 min.

Say, "The world is full of refugees—people who have been forced to leave their homeland and go to a new country. Many people throughout history have been refugees. Some people have come to this country when they were in danger because of religious persecution. Some have come because there was a famine in their homeland and they were in danger of starving. Some people have come because there was a war in their country and they were in danger of being killed. As long as people are in danger, there will continue to be refugees."

Engage the children in a discussion of the following questions. Have you ever moved from your house? Town? State? Country? What did it feel like? How would you have felt if you had to go to a strange place because your life was in danger?

Then say, "Hebrew scripture told many stories of times when the Hebrew people were refugees. You might remember that Joseph's family went to Egypt because of famine in their land of Canaan, which was later called Israel. At another time, after many battles, the Hebrews were forced to be refugees in Babylon. Today's story of the early life of Jesus, from Christian scripture, is another story of a family forced to be refugees."

Definition

homage respect

Read the Story   5 min.

Discussion   15 min.

Show the children the map of Egypt and Israel, and point out the distance between the two. Then discuss the story guided by the following questions.
1. Do you think Joseph was wise to leave Israel and take his family to Egypt? Why? Was he wise to come back? How do you think he and Mary felt about having to leave? If you know about people who had to leave their country because their life was in danger, tell us about them. (Be sensitive to the children's fears in relation to the massacre of the infants and allow time to talk about them.)
2. People in biblical times believed that dreams were important. The wise men and Joseph paid attention to the warnings they got in dreams. Many people today believe dreams are important. What do you think dreams mean?
3. Sometimes the warnings in the story were given by an angel in a dream. Angels were believed to be messengers from God. What do you think angels are?

Song   10 min.

Teach, or have someone teach, "Mary Had a Baby," or one of the other songs if you prefer. One option might be a Christmas carol from your guest's country: have him or her help teach it and join in the singing.

Meeting Your Guest(s)   15 min.

Welcome and introduce your guests. Ask them to tell the children about their experience of having to leave their home. Invite the children to ask their questions.

Having a Party Together   10 min.

Put the music on and serve refreshments!

Closing   5 min.

Gather everyone in a circle, light the chalice or candle, and close by saying, "A place to call home is very important for people. For many of us it is hard to leave and move to a new home; it is especially hard if we must leave because we feel our lives are in danger. The good thing is that wherever we live, we can always make new friends."

The Stories in Timeless Themes

Stories from the Hebrew (and Christian) Bibles
Adam and Eve, Cain and Abel, Noah, The Tower of Babel, Sodom and Gomorrah, Abraham and Isaac, Jacob and Esau, Joseph and His Brothers, Joseph and the Dreams, Moses in the Bulrushes, Moses and the Burning Bush, Let My People Go, The Ten Commandments, And the Walls Came Tumbling Down, Samson and Delilah, Wise King Solomon, Jonah and the Large Fish, Job, The Religion of Ruth, Fiery Furnaces and Roaring Lions.

Stories from the New Testament of the Christian Bible
The Flight to Egypt, John the Baptist, The Temptations of Jesus, Jesus and the Temple, Jesus and the Law, It's a Miracle, The Healing Power, Mary and Martha, The Teachings of Jesus, The Crucifixion of Jesus, Mary Magdalene, The Good Samaritan.

The Flight to Egypt

IN THE DAYS OF THE ROMAN emperor Augustus, Israel was occupied by the Romans. Augustus commanded everyone in Israel to return to his or her hometown to register. Joseph, and Mary to whom he was engaged, went from Nazareth in Galilee to Bethlehem in Judea. While they were in Bethlehem, Mary gave birth to her first son, Jesus.

After Jesus was born, three wise men from the east came to Jerusalem asking, "Where is the child who has been born King of the Jews? For we have seen his star at its rising, and have come to pay him homage."

King Herod, who was the king of Israel at the time, asked his chief priests and scribes where the new king was supposed to be born. They replied, "In Bethlehem of Judea; for so it is written by the prophet."

Herod secretly called for the wise men and learned from them when the star appeared. Then he sent them to Bethlehem, saying, "Go and search diligently for the child, and when you have found him bring me word so that I may also go and pay him homage."

When the wise men had heard Herod they set out; and there, ahead of them, went the star that they had seen at its rising, until it stopped over the place where the child was. On entering the house they saw the child with Mary, his mother; and they knelt down and paid him homage. Then, opening their treasure chests, they offered him gifts of gold, frankincense, and myrrh. And having been warned in a dream not to return to Herod, they left for their own country by another road.

Next, an angel of God appeared to Joseph, Jesus' father, in a dream. "Get up, take the child and his mother, and flee to Egypt, and remain there until I tell you; for Herod is about to search for the child, to destroy him." Joseph and Mary got up and took the child by night, and went to Egypt.

When Herod saw that he had been tricked by the wise men, he was infuriated, and he sent and killed all the children in and around Bethlehem who were two years old and younger.

When Herod died, an angel of God suddenly appeared in a dream to Joseph, who was still in Egypt, telling him to return to Israel. Joseph, Mary, and Jesus moved back, but they moved to the town of Nazareth in Galilee because they were now afraid of Herod's son, who was king.

JOHN THE BAPTIST

Sources: Matthew 3, 4:12; Mark 1:1-14; Luke 3:1-21

Theme: Repenting and Resolving to Lead a New Life

Goals for Participants

- to become familiar with the stories of John the Baptist
- to explore the meaning of repentance
- to discover other themes in the stories, such as baptism and other naming ceremonies, and symbols such as the dove, water, and flowers.

Background

You will find the story of John the Baptist in all four gospels, and there is mention of him also in the writings of the Jewish-Roman historian Josephus. Luke offers a nativity legend in which an angel announces John's conception. All four gospels give witness to John's simple life in the wilderness, his call for repentance and baptism, and his arrest; all four characterize him as one who prepares the way for someone mightier. Matthew and Mark describe how Herod Antipas puts him to death at Salome's request. Josephus' short reference to John explains that the Jews believed the defeat of the armies of Herod Antipas was God's punishment for John's death.

Though John is described as being born into a priestly family, he emerges later as a prophet preaching in the wilderness. It is possible that he had contact with the Essene "Dead Sea Scroll" community; his teachings and actions reflect some elements of their beliefs and practices. But even more, John's teachings are grounded in Jewish traditions and ethics. Like Jesus, he had a following of disciples, and it is likely that

portions of the gospel writings about him were handed down by them. In Iraq today there is a sect called Mandeans who continue to keep alive the Baptist tradition. The early Christians, however, understood John to be not a prophet in his own right, but one who prepared the way for the coming of Jesus.

Water is an obvious symbol for use in rites of purification. It was used by Jews before John's time in a baptism of converts; the Essenes had a ritual that included repentance and washing; and Hellenistic mystery cults had similar ceremonies. For John, the meaning seems to be related to repentance, forgiveness of sins, receiving God's Spirit, and the coming of a new order, the Kingdom of God. In the early church it served these purposes too, but it also marked an acceptance of the gospel and initiation into the church.

The Hebrew word that is translated *repentance* carries the meaning of "turning" or "returning," and signifies a turning away from wrongdoing and toward an active ethical life—a returning to God. The Greek word used in the New Testament means "change of mind," along with sorrow for errors. In both cases some concrete action or ritual usually accompanies the mental and spiritual conversion. The dove symbolizes various things in the Hebrew Bible: gentleness, innocence, nesting in rocks, flight, Israel (the name Jonah means dove), and cessation of hostilities and the coming of peace (as in the story of Noah). Later it comes to symbolize the presence of the powers of the divine.

Unitarian Universalist congregations celebrate baptisms, christenings, and dedications, and mid-elementary-aged children are likely to have experienced one or more of them either as a witness or a participant.

Unitarian Universalist children of this age are not likely to understand the yearning to repent and turn toward a whole new way of life which is represented in the story of John and the ritual of baptism. They will, however, be able to think of times when they have done wrong and wanted to start over. They may have made a few resolutions at the New Year. They will probably be more comfortable working together on a group list of wrongdoings and actions for a good life than sharing personal ones.

Eight- and nine-year olds are very interested in joining clubs and groups that have ceremonies of initiation. Most will have heard of baptisms and will be curious about them.

Materials

- Copies of Song 29, "Amen," and/or Song 30, "When Jesus Went to Jordan"
- Newsprint and marker
- Black construction paper, 8 1/2" x 11"
- Tissue paper or cellophane, in at least four colors
- Glue, scissors, and needle and thread
- Cardboard patterns of the dove (see Resource 5)
- Cardboard patterns of the inner spaces
- Hole punch
- Bowl (to be filled with water)
- Vase of flowers, with one flower for each child
- A world globe

Preparation

- For this and forthcoming sessions, it will be helpful to prepare by reading the three New Testament versions in *Gospel Parallels*, in which they appear side by side. Your minister or the public library may have it.
- Think through your own answers to the motivating and discussion questions.
- Become familiar with the customs of your congregation concerning baptisms, christenings, and dedications. If one is scheduled around this time, perhaps you can arrange for the children to attend.
- Decide which version of the dove you will make. Version 1 is more complicated and may be difficult for some groups. Version 2 is much simpler. Make several copies of the stained-glass dove pattern in cardboard. Make a sample dove (see Resource 5). Set out the

materials for this activity.
- Think through the steps involved in the Ceremony of Repentance and Resolution.
- Arrange the Ceremony space, with a semicircle of chairs preferably facing a window on which the stained-glass doves will be hung. Place the globe, flowers, and bowl of water on a small table in front of the window.
- Learn the song "When Jesus Went to Jordan," and/or "Amen," or arrange for someone else to lead the group singing.

Session Plan

Gathering   Varies

As the children arrive, begin work on the stained-glass doves. When everyone has arrived, set the project aside and move to the next activity. If your group arrives all at once, begin with the Motivating Questions.

Motivating Questions   10 min.

Say, "At the beginning of a new year, many people make resolutions—promises to do things in the new year that will make them better persons." Ask the children, "Have any of you made resolutions at New Year's? What were they?"

Continue by saying, "Birthdays are another time we make resolutions to be better. Still another is when people take part in certain religious ceremonies. Baptism is one of these religious ceremonies. Baptism is when a person is dipped in water or sprinkled with water. It was an ancient Jewish custom that symbolized the washing away of bad thoughts and deeds, thereby purifying the person. She or he is then clean and whole. Has any of you ever been baptized, christened, or dedicated or seen someone who was? Was it a child or an adult? What was it like? How are baptisms, christenings, and dedications alike? How are they different?

"Today's story from Christian scripture is about the ceremony of baptism."

Read the Story   5 min.

Discussion 15 min.

Lead a discussion of the story guided by the following questions.

⚜ 1. John's baptism was for people who "repented" from wrongdoing. To repent means to realize you have done something wrong, to be sorry, and to turn instead toward a new life of goodness and right. What kinds of things should people repent of? (List the children's answers on newsprint.) If they repented, then how would people lead their lives afterward? (Write these responses on another piece of newsprint.)

2. In the days of Jesus, only adults were baptized. Today, baptism and dedication ceremonies are often for babies or young children. Do you think these ceremonies should be for children or adults? Why?

3. Symbols are things we can see and touch that make us think of things that are not so easy to see or touch, like a red heart being a symbol for love. The water used in baptism is a symbol. What would it be a symbol of? Flowers can be symbols too, and we use them in our dedication ceremonies. What might flowers be symbols of?

4. When John baptized Jesus, God's spirit came to Jesus in the form of a dove, another symbol. What do you think it means that God's spirit came to him? Why would it come in the form of a dove?

Making Stained-Glass Doves 15 min.

Gather in your work space and guide the children in making their doves. Fold the black construction paper in half. Place the dove pattern on the construction paper with the bottom of the dove on the fold. Draw around the outside and around the inner spaces with a pencil.

Cut around the outer edges of the dove, through both layers of paper. Then make a small cut in the center of each inner space. Using that cut as a starting point, cut away both layers of the inner sections. Paper-punch the eye hole.

Cut a piece of tissue paper or cellophane for each inner space, using the patterns as guides. Open the construction paper and glue the tissue paper or cellophane inside. Glue the paper down. Trim off any pieces that stick out. Glue dove back together.

Run the needle and thread through the top of the dove's wing (for a descending dove), tie into a loop, and hang by the window.

Ceremony of Repentance and Resolution 10 min.

Ask the children to sit in a semicircle on chairs or a rug facing the window with the hanging doves and the table with flowers and bowl of water. Post the children's responses to discussion Question 1 where they can be seen.

Describe the ceremony you are about to carry out saying, "We have heard the story of a man named John who baptized people. Some of us have been baptized or seen baptisms. Some of us have seen Unitarian Universalist dedication ceremonies, and some of us have been dedicated. Today we are going to have a 'Ceremony of Repentance and Resolution for the People of the World.' First we will read the list of things for which we wish the people of the world would repent. Then we will each go forward and sprinkle water on the globe as a symbol of cleansing," or use some other word or phrase that the children have suggested. "Then we will read the list of things that those who turned toward a new life of goodness and right would do. After that we will each go forward and take a flower as a symbol of hope."

Read the first list, for each item saying: "We wish that we, the people of the world, would repent and no longer . . . " At the end of the list, say "So be it!" Invite each child to go forward and sprinkle water on the globe.

Then read the second list, for each item saying: "Turning toward a new life of goodness and right, we wish that we, the people of the world, would resolve to . . ." Again, close with "So be it!" Ask each child to go forward and take a flower.

Closing 5 min.

Teach the children "When Jesus Went to Jordan" or "Amen," singing the verses about Jesus as a baby and John the Baptist. If you sing "Amen," say that it has more verses about Jesus which you will sing in the weeks to come.

If Your Time Is Limited

- Cut out the dove "frames" ahead of time, so that the children need only place and glue the tissue paper or cellophane.
- Or have the children cut out the dove frames while you are reading the story.

If You Have More Time

- Teach both songs.

John the Baptist

JOHN THE BAPTIST was a man who lived in the wilderness and wore clothing of camel's hair with a leather belt around his waist. He ate locusts and wild honey, and proclaimed, "Repent, for the kingdom of heaven has come near."

Many people came to be baptized by John in the River Jordan. One day, John's cousin Jesus of Nazareth came to be baptized. As Jesus was coming up out of the water, suddenly the heavens were opened to him and he saw the spirit of God descending like a dove and alighting on him. And a voice from heaven said, "This is my son, the beloved, with whom I am well pleased."

Then Jesus was led up by the spirit into the wilderness to be tempted by the devil. After forty days and forty nights, Jesus heard that John had been arrested because the town leaders felt he was getting to be too popular with the people. So Jesus came back from the wilderness and started preaching, as John had, "Repent, for the kingdom of heaven has come near."

Jesus went throughout Galilee, gathering his first four disciples, Simon Peter, Andrew, James, and John. He also taught in the synagogues, preached, and healed every disease and every infirmity among the people. Jesus' fame spread, and great crowds followed him. Soon he had more followers than John had had before he was arrested.

The people who arrested John the Baptist now thought Jesus was a danger, too. From this time on the leaders had Jesus spied upon, just as they had had informers follow John the Baptist.

SESSION 25

THE TEMPTATIONS OF JESUS

Sources: Matthew 4:1-11; Luke 4:1-13; Mark 1:12-13

Theme: Temptations

Goals for Participants

- to become familiar with the story of the temptations of Jesus
- to gain an understanding of the concept of temptation
- to consider things which might tempt them personally
- to explore the issue of moral decision-making.

Background

The temptations of Jesus occur after 40 days in the wilderness. The rains in the story of Noah lasted 40 days and 40 nights (Genesis 7:12). The Israelites spent 40 years in the wilderness before arriving in the "promised land." Forty represented a large number for biblical writers—40 years was two generations, and 40 days was certainly longer than any rain storm of human memory. To live in the wilderness for 40 days with nothing to eat would have been remarkable.

Deprivation is the basis of most temptation. Poverty may tempt one to acquire wealth illegally. Deprived of food, one may be tempted to set aside traditional values or laws to obtain sustenance. Deprived of power, one may seize upon violent or extraordinary means to demonstrate one's importance. All of these temptations are illustrated in the story of Jesus.

But there is another perspective on the temptations—a theme that we have found in earlier stories. Biblical writers regarded the process of temptation as a test of an individual's devotion to and trust in God. Just as Abraham was tested by God, and Job by Satan, Jesus is put to the test. Thus today's story shows Jesus not only resisting temptation but also demonstrating his trust in God.

Children in the middle elementary years will have personal experience with both of these ideas. Deprivation comes in degrees, and all children have some sense of one or more of the deprivations portrayed in the story of Jesus—hunger, powerlessness, poverty. Loyalty and devotion to friends are also a major issue for children this age. Clubs and clubhouses symbolize a trusted group; friendship pins and bracelets hold great meaning for both givers and receivers. Children may be able to identify times when a trusting relationship of their own has been tested, and although this is not the same as Jesus' trust in God, it is the beginning of an understanding of trustworthiness.

Devil, as used in this story, is virtually the same word as the Hebrew *Satan.* The 27 books of the New Testament were written in Greek, and the writer of Luke used the word *diablos* in this account, the same word that Greek translators of the Hebrew Bible used for Satan in the story of Job.

Materials

- Glue, scissors, and markers or crayons
- Large sheet of paper or posterboard
- Old magazines to cut up
- Brown paper lunch bags
- Scraps of yarn, fabric, colored paper
- Table or other "stage"
- Copies of Songs 29 and 30, "Amen" and "When Jesus Went to Jordan"
- Sheet

Preparation

- Think through your own answers to the motivating and discussion questions.
- Make a sample paper-bag puppet.
- Practice verses 1-5 of the song "Amen" and/or "When Jesus Went to Jordan," or ask your song leader to do so.

Session Plan

Gathering   Varies

As the children arrive, ask each one to find in a magazine a picture of something that is very tempting to them. It might be a special food, a skateboard or tape deck, a special athletic or musical ability. Have markers available so that children can "doctor" the magazine pictures. Tell them to cut out their pictures and glue them on a large piece of paper or posterboard, writing their names with a marker beneath the items. In addition to their own temptations, the leaders might add symbols for the temptations of Jesus—bread, the world, and an angel.

When everyone has finished, display the poster for all to see.

Motivating Questions   5 min.

Gather on a rug or around a table. Say, "Looking at the items on our poster, ask yourself, 'Would I do something I know is wrong in order to have that?'" Allow the children to share their responses, if they wish. Ask, "What types of things have tempted you in the past? Did you resist the temptation or did you give in? What happened?"

Then say, "At times, everyone has been tempted to do what they know they should not do. Children are tempted, and so are adults. The only thing that changes with age is the kinds of things that tempt us.

"We heard stories from Hebrew scripture about people being tempted. Remember how Adam and Eve were tempted to eat the fruit from the tree of knowledge of good and evil? And how Lot's wife was tempted to look back at the destruction of Gomorrah?

"Today's story from Christian scripture is about Jesus' being tempted by the devil, another name for Satan, after 40 days in the wilderness."

Definition

the devil   another name for Satan

Read the Story   5 min.

Discussion   10 min.

Lead a discussion of the story guided by the following questions.

1. According to the story, with what did the devil try to tempt Jesus? Why would they have been tempting to Jesus? Why do you think Jesus resisted temptation? What makes you able to resist temptation?
2. *Devil* is the word used in the New Testament of the Christian Bible to translate the Hebrew word *Satan*. Can you remember another story we have heard where Satan played a part? (Adam and Eve; Job, when Satan tested Job's trust on God.) Why do you think the devil is tempting Jesus in this story?
3. Jesus quotes some words from the Hebrew Bible as he resists the devil's temptation. When he says, "People do not live by bread alone," what does he mean? This passage is most often translated "Man does not live by bread alone." Do you think Jesus' words refer only to men?

Making Paper-Bag Puppets   10 min.

Give each child a paper bag. Invite the children to experiment with it as a puppet by inserting a hand into the bag and moving their fingers. Engage them in making puppets of Jesus, the devil, or any person they choose, using markers, crayons, and scraps of yarn, fabric, or colored paper. Remind the children that the devil is not a person; that they can use their imagination in creating a puppet to represent the devil. Encourage at least one child to make a Jesus puppet, and one a devil, so that the story can be effectively reenacted.

Act Out the Story   10 min.

Using puppets for Jesus and the devil, act out the story of the Temptations. Some children who finish their puppets early might improvise props such as a tower and a stone. A sheet draped over a table will provide an instant puppet stage. One child can narrate or tell the story while two others act it out, or the characters can make up dialogue to tell the story.

A Moral Dilemma   10-15 min.

Read the following moral dilemma aloud. Be sure the children understand the problem.

"You want to see a certain movie. Many of those in your group have seen it and say it's hilarious. Your parents think it's too 'adult' for you, and refuse to allow you to see it. Your best friend, who is having the same argument at home, suggests a plan. Each of you will tell his or her parents that you will be at the other's house on Saturday afternoon. But instead, you'll really be going to the movies. The plan works—at least until you're coming out of the movie. Your mother is driving home from grocery shopping. She stops the car and tells the two of you to get in. No one says a word all the way to your house. Both you and your friend are nervous and scared."

Lead a discussion using the following questions as a guide.
1. What is your dilemma (problem)?
2. What will you say to your mother?
3. Your mother says, "No movies for a month." Is that fair? Why?
4. Your friend receives only a scolding when her (his) parents find out. Is that fair? Why, or why not?
5. Are there other temptations in this story? What are they?

Closing   5 min.

Light a candle or chalice, and close by saying, "May we feel strong enough to resist the temptation to do things we know are not right." Close by singing "Amen," verses 1-5, or "When Jesus Went to Jordan."

If Your Time Is Limited

- Sing only the chorus of "Amen" or one verse of "When Jesus Went to Jordan."
- Omit the reenactment of the story.

If You Have More Time

- Discuss another moral dilemma—perhaps one suggested by the children, or one of the following:

A heavy rainstorm has caused the creek near you to overflow. Several of your friends have gone down to see how high the water has risen despite their parents' warning not to. They have been gone for two hours, and, frankly, you're getting worried. What do you do? Do you go after them? Do you tell an adult? Why? How do you choose between loyalty to your friends and their safety? Is a choice necessary? What tempts you in this dilemma?

OR

A supermarket shopping cart appears on your front lawn one morning. You and your family don't know how it got there. The name of a local store is printed on the cart, so probably a neighbor has used it to bring groceries home. You discuss what to do with the cart. Dad says he could use it to help move bags of topsoil and mulch for the garden. Your brother thinks he could use the wheels to make a go-cart. Mom thinks it would be handy as a laundry cart, but feels a little uneasy about keeping it. Your sister insists that the only thing to do is to return it to the store. What do you think? Why? What would you do? Name the temptations involved for each member of your family.

The Temptations of Jesus

JESUS FASTED forty days and forty nights in the wilderness, and he was famished. The devil came and tempted him, saying, "If you are the son of God, command these stones to become loaves of bread."

But Jesus answered, "It is written, 'One does not live by bread alone, but by every word that comes from the mouth of God.'"

Then the devil took Jesus to the Holy City of Jerusalem and placed him on the highest point of the temple, saying to him, "If you are the son of God, throw yourself down; for it is written, 'God will command God's angels concerning you,' and 'On their hands they will bear you up, so that you will not dash your foot against a stone.'"

But Jesus said to the devil, "Again it is written, 'Do not put the Lord your God to the test.'"

Again, the devil took Jesus to a very high mountain, and showed him all the kingdoms of the world and their splendor, and the devil said, "All these I will give you, if you will fall down and worship me.'"

Then Jesus said to the devil, "Away with you, Satan! For it is written, 'Worship the Lord your God, and serve only God.'"

All of the answers which Jesus gave he had learned from the Hebrew scripture. When the devil saw how strong Jesus' faith was, the devil left, and suddenly angels came and waited on Jesus.

JESUS AND THE TEMPLE

Sources: Luke 2:41-50; Mark 11:15-19; Matthew 21:10-17; Luke 19:45-46

Theme: Anger

Goals for Participants

- to understand the New Testament stories of Jesus and the temple
- to strengthen their sense of identity with their Unitarian Universalist congregation
- to explore the issue of anger, in relation to the story and in their own lives
- to learn the use of nonviolent responses to anger.

Background

The first portion of today's story is the only incident from Jesus' childhood recorded in the four gospels. The story was most likely included by Luke to establish without a doubt Jesus' Jewish upbringing. We are told of his family's Passover pilgrimage, and we witness Jesus with the elders of the Temple. His age is clearly important here, for 12 was the age of bar mitzvah ("son of the law"), when boys assumed adult responsibilities toward the observance of the law. The story further establishes that Jesus is thoroughly at home in the temple, and that even at this young age he assumes that others must recognize his special relationship with God.

Though not entirely surprising that a boy might not be missed immediately in a throng of pilgrims, the reaction of Jesus' parents is remarkably mild. Almost all children experience being "lost" temporarily, and discussion question 2 may evoke some strong memories.

Questions 3 and 4 may present problems for some children. If they have absorbed a cultural image of Jesus as holy and perfect, it may seem wrong to ask how Jesus might have handled his anger differently. This is a good opportunity to emphasize Jesus' humanity. Stress that he faced the same kinds of struggles that all human beings face; and point out that questioning someone's actions does not devalue that person, but helps us to understand the person more completely.

Anger is a universal emotion, in itself neither good nor bad. The important thing is not that one is angry, but what one does with that anger.

Out-of-control anger can be terrifying, both for the person experiencing it and for those at whom it is aimed. Learning to control this powerful emotion and to use it productively is part of the maturation process. Children in the middle elementary grades generally understand that there are many ways to act when they are angry, though they often act without considering the options. Adults can help by identifying nonviolent ways of acting and by modeling them in their own lives.

Perhaps the most important thing we can convey to children is that anger need not lead to rage and aggression, that we can choose to respond constructively to angry feelings, and use the anger to correct an unjust situation. "When I am angry I can write, pray, and preach well, for then my whole temperament is quickened, my understanding sharpened, and all mundane vexations and temptations gone." (Martin Luther King, Jr., quoted in Tavris, *Anger, the Misunderstood Emotion,* p. 83)

To understand the second part of today's story, children may need to be reminded about sacrifice (see Session 7, "Abraham and Isaac") and told that birds and small animals were used as offerings in the temple. The issue in the story seems to be that of cheating people who were buying animals for sacrifice, but the money-changers may also have been collecting a prescribed tax collected annually at the time of Passover. Since money-changers sometimes acted as bankers and loan agents, it is possible that they were violating the Jewish laws against usury (collecting interest on loans). Because of abuses such as those implied in this story, the number of obligatory sacrifices was greatly reduced; by the middle of the first century C.E. they were eventually eliminated.

The Temple in Jerusalem played an important role in Jewish religious life during the time of Jesus. It was the center of worship, and large crowds came there to celebrate three major feasts each year—Passover, Pentecost, and Succoth. Pilgrims often traveled in groups, as described in today's story, and even after the Temple was destroyed in 70 C.E., Jews continued to come to Jerusalem. Today Jews still visit the remaining western wall of the Temple—once referred to as the Wailing Wall because of the prayers offered there bemoaning the Temple's loss.

Materials

- Colored markers or crayons, tape or glue, and pencils
- Picture of your congregation's building, labeled with the official name of your congregation
- Pictures of other churches and temples
- Notepapers with adhesive
- Drawing paper
- Newspaper articles related to anger
- Copies of Song 29, "Amen"
- Several building sets such as Legos, Tinkertoys, Lincoln Logs, blocks

Preparation

- Think through your own answers to the motivating and discussion questions.
- If possible, read Charlotte Zolotow's contemporary story *The Hating Book.*
- Obtain and hang in your room pictures of your church and of other churches and temples.
- Practice verse 10 of the song "Amen."

Session Plan

Gathering   Varies

As the children arrive, call their attention to the pictures of your church and other places of worship. Ask them to label the various types of buildings with adhesive notes. Point out how many very different places of worship are called "temple." Discuss informally the different types of places of worship the children have visited and how they compare to yours. Be sure that the children know the official name of your congregation.

Motivating Questions   5 min.

Say, "Everyone gets angry sometimes. We all know we should keep our temper under control, but sometimes it just gets away from us. Have you ever been angry? What made you angry?

"Today's stories from Christian scripture tell about two visits Jesus made to the Temple in Jerusalem. Duing the second visit, Jesus got very angry."

Read the Story   3 min.

Discussion   15 min.

Lead a discussion of the story guided by the following questions.

1. Jesus felt that the Temple was a special place for him, that it felt like a home. Is our church a special place for you, like a home, as the Temple was for Jesus? Why?
2. When Jesus' parents discovered he was missing from the group returning from Jerusalem, they were concerned and went back in search of him. When they found him, his mother said, "Child, why have you treated us like this?" Do you think she was angry? Why? How else might she have reacted?
3. Jesus dealt with his anger by turning over the tables in the Temple. Why was he angry? Is it all right to be angry sometimes? Is there a "good" way to deal with anger? How have you handled your anger?
4. Some people praised Jesus for what he did,

while others were upset at him. What do you think about the way Jesus expressed anger? How else might he have handled it?

A Better Way   10 min.

Gather the children at a table and distribute drawing paper to each. Say, "All of us have been angry sometimes. Think about a time when you, or someone you know, was really angry. Think about what happened as a result of that anger. Now divide your drawing paper into two sections. Label one section "The Way It Was," and the other section "A Better Way." Think about how it felt to be that angry person, and see if you can figure out a better way to handle your anger. Draw a picture that shows that 'better way,' or, if you prefer, write a new ending to the incident. If it's hard to think of a better way, feel free to ask your friends for ideas. And, of course, I'll be happy to help you."

When the children have finished, post their papers and ask for a few volunteers to briefly tell their "better way." If you have time, have everyone tell his or her story.

Building a Temple   15 min.

Gather in your work space. Say, "Often when congregations are new, they don't have buildings of their own." Relate this more specifically to the history of your own congregation. "Usually, as they get larger and better established, they begin to think about 'a building of our own.' Let's imagine that we—our group—are a fairly new congregation and have decided that it's time to have a building of our own."

Divide the children into groups of two or three, and invite each group to build a "temple" for their congregation, using building materials such as Legos, blocks, Tinkertoys, etc. When all the groups have finished, or your time is up, take a tour of all the temples, letting each group explain its work.

Closing   5 min.

Gather the children together. Light a candle or chalice, and say, "Churches, temples, mosques, and meeting houses are religious homes. But they are more than the building. They are the people who worship in them. It is the people, the ideas, and the feelings inside these buildings that are important, not the buildings themselves. They are places where people take time to think about their lives, and about feelings such as anger. They are places where people come to find a better way." Close by singing "Amen," verse 10.

Jesus and the Temple

IN THE DAYS OF JESUS, the Temple in Jerusalem was the place where all of the faithful Jews wanted to worship. Those who could came from all over Palestine to worship and to make sacrifices to their God. When Jesus was twelve years old, he and his parents, Mary and Joseph, journeyed to Jerusalem at the time of Passover. When Mary and Joseph left Jerusalem to return home, they assumed that Jesus was with the group of travelers. After a day's journey, they did not find him, so they returned to Jerusalem to search for him. After three days they found him in the Temple, sitting among the teachers, listening to them and asking them questions. All who heard him were amazed at his understanding and his answers.

When his parents saw him they were astonished; and his mother said to him, "Child, why have you treated us like this? Look, your father and I have been searching for you in great anxiety."

Jesus said to them, "Why were you searching for me? Did you not know that I must be in my Father's house?"

When Jesus became an adult he still felt that the temple was a special place. When he and his disciples went to the Temple, they found people making money in the Temple by selling animal sacrifices and changing money. Jesus became very angry, and he went into the temple and drove out all of the people who were buying or selling sacrifices. Then he overturned the tables of the money-changers and the seats of those who sold doves.

He said to them, "It is written, My house shall be called a house of prayer for all the nations; but you have made it a den of robbers." This made the people who had been cheated by the money-changers and the animal sellers very happy. The crowd was spellbound by Jesus, which upset the leaders of the Temple. They kept looking for a way to get rid of him. For his own safety, Jesus decided to sleep outside Jerusalem that night.

JESUS AND THE LAW

Sources: Matthew 12:1-8, 22:15-22; Mark 2:23-28, 12:13-17; Luke 6:1-5, 20:20-26

Theme: Laws

Goals for Participants

- to think about laws and obedience to them
- to become familiar with stories about Jesus' beliefs about laws
- to discover other themes in the story, such as "higher laws" or "God's laws."

Background

The story of plucking grains on the Sabbath and the story about Caesar's tribute coin are found in all three synoptic gospels with differing emphases. How much of the stories' content is from Jesus and how much is additions and interpretations of the gospel writers is difficult to determine.

The statements and stories concerning "Jesus and the Law" reveal a tension between affirmation and criticism. In statements such as "Do not think that I have come to abolish the law or the prophets; I have come not to abolish but to fulfill," Jesus clearly affirms his belief in the Law. Stories like that of his plucking of the grains on the Sabbath, however, and of healing on the Sabbath (Matthew 12:9-14), criticize the Law for being unresponsive to human needs. While Jesus does not suggest that the Law be abolished, he appeals to a broader and higher truth: "So it is lawful to do good on the Sabbath."

The story about Caesar's tribute coin demonstrates another kind of ambiguity, as Jesus cleverly avoids having to make a public statement in the conflict between secular and religious law. In this story, one side is represented by the Herodians, who support the Roman government and its tax laws, the other by the Pharisees and Zealots, who wish for independence and further believe that Jewish religious law is affronted by the graven image of the Caesar on the coin. Roman taxes could be paid only with this special silver coin, which was the property of the monarch. The question posed to Jesus in this story is really an attempt to entrap him. If he answers that his questioners should pay the tax, then he negates Jewish law, but if he answers that they should not pay, he will be in trouble with Roman law and may even be arrested. But by demonstrating that they already support the Roman government by having the coin at all, and by making the distinction between Caesar's and God's laws, Jesus sidesteps the question, or perhaps raises it to a different level. It is also possible that since he believed that a new order was imminent, Jesus simply considered the entire issue unimportant.

In the story of plucking of the grains on the Sabbath, Jesus is confronted with concern about a central Jewish law—that any sort of work is forbidden on the Sabbath. Though people are allowed to pick grapes or grain to eat, they are not allowed to harvest it, which they are considered to be doing by rubbing it with their hands, as the version in Luke explains. In this case, Jesus appeals to places in the Hebrew scriptures themselves where human need became more important than observing the letter of the law. He points out that King David ate the bread of the presence in the temple, which was unlawful, and he paraphrases Hosea 6:6, "For I desire steadfast love and not sacrifice, the knowledge of God rather than burnt offerings."

It is important to remember here that within Judaism there are a number of different understandings of the meaning of the Law. In general, however, most Jews consider observance of the Law, including the keeping of the Sabbath, not as an onerous duty but rather as a joyous and sacred celebration of their relationship with God. From this point of view, the Law is not in conflict with human needs but instead provides the ultimate source for meeting them.

Children of this age understand the importance of rules and laws, not only at home but also in school, games, and organizations they belong to. At times they may fuss about particular rules, but in general rules are important to their sense of security. On the other hand, children are capable of understanding that some laws may be wrong or unjust, that there are ways to change them, and that, on rare occasions, it may be necessary to break an unjust law. They also can begin to understand the idea of a higher law or God's Law. Should your group get stuck on bemoaning the injustice of relatively trivial school rules, help them to move on to an understanding of more serious kinds of unjust laws.

Materials

- Newsprint, markers, and masking tape
- Self-hardening clay
- A selection of pointed objects for incising the clay: pencils, old ballpoint pens, wire, skewers, opened-up paper clips
- Gold and/or silver tempera paint
- Small watercolor brushes
- A jar of water
- Paper towels and waxed paper or aluminum foil
- Tongs
- Turpentine, for cleaning brushes and tongs
- Copies of Song 32, "The Teachings of Jesus"

Preparation

- Think through your own answers to the motivating and discussion questions.
- Make a sample coin so you will be familiar with the process.
- Learn the song "The Teachings of Jesus," or arrange for someone else to teach it.

Session Plan

Gathering   Varies

As the children arrive, invite each to form a small portion of clay into the shape of a large coin, and cover it with a damp paper towel.

Motivating Questions   10 min.

Gather the children onto a rug or around a table and say, "Throughout history, people have known that some laws are just, and some laws are unjust. While it is possible to change a law, it is usually a very long process. It is even much more difficult if the people in power like the law the way it is.

"In the United States, civil rights leader Reverend Martin Luther King, Jr., always urged lawmakers to make just laws and to change unjust ones. But if he could not get an evil law changed, he did not hesitate to disobey that law. He believed he should obey the laws of God before he obeyed the laws that people made. God's laws are usually referred to as a 'higher law.'"

Ask the children, "Do you think we need laws? Why? What would life be like without laws? Are all laws good? Can you think of a law that you think should be changed? Why do you think it should be changed?"

Then say, "Jesus, and many other Jews, believed that the Jewish religious laws should be followed less strictly. In today's stories from Christian scripture, Jesus gave his opinion about the laws of his day."

Definition

Pharisee strict follower of Jewish law

Read the Story   3 min.

Discussion   15 min.

Lead a discussion of the story guided by the following questions.

1. Roman law said that the Palestinians were supposed to pay taxes to the emperor. What do you think Jesus meant when he said to give to the emperor the things that are the emperor's, and give to God the things that God's? What kind of things should be given to the emperor? What kinds of things should be given to God? When Jesus said this, was he telling them to obey the law or not?

2. One example of people breaking a law because of a higher law or "God's law" was blacks who sat wherever they wanted to on buses or drank from any water fountain, when to do so was against the law in their state. What do you think of this? What was the "higher law"?

3. Jesus broke a religious law by harvesting grain on the Sabbath. Do Unitarian Universalists have anything that is against their religion to do? What?

4. Most people want to obey the law. If their conscience tells them they must break a wrong or unjust law, it can be difficult and scary for them. Why would it be hard or scary? Do you think it was hard or scary for Jesus? Why?

5. In the United States and Canada, we elect people to make our laws. Do all other countries make laws this way? How else might laws be made? How are laws made where there is a dictator?

Important Laws, Laws to Change, and Higher Laws   10-15 min.

At the top of the a sheet of newsprint write: "Important Laws." Ask the children to name some laws that they consider important. List them. On a second sheet of newsprint write: "Laws I Would Change." Make a similar list here. On a third sheet write: "Higher Law or God's Law." Invite the children to consider what these laws might be, and write down their answers.

Making Higher-Law Coins   20 min.

Gather the children, with their clay coins, in your work space. Ask them to choose a "higher law" and incise it on one side of their coin. On the other side, if they wish, they can make a design or symbol to illustrate it. (If they work on both sides, caution them not to damage or erase the underside markings.) Show them how to mold an edge for the coin, then poke a hole through the top. Invite them to paint their coins in silver or gold. (Let one side dry for a few minutes, then use tongs to turn the coin over, and paint the other side.) Put the coins in a safe place to dry during the week. At the next session, the children can run string through the holes to make pendants.

Clean up and gather for the Closing.

Closing   10 min.

Light your chalice or candle and say, "Most of the time, laws are made to help people or to protect the environment, but occasionally laws are wrong or unjust. Those laws can usually be changed by our votes or by working with our elected officials. Every once in a while, though, it becomes necessary to break a law that is wrong or unjust, because we believe in a 'higher law.' These are some possible 'higher laws.'" Invite the children to share the "higher laws" they wrote on their coins.

Close by singing "The Teachings of Jesus."

Jesus and the Law

THERE WAS A RELIGIOUS LAW that forbade anyone to work on the Sabbath, for it was supposed to be a day meant for rest and prayer only. One Sabbath Jesus and his followers were walking through a grain field, and his followers, who were hungry, began to pluck heads of grain and to eat.

When the Pharisees saw it, they said to Jesus, "Look, why are they doing what is not lawful on the Sabbath?"

Jesus replied, "Have you never read what David did when he and his companions were hungry and in need of food? He entered the temple and ate the bread, which it is not lawful for any but the priests to eat. If you knew the meaning of the saying 'I desire mercy and not sacrifice,' you would not have condemned the guiltless." And Jesus said to the people, "The Sabbath was made for humankind, not humankind for the Sabbath."

Another time some leaders from the temple and from the palace came to Jesus, trying to trap him into saying something for which they could arrest him. They asked, "Teacher, we know that you are sincere, and won't bow to any person; for you are not impressed with people's position, but truly teach the way of God. Is it lawful to pay taxes to the emperor, or not? Should we pay them or should we not?"

Jesus knew they were trying to trick him. Caesar was the Roman emperor, and Caesar's troops had taken control of Palestine. The Romans would arrest anyone who told the people to break the law by not paying their taxes.

Jesus replied, "Why are you putting me to the test? Bring me a coin and let me see it." They brought one, and he said, "Whose head is this, and whose title?"

"The emperor's," they answered.

Jesus said to them, "Give to the emperor the things that are the emperor's, and to God the things that are God's."

SESSION 28

IT'S A MIRACLE

Sources: Wine at Cana—John 2:1-11; Man with Unclean Spirit—Matthew 8:28-34; Mark 5:1-20; Luke 8:26-39; Fishes and Loaves—Matthew 14:13-21; Mark 6:30-44; Luke 9:10-17; John 6:4-14; Walking on Water—Matthew 14:22-33; Mark 6:45-52; John 6:16-21

Theme: Amazing Happenings

Goals for Participants

- to become familiar with four stories concerning Jesus and miracles
- to explore the concept of miracles.

Background

The miracle stories that appear in all four gospels serve several purposes: to convince the Jews (and Gentiles) that Jesus was the Messiah; to indicate that the Kingdom of God had come; to connect Jesus' actions with the sacrament of the Eucharist.

Although Jesus rejects the devil's challenge to turn stone into bread (Matthew 4:3-4; Luke 4:3-4), in several other stories he does accomplish something extraordinary. These extraordinary events have been classified as either healing miracles or nature miracles. Turning water into wine, walking on water, and feeding 5,000 or more people with five loaves and two fish are nature miracles; ridding a demoniac of unclean spirits is a healing miracle. (More stories of healing miracles are found in Session 29: raising a girl from the dead; causing the deaf to hear and the blind to see.)

In general, Jesus' miracles are not meant to dazzle and impress but rather are another way, along with preaching and teaching, of conveying the message of the gospel, which brings new life.

In the first century B.C.E., stories of miracle workers were common in both Jewish-rabbinical and Hellenistic circles. Most descriptions of healing miracles followed a prescribed form: first, the disease was described; often the next thing was to tell its duration; then the cure was described; and finally, the reactions of witnesses were reported. Many of Jesus' healing miracles were described in this manner. By comparison, the stories of nonhealing miracles are far more varied in both content and form.

Unitarian Universalists place great trust in the power of reason and thus bring considerable skepticism to these miracle stories, although some may feel comfortable explaining the healing miracles by appeal to psychosomatic processes. In general, however, we feel much more secure applying the word "miracle" to what Forrester Church calls "everyday miracles." Dr. Church describes such miracles as our ordinary opportunities for self-acceptance, forgiveness, courage, and love.

Another perspective on the concept of miracles was promoted in a Unitarian Universalist curriculum from the 1940s entitled "How Miracles Abound." Here such wondrous natural events as trees, shells, water, and the human hand were explored by eight- and nine-year olds.

Third- and fourth-grade children are likely to be skeptical yet intrigued by the idea of the extraordinary. It is important that they have an opportunity to discuss openly all possible explanations and meanings, with those who believe that the miracles could have happened feeling comfortable to say so.

Materials

- Drawing or manila paper
- Watercolors, poster paints, or colored markers

- Water jars for cleaning brushes, if necessary
- One can of tuna fish, one loaf of bread, and mayonnaise
- Table knife, wooden spoon, and can opener
- Clear pitcher of water
- 12-ounce can(s) of frozen pink lemonade
- A bowl in which to mix tuna and mayonnaise
- Hand-lettered sign reading "Miracle Meal"
- Paper cups, a bread board, and a serving tray
- Copies of Song 33, "Hold the Wind"

Preparation

- Think through your own answers to the motivating and discussion questions.
- Decide to whom you will serve the Miracle Meal—parents, another class, some other small group in your congregation, and make arrangements with that group.
- Learn the song "Hold the Wind," or arrange for it to be taught by your music leader.

Session Plan

Gathering   Varies

As the children arrive, invite them to help make tuna sandwiches. Set the lemonade out to thaw. Tell the children they will find out later what you will be doing with the food.

Motivating Questions   10 min.

Gather the children together around a table or on the rug and say, "When things happen that are especially hard to explain, they are often called miracles. Some people think quite ordinary events, such as the birth of a baby or the return in spring of the birds and the flowers, are miracles. Others save the word *miracle* for those events that seem unnatural—like a person being under water for a long time and not drowning.

"There are many miracle stories in both the Hebrew and the Christian scriptures. We have heard some of the stories in which miracles happened. Remember the stories of Shadrach, Meshach, and Abednego in the fiery furnace; Daniel in the lion's den; and the Hebrews' escape from Egypt through the Reed Sea? What hap-

pened in those stories that could be called miracles? What do you think a miracle is?

"Here are some from the Christian scripture about miracles that Jesus performed."

Definition

denarii money worth about one day's wages

Read the Story   5 min.

Discussion   15 min.

Lead a discussion of the story guided by the following questions
1. Of the miracles Jesus performed, which is your favorite? Why? Do you think these miracles could have happened? If not, why did people tell these stories? Why have they continued to be told for nearly 2,000 years?
2. What are some other types of miracles? Do you think seeds growing into flowers, or the birth of a baby, or forgiving someone is a miracle? What other things might be considered everyday miracles?
3. How would you react if you saw a miracle like the unclean spirit going into the pigs or someone walking on water?
🕯4. If you were a miracle worker, what kind of miracle would you perform?

Drawing Miracle Pictures   10 min.

Put out paper and paint and brushes or markers, and invite the children to make a picture of themselves performing the miracle they would like to do.

The Miracle Meal   15 min.

Explain to the children that they will offer a Miracle Meal to the group you've invited. Place the sandwiches, water, lemonade, paper cups, and knife and spoon on the tray. Take everything to the area where you will be serving. Place a sign saying, "Miracle Meal" nearby. When you are ready, have the children put the lemonade into the water, cut the sandwiches into tiny servings, and serve. As they serve the meal, encourage the children to explain to the guests the meaning of "water to wine" and the "loaves and fishes."

Play the song tape quietly in the background while the meal is going on.

Closing   5 min.

Light your chalice or candle and invite the assembled children and guests to join you in saying, "We give thanks for our food, special friends, and a loving community." If time permits, lead the group in singing "Hold the Wind."

It's a Miracle

ONE DAY JESUS, his mother Mary, and his followers were at a wedding in the town of Cana. When the wine was all gone, Mary asked Jesus to do something about it. He told the servants to fill six stone jars with water, and then to take some of that water out of one of the jars and give it to the host.

The host tasted the water, which had become wine, and declared that it was even better than the wine they had been drinking earlier.

Another time Jesus was out in the countryside and a man of unclean spirit ran up to him and bowed down. This man lived among the tombs, where dead people were buried. No one could restrain him, even with a chain. Every time they tried, he would wrench apart the chain and break the shackles to pieces. Night and day among the tombs and on the mountains he would howl and bruise himself with stones.

Jesus said, "Come out of the man, you unclean spirit!" The unclean spirit came out the man and entered a herd of pigs that was feeding nearby. The 2,000 pigs, crazed by the spirit, rushed down a steep bank into the sea and were drowned. Then the people came to see what had happened and saw the man sitting there, in his right mind.

Wherever Jesus went crowds followed him to hear him preach. Late one day Jesus found himself surrounded by 5,000 people. When he told his disciples to feed the crowd, they asked, "Shall we go and buy 2,000 denarii worth of bread to give to them to eat?"

"How many loaves have you?" Jesus asked. "Go and see."

When they found out, they came back and said, "Five, and two fish."

When Jesus told the crowd to sit down on the green grass, they sat in groups of hundreds and fifties. Jesus took the five loaves and two fish, looked up to heaven, and blessed them. He broke the bread into pieces and divided the fish and gave them to his disciples to set before the people. Everyone ate until he or she was full. When they finished they found there were still twelve baskets of broken pieces of bread and fish left.

Perhaps the best-known miracle story about Jesus took place in the middle of a lake. His disciples were out in a boat during the night, and a storm developed. Jesus, who was on the shore, walked out to them across the water. When they saw him they were afraid, because they thought it must be a ghost, and they cried out.

When he saw they were terrified, he spoke to them and said, "Take heart, it is I; do not be afraid." He got into the boat with them, and the storm stopped.

SESSION 29

THE HEALING POWER

Sources: Jairus' Daughter—Matthew 9:18-19, 23-26; Mark 5:21-24, 35-43; Healing the Deaf Man—Mark 7:31-37; Healing the Blind Man—Mark 8:22-26

Theme: The Power of Faith

Goals for Participants

- to consider sickness, healing, and faith
- to become familiar with stories about Jesus' healing power.

Background

The early Hebrews considered illness to be divine punishment for sin, even believing that the sins of parents could cause illness in their children. Thus they believed the only cure was to regain a right relationship with God. Unlike their contemporaries in nearby territories, they did not compile lists of herbs and potions to be used on various illnesses, nor did they make use of magical phrases and objects such as amulets. There is no mention of laying on of hands in the Hebrew Bible or in the rabbinical writings. Only in the writings from Qumran is such a form of healing mentioned.

Under the influence of Persian beliefs, by the time of Jesus, disease had come to be attributed to evil or unclean spirits or demons, and Jesus' understanding of the coming of the Realm of God included triumph over such evil spirits. The exorcism of demons was accomplished in a variety of ways: by incantation of formulas such as "I know who you are" and "I adjure you by God," by causing the demon to disclose its name, or by keeping the name of the exorcist from the demon. The vast majority of illnesses that Jesus heals are attributed to such spirits, and they are healed by a combination of the usual exorcisms, by touching and being touched, and by faith. In one case Jesus heals by putting spittle, which was believed to have medicinal powers, on a blind man's eyes. And on one occasion, he heals a paralytic by forgiving his sins.

Many of these healing acts would undoubtedly have been seen as proof of the coming of the Messiah prophesied in Isaiah 35:5-6:

Then the eyes of the blind shall be opened,
and the ears of the deaf unstopped;
then shall the lame man leap like a hart,
and the tongue of the dumb sing for joy.

Jews in the first century C.E. would have been familiar with this passage and would have seen a connection between the words of the prophet and Jesus' healing.

A good number of the diseases Jesus healed could have had psychosomatic causes, so that a strong faith in the healer and his powers might have brought about remission of the disease. There is much interest today in the interrelationship between the physical, mental, and emotional aspects of disease. Books such as Norman Cousins' *Anatomy of an Illness,* in which laughter cured where modern medicine could not, and Bernie Siegel's *Love, Medicine, and Miracles,* which highlights the importance of faith and love, offer new insights into what may have been ancient understandings. As Siegel says, "Remember that one generation's miracle may be another's scientific fact. Do not close your eyes to acts or events that are not always measurable. They happen by means of an inner energy available to all of us" (p. 6).

Children of this age are likely to be more comfortable than adults with the idea of making things happen by wishing them to be so. Although their powers of logic can be quite impressive, third- and fourth-graders will still fall back on earlier modes of thinking which rely more on fantasy and magic. A child of this age will sometimes make inappropriate causal connections—believing, for example, that someone died or his or her parents divorced because of his or her own bad behavior.

Materials

- Blindfolds
- Cotton balls
- Sticks for canes
- A sleeping bag or two
- A bathrobe
- Drawing paper and envelopes
- Colored markers, crayons, and colored pencils
- Gifts of cookies and/or flowers
- Boxes or tins for cookies
- Wrapping paper and ribbon
- Copies of Song 34, "I Know That Jesus Laid His Hand on Me"

Preparation

- Think through your own answers to the motivating and discussion questions.
- Find out from your minister or caring committee who in your congregation is sick or shut-in and would enjoy a cheering visit. If it is feasible for the children to visit, make the necessary arrangements, such as contacting the person and recruiting drivers. If such a visit is not practical, an alternative is to deliver the children's cards and cookies yourself later.
- Send a note to parents early in the week asking that the children bring flowers and/or cookies, explaining your plans for the session, the length of the visit, transportation arrangements, and so on.
- Become familiar with the song "I Know That Jesus Laid His Hand on Me." Practice it or arrange with someone to lead it.

Session Plan

Gathering   Varies

As the children arrive, engage them in filling boxes and/or making bouquets with the cookies and flowers they have brought. Wrap the gifts with paper and ribbon, and set them aside.

Motivating Questions   10 min.

Gather the children around a table or on a rug and say, "Throughout history, there have been people who seemed to have the power to heal sick people. Some people claim that only God or the devil has the power to make this happen. Others say it is having a strong faith that heals a sick person. Whatever the explanation, for as long as stories have been told, there have been stories of people who were very ill and were somehow made well.

"Think about the times you have been sick. What made you get better? Are there other things that can help sick people get better?

"Do you think we can make things happen by really believing that they will? Has this happened for you? Tell us about it. Was there a time when you really believed something would happen but it didn't? Tell us about it.

"There are many stories in Christian scripture about the healing power of Jesus. Here are a few of them."

Read the Story   5 min.

Discussion   15 min.

Lead a discussion of the story guided by the following questions.
1. What were some of the ways that Jesus healed people? (Remind the children of the story they heard in Session 28 of Jesus healing the man with the unclean spirit.)
2. What are some of the ways that people are healed today?
3. In many of the healing stories about Jesus, an important part of getting well was that people had faith in him—they really believed that he could heal them. Do you think we can be

healed by believing that another person can heal us? Can we heal ourselves that way?

4. Do most patients have faith in their doctors? Why do you think that is so?

⚶ 5. What is faith? Can we have faith in people? What or whom do you have faith in?

6. If you can't heal others, how can you help them feel better?

Song   5 min.

Play the tape of the song "I Know That Jesus Laid His Hands on Me," and then lead the children in singing it.

Smile or Laugh Yourself Well   10-15 min.

Choose one person to be the healer. Tell the children that several people will have a chance to be the healer as the game goes on. Have the healer wear a bathrobe.

Invite each of the other children to choose a sickness, and give them appropriate garb or props. The blind can wear a blindfold, the deaf can put cotton in their ears, the lame can use a cane, the "person in a coma" can lie on the sleeping bags.

Play the game. The healer goes up to a sick person and does whatever she or he can to make that person smile or laugh. For the "deaf," it will be visual; for those with blindfolds, it must be audible. The leader moves from person to person until he or she makes someone smile or laugh.

When a sick person smiles or laughs, the healer says, "You're healed!" The sick person then puts on the robe and becomes the healer, and the healer takes a symbol of sickness and joins the circle. Continue until everyone has a turn being healer or until time runs out.

Get Well Cards   10 min.

Gather the children around a table. Tell them a little about the people for whom they are making the cards, and then give them simple directions: Fold a piece of drawing paper in half once, then in half again; decorate the cards with crayons or markers. When they are finished, put the cards in envelopes and address them.

Closing   5 min.

Light the chalice or candle, and say, "There are many ways to be healed when we are sick. Resting in bed and drinking lots of liquids can help. Doctors and medicines and operations can help. Having faith in our bodies and in those who heal us can help. Knowing that others care about us through cards and flowers and cookies can help. Smiling, laughing, and believing in life can help. May we help each other to be well."

If You Have More Time

• Take the children on a short visit or visits to deliver their cards, gifts, and good cheer to sick or shut-in persons. An alternative is to let the children know that you will deliver their cards, gifts, and best wishes.

The Healing Power

JAIRUS, ONE OF THE RULERS of the synagogue, came to Jesus and fell at his feet, crying, "My little daughter is at the point of death. Come and lay your hands on her, so that she may be made well, and live." Jesus went with him.

As they got close to the house, people came up to Jairus and said, "Your daughter is dead. Why trouble the teacher any further?"

But Jesus said to him, "Do not fear, only believe."

When they got to the home, people were weeping and wailing loudly. Jesus said to them, "Why do you make a commotion and weep? The child is not dead but sleeping." But the people laughed at him.

Jesus sent everyone outside but the child's mother and father, then took them into the room where the child was. Jesus took the girl's hand and said, "Little girl, get up." Immediately the twelve-year-old girl got up and began to walk about. Jesus told her amazed parents to give her something to eat.

Another time some people brought a blind man to Jesus in Bethsaida and begged Jesus to touch him. Jesus took the blind man by the hand and led him out of the village; and when he had put saliva on the eyes and laid his hands upon him, Jesus asked, "Can you see anything?"

The man looked up and said, "I can see people, but they look like trees, walking." Jesus laid his hands upon the man's eyes again; and the man looked intently and his sight was restored, and he saw everything clearly.

Yet another story tells of a deaf man who had an impediment in his speech. People brought him to Jesus and begged him to heal the man by laying his hands upon him.

Jesus took the man to a private place. He put his fingers in the man's ears, and he spat and touched the man's tongue. Looking up to heaven, Jesus said, "Be opened." Immediately the man's ears were opened, his tongue was released, and he spoke plainly.

During the three years of Jesus' ministry, word about his healing powers spread around the country. People came from all over, in villages, cities, or country. They had faith, or believed, that Jesus could heal them. They tried to touch him, or have him touch them, so that they would be healed. The Scripture says that as many people as were touched was the number of people who were made well.

SESSION 30

MARY AND MARTHA

Source: Luke 10:38-42

Theme: Choosing What Is Most Important

Goals for Participants

- to consider how we can best honor another person
- to become familiar with the story of Mary and Martha
- to discover other themes in the story, such as timing and making decisions.

Background

This brief story of Mary and Martha is found only in Luke and comes from Luke's special L source. There is, however, a different story about what seems to be the same two women in John 11 and 12. Here they are described as the sisters of Lazarus, whom Jesus brings back to life. Once again, Martha serves a meal and Mary is seen in devotion to Jesus, in this case anointing his feet. John tells us they lived in Bethany, near Jerusalem.

A number of Marys are mentioned in Christian scripture. The most familiar are Jesus' mother and Mary of Magdala, the woman "from whom seven devils had gone out," who traveled with Jesus and was the first to behold him after his crucifixion. A third Mary is the one described in Luke 7:37-38 as a woman "of the city, who was a sinner." Although this third Mary also anointed Jesus' feet, she is not the woman in this story.

This story is interesting for its portrayal of Mary sitting at Jesus' feet, in the posture typical of a disciple or learner. Although all of Jesus' known apostles were men, and although Jewish teaching of the time was opposed to the education of women, Jesus clearly demonstrated in this story that he approved of a woman's learning from him.

There are several translations of Luke 10:42. The RSV chooses "one thing is needful" but in a footnote explains that it could be translated either "few things are needful" or "only one thing is needful." The New RSV (1989) translates it as "there is need of only one thing." These variants express slightly different meanings, and there seems to be no way to be sure which is correct. All of them, however, carry the double meaning of applying both to the food being served and to honoring Jesus. There is a similar double meaning in "Mary has chosen the good portion"; while "portion" most often refers to servings of food, here it also seems to mean choosing how to apportion her time.

Honoring people by being quiet and really listening to them is difficult for adults and even more difficult for eight- and nine-year olds. The exercise is worth a try, however. Just keep the amount of time short, and allow for discussion of how difficult it is to do. Reassure the children that it is hard for everyone, but also that it is a wonderful gift, since we all like to have someone give us their undivided attention. In "Making the Special Meals," the recipients may wish their meal had been different, and this too should be discussed if the issue arises.

Materials

- Slips of paper for each child, half numbered 1 and half numbered 2
- List of questions (see Preparation) on newsprint and masking tape
- Selection of nuts, raisins, crackers, fruit, peanut butter, cheeses, juices, etc.
- Plain paper plates, cups, and napkins
- A place card for each person

- Crayons or markers
- Decorative stickers (optional)
- Copies of Songs 35 and 36, "Turn! Turn! Turn!" and "Mary and Martha"

Preparation

- Think through your own answers to the motivating and discussion questions.
- Learn the song "Turn! Turn! Turn!" and/or "Mary and Martha," or arrange for someone else to teach them.
- Set up the Special Meal area.
- Print the following questions on newsprint:
  1. What should people do to be sure there is peace in the world?
  2. What is the most important thing to learn in school? Why?
  3. What causes fights at school, and what can be done to keep fights from happening?
  4. What kinds of things make you mad at another person? What do you do when you are mad? How do you get over it?

Session Plan

Gathering   Varies

As the first children arrive, gather them around you and begin playing and singing "Turn! Turn! Turn!" Invite newcomers to join as they arrive, and continue the "sing-along" until all the children have gathered and sung the song a few times. If you prefer, teach the song after the discussion of the story.

Motivating Questions   10 min.

Gather the children around a table or on a rug and say, "There is a poem in Hebrew scripture, in the book of Ecclesiastes, that states, 'For everything there is a season, and a time for every matter under heaven: a time to be born and a time to die.' It is often hard for us to remember that we need to take time for many different activities, especially if there is one that we like the most or do the best." Then engage the children in a discussion of the following.

Does the time you choose to do something matter? Can you think of a time you did something that was a perfectly good thing to do but you chose the wrong time to do it?

Have you ever had to choose between doing two things, both of which seemed important to you? What were the two things? Which did you choose? Why did you choose that and not the other?

Say, "Today's story from Christian scripture is about two sisters—each had a different idea about what was important to do."

Read the Story   2 min.

Discussion   15 min.

Lead a discussion of the story guided by the following questions.
1. What do you think Jesus meant when he said, "Martha, Martha, you are worried and distracted by many things; there is need of only one thing"? What did he mean when he said, "Mary has chosen the better part, which will not be taken away from her"?
2. How were Martha and Mary different? What did each want to do to honor Jesus? Which thing would you have chosen to do?
3. Did Martha choose the wrong time to cook a fancy meal, when she could have been listening and learning from Jesus instead? Would you have been angry if you were cooking and your sister wasn't helping?
4. Would you rather be honored with a fancy meal or with someone listening closely to what you have to say? Why?

Close the discussion by singing one or two verses of "Turn! Turn! Turn!" If the group did not learn it at the beginning of the session, take time to teach it here.

Honoring Others by
Listening and Learning   15 min.

Post the newsprint list of questions which you prepared in advance; put the paper slips numbered 1 and 2 on a table, and ask each participant to take one. Tell the participants that they will now have an opportunity to honor and be honored by one another. Tell those who are number 1s to pair off with number 2s and find a comfortable place to sit together. Tell the children that first the 1s are to choose one of the questions on the newsprint and talk about it to her or his partner. Their partners will honor them by listening carefully. At the end of three minutes you will signal that it is time to switch, and the 2s will choose a question and talk about it while the 1s listen carefully. Say that when all have been honored by being listened to, the group will come together for a brief sharing.

When the time is up, gather the group in a circle and ask for a few volunteers to finish the sentence, "One thing I learned from listening to my partner was . . . "

Honoring Others with a Special Meal   15 min.

Invite the children to the table on which you have placed the supplies for the meal. Say that they will now have a chance to honor their partners by serving them a Special Meal. Each will decorate a plate and make a place card for her or his partner with the markers, crayons, and stickers, and choose the food they think will please the partner. When the plates of food are ready, they are to set a place for the partner at the table, complete with place card, napkin, cup, and plate of food. Specify the amount of time they have to do this. When ready, all will sit down to enjoy the Special Meal with which they have been honored.

While they are eating, ask, "Did you feel more honored by being listened to or by having a special meal prepared for you? Why?" When the food is consumed and the discussion over, ask all to thank their partners.

Closing   5 min.

Gather in a circle, light the chalice or candle, and say, "There are many things that are good to do, and sometimes we have to decide which is the most important at the time. People are different and they will make different choices." If time permits, sing "Turn! Turn! Turn!" or "Mary and Martha" one more time.

Mary and Martha

MARTHA AND MARY were sisters who lived together in Bethany. One day Jesus and his followers were visiting their village, and Martha welcomed them into her home.

Jesus was talking to the crowd of people who were gathered at the house of Martha and Mary. Mary sat at Jesus' feet and listened to what he was saying, for this is what Mary thought was important. Martha was busy cooking and taking care of their house, being especially anxious that everything be just right for Jesus and all of his followers, for this is what Martha thought was important.

Martha, who was distracted with the many tasks she felt she had to do, got angry. She went to Jesus and said, "Do you not care that my sister has left me to do all the work by myself? Tell her then to help me."

But Jesus answered, "Martha, Martha, you are worried and distracted by many things; there is need of only one thing. Mary has chosen the better part, which will not be taken away from her."

Jesus knew that there was a time for everything, and that this was the time to learn.

THE TEACHINGS OF JESUS

Sources: Eye for an Eye—Matthew 5:38-39; Love Your Enemies—Matthew 5:43-44; Judge Not—Matthew 7:1; Golden Rule—Matthew 7:12; Luke 6:31; Great Commandment—Matthew 22:34-40; Mark 12:28-34; Luke 10:25-28

Theme: How We Treat Others

Goals for Participants

• to consider the various ways that we treat each other and what Jesus had to say about this
• to become familiar with some of the sayings of Jesus.

Background

The first four of these teachings of Jesus are found in the section of Matthew called the Sermon on the Mount. Luke has a similar but shorter section called variously the Sermon on the Plain or the Great Discourse. These sections are really a collection of sayings, not a sermon, and scholars surmise that they were taken from an earlier collection of such sayings which they call Q (for the German *Quelle*, meaning source). It has been suggested that the author of Matthew chose a mountaintop setting in order to compare Jesus and his proclamations with Moses receiving the Ten Commandments on Mount Sinai.

There are similarities in these sayings to Jewish wisdom literature, to the teachings of Hillel (25 B.C.E.), to material found in the Dead Sea Scrolls from Qumran, and to the rabbinical thought from Jamnia in the late 1st century C.E. Jesus' so-called Golden Rule, for example, gives a more positive, active thrust to Hillel's earlier teaching that what is hateful to oneself one should not do to others.

But there are important differences as well.

For example, though these other teachings make clear the need to love one's fellow Jew and even resident aliens, there seems to be no precedent for the idea that one should "love one's enemies." Near Eastern ethics had always allowed for the law of revenge, and "an eye for an eye and a tooth for a tooth" was in fact a limitation on that law. Jesus was teaching something new in suggesting nonresistance.

In the Hebrew scriptures there are 613 commandments. The question of which was the greatest, the first, or the "parent commandment" was often debated by the rabbis. Jesus' answer is a combination of Deuteronomy 6:4-6 and Leviticus 19:18. These had actually been combined in one other piece of writing (the Testament of Issachar), but only Jesus gave this response to the question of which was the greatest commandment.

Scholars have classified the literary form of the Sermon on the Mount as being something like proverbs, but proverbs that are also proclamatory. Like all proverbs, they give a brief statement of how to live wisely, but at the same time they proclaim that wisdom to be a part of a whole new radical way of living. Together they present a philosophy of life that, though it might inspire us, we might have trouble living up to.

In discussing these teachings with children, it is important to keep in mind the radical nature of these sayings and to encourage open discussion of their merits and applications. Children of this age are very concerned with a one-to-one kind of fairness, while Jesus' teachings point the way toward a transcendence of that ordinary sense of fairness. This may be difficult for third- and fourth-graders to understand and accept. On the other hand, the opportunity to grapple with these teachings in a tolerant atmosphere in which questions are encouraged may allow children to stretch their understanding of what constitutes "right living."

Materials

- Handout 5, one for each child
- "The Teachings of Jesus" on newsprint or a chalkboard (one version with the biblical words and one short version; see Handout 5)
- A piece of wood, 1" x 5" x 10", per child (use an inexpensive piece of 1" x 5" pine board cut into as many 10" lengths as you need; the size will actually be 3/4" x 4 1/2" x 10")
- Sandpaper, wood stain, yellow shellac, and brushes
- Glue
- Drawing paper, cut to 3 1/2" x 8"
- Slim colored markers, crayons, colored pencils, and calligraphy pens (if available)
- Old newspapers
- Turpentine, jars, and old rags for cleaning brushes and fingers
- Two cuphooks for each plaque
- Cord
- Copies of Song 37, "The Golden Rule"

Preparation

- Think through your own answers to the motivating and discussion questions.
- Make a sample plaque.
- Become familiar with the song "The Golden Rule," or enlist help for teaching it.
- Set up area for staining and shellacking. Cover a table with newspapers, and put out materials. Put materials for writing and drawing on another table.

Session Plan

Gathering   Varies

As the children arrive, invite them to the table with the wood. Start them on the plaque-making project by having them each sand the rough edges of a piece of wood and then stain its top and sides. Clean fingers with turpentine and then soap and water. Leave the wood to dry. Put the brushes in turpentine to clean so they can be used next for the shellac.

Motivating Questions   5 min.

Gather the children around the table or on a rug and say, "Sometimes it is hard to understand why someone treats us badly. Often we can't think of anything we did to deserve such treatment. At these times, it seems clear to us that we would never treat someone else like that. And then there are other times when we treat someone badly. We don't really understand why we behaved the way we did, and are sorry about the hurt we caused.

"What do you think the world would be like if you, and everyone else, treated each other the way you would like to be treated? Jesus taught that we should do this. In Christian scripture there are many well-known teachings that are supposed to have come from Jesus. Usually these teachings came from times when Jesus was meeting with a large group of people and was teaching them how best to live their lives. Today we will be hearing some of the teachings."

Read the Story   5 min.

Discussion   15 min.

Refer the children to the newsprint (or chalkboard) where you have written out the teachings of Jesus. Lead a discussion guided by the following questions.

1. When someone hurts us, most of us know what it feels like to want to hurt that person back. "An eye for an eye and a tooth for a tooth" means "getting back in a fair way." For example, if someone poked you in the eye, you would poke him in the eye, not kick him. If someone said something mean to you, you would say something mean back, not hit her. That's what "an eye for an eye and a tooth for a tooth" means. But look at what Jesus said. What do you think he means when he says, "If anyone strikes you on the right cheek, turn to him the other also"? What do you think you ought to do when someone hurts you? Why?

2. If a person hits back, the violence can just keep going on and on. "Turning the other cheek" can stop the violence; it is nonviolence. Nonviolence works because it causes the violent energy to drain away from the one who is violent. Have you ever used nonviolence

to respond to someone who was being violent? How did it work?

3. Do you think people usually notice the faults of others more than their own? Why do you think that is? Is it a good idea to "judge not"?

4. In the Great Commandment, Jesus taught that we should love our neighbors as ourselves. When Jesus says "neighbor" he means family, friends, and people in your neighborhood or in your town or country. What would be an example of loving your neighbor?

⚶ 5. Jesus taught that not only should we love our neighbors but we should love our enemies also. What do you think of this idea? What would be an example of loving your enemy?

⚶ 6. What do you think of the Golden Rule? Do you think it would be a good rule for people to follow? Would it be a good rule for leaders of countries to follow?

Making a Plaque   20 min.

While the stain continues to dry, gather the children at the table with the paper and other writing materials. Invite them to choose one of the short forms of Jesus' sayings to put on their plaque. Suggest they copy it onto the paper with their best handwriting or printing, using any of the writing materials and adding decorations or pictures if they wish. When finished, they can glue the paper onto their piece of wood, trying to keep it in the center of the wood with a small border around each edge.

Then, at the staining/shellacking table, help the children screw in the cuphooks and tie on a piece of cord for hanging their plaque. Finally, have them brush shellac over the plaque. (If the plaques are not dry enough to take home, set them aside until next week.) Distribute Handout 5 to take home.

Closing   5-10 min.

Gather the children in a circle, and light the chalice or candle. Teach them "The Golden Rule," and sing it in a round.

If You Have More Time

• Sing "The Teachings of Jesus," which was introduced in Session 27.

The Teachings of Jesus

JESUS WENT THROUGHOUT GALILEE, teaching in the synagogues, and proclaiming the good news of the kingdom and curing every disease and every sickness among the people. And great crowds followed him from Galilee, and from beyond the Jordan.

When Jesus saw the crowds, he went up the mountain; and after he sat down, his disciples came to him. Then he began to speak, and taught them, saying: "You have heard that it was said, 'An eye for an eye and a tooth for a tooth.' But I say to you, do not resist an evildoer. But if anyone strikes you on the right cheek, turn the other also; and if anyone wants to sue you and take your coat, give your cloak as well; and if anyone forces you to go one mile, go also the second mile."

Jesus continued in his teaching, "You have heard that it was said, 'You shall love your neighbor and hate your enemy.' But I say to you, love your enemies and pray for those who persecute you." He said, "Do not judge, so that you may not be judged."

And he asked, "Why do you see the speck in your neighbor's eye, but do not notice the log in your own eye?"

One of Jesus' teachings has been called The Golden Rule. It is, "In everything do to others as you would have them do to you; for this is the law and the prophets."

Another teaching of Jesus is called The Great Commandment. Some people in Jerusalem were trying to test Jesus and make him say something that would get him in trouble. A lawyer asked Jesus, "Teacher, which commandment in the law is the greatest?"

And Jesus answered, "You shall love the Lord your God with all your heart, and with all your soul, and with all your mind. This is the greatest and first commandment. And a second is like it, you shall love your neighbor as yourself. On these two commandments hang all the law and the prophets."

Jesus knew that if everyone kept just these two commandments all wars and hatred would disappear from the earth.

SESSION 32

THE CRUCIFIXION OF JESUS

Source: Mark 11-15

Theme: Death and Sorrow

Goals for Participants

- to become familiar with the events leading up to the death of Jesus
- to learn the meanings of key words and concepts that are central to to the message of the Christian Church: crucifixion and resurrection
- to explore the meaning and importance of symbols in their lives.

Background

In this session we focus on one of the most important theological concepts in Christianity—the crucifixion. For almost 2,000 years people have struggled to understand its significance. The most common interpretation is that Jesus died on the cross as a sacrifice for the sins of humanity, so that individuals might experience the saving grace of God. This is a very difficult concept for third- and fourth-graders, and it may not represent the views of their parents or their Unitarian Universalist congregation. As with previous stories, we have presented the story of the crucifixion in narrative form, without seeking to interpret the meaning of the events. Children are free to derive their own meanings, to question, and, through the Tenebrae activity, to experience the powerful feelings associated with the story, feelings of sadness, loss, hope, and joy.

Though our children have heard the life and teachings of Jesus, this may be the first time the death of Jesus has been addressed with them directly. It is a rich and meaningful story on

many levels, and children will need time to discuss it thoroughly and ask their own questions. The session has been structured to allow the drama of the story full expression.

In our Tenebrae Service, 13 candles are used to represent Jesus and his twelve disciples. Modeled on an ancient liturgical form, our service is appropriate to the age of the children and provides an opportunity to retell the story of the crucifixion. In the next session (Mary Magdalene) the story continues as we learn of the resurrection of Jesus.

Although death has been a part of many of the stories told in *Timeless Themes*, the focus on death is more intense in this session. It is Jesus who is being put to death, and children will recognize that this is a very important story about an important person. As the children listen to today's story and retell it in their activities, it is possible that some personal sorrow may be evoked, such as the death of another important person in a child's life. Reassure children that sad feelings are an important part of our lives—that no one goes through life without some sorrow. Reassure them also that there are adults who care about them and who can help them through the painful times. If any child seems to need special attention, be sure to alert a parent, your minister, or your religious educator, so that additional help may be offered if necessary.

Materials

- Books of Christian symbols, especially crosses
- A variety of crosses and crucifixes
- "Tenebrae List," photocopied and cut into its 13 parts (see Resource 6)
- A box or table for altar
- Cloth to cover altar
- 13 votive candles, a candle snuffer, and matches

- Small box or bowl (to raise center candle)
- Copies of Song 29, "Amen," and Song 31, "The Seven Joys of Mary" (see "Tenebrae Service")
- Taped music to use as a prelude
- Palm frond, scissors, and string or thread (optional)

Preparation

- Consider the meaning the story has for you. Depending on your personal religious backgrounds, you and your teaching partners may have different views of this story. It would be wise to discuss this in advance.
- Think about your own answers to the motivating and discussion questions.
- If you plan to make palm crosses, construct one in advance so that you are comfortable with the materials. See end of this session.
- Practice "Amen," verses 11 and 12, or "The Seven Joys of Mary," verses 6 and 7, or arrange for a music assistant.

Session Plan

Gathering   Varies

As the children arrive, have on display of a variety of crosses. These may be pieces of jewelry, altar or home crosses, rosaries, or pictures in books of Christian symbols. Use this time to discuss the power of symbols, and how important the symbol of the cross is to Christians. You can point out the chalice used in many Unitarian Universalist churches and ask the children about its importance to them. Explain that symbols such as the chalice and cross are reminders. They help us remember the places and times where we have seen that symbol before. They help us remember the stories associated with the symbol. And they remind us to act in a certain way. Today we will be focusing on the story behind the symbol of the cross.

Motivating Questions   10 min.

Tell the children, "Everyone who lives eventually knows sorrow as well as joy. Has anyone you loved died, or someone you know? How did it feel when this happened?

"In today's story from Christian scripture, Jesus' followers felt great joy when they entered Jerusalem on Sunday; but by Friday, they felt great sorrow."

Definitions

crucifixion   death by being nailed or tied to a cross; Jesus died by crucifixion

resurrection   coming back to life, rising from the dead; in the Christian church, Easter is the celebration of the resurrecton of Jesus

Read the Story   5 min.

Discussion   15 min.

1. Why do you think Jesus went from being greeted joyfully by large crowds to being crucified in less than a week? Do you think he should have been executed?
2. In the story, Jesus seemed to know what Judas was up to. What are some ways we can tell when someone is "up to no good"? Have you ever been betrayed by a friend? How did it feel?
3. After Jesus was arrested, but before he was crucified, one of his disciples, Peter, denied knowing him for fear that he, Peter, would be arrested, too. Have you ever denied a friendship for fear that something bad would happen to you? How did you feel afterward? Would you do it again? Why?

Tenebrae Service and Closing   20 min.

Explain to the children that a tenebrae service is a way of telling the events of "Holy Week" using candlelight and darkness. The Latin word means darkness or shadow. During the service each participant will tell of an event and extinguish the candle. In small groups, children may need to take more than one turn.

Give one section of the Tenebrae Service to each child. Explain that these are their parts in the service. Move among the children and help them to read what is on their slip of paper. Explain that they may either read or tell what is on the slip during the Tenebrae worship service, whichever is more comfortable. Depending upon your group, you may wish to rehearse the story.

Show them a candle snuffer, explain how it is used, and allow the children to try it out if necessary.

Prepare a worship center or altar. Use one or more of the crosses that you brought in for the gathering time. Arrange 13 votive candles across the front of the altar, with the one in the middle slightly raised on a box or overturned cup or bowl. Lay the candle snuffer on the table in front of the candles. Darken the room, if possible.

Select a song and practice it. Some suggestions are "Amen" (verses 11 and 12) or "The Seven Joys of Mary," both in the songbook; "Alleluia" from *Holidays and Holy Days* (by Brotman Marshfield); "Lo the Earth Awakes Again," Hymn 318 in *Hymns for the Celebration of Life*.

Once the preparations have been made, gather the children on the floor or chairs in the worship area in front of the altar. Use taped or live music to help set the mood, and encourage them to sit quietly and thoughtfully. (If you have a willing young musician in your group, ask him or her a week or two in advance to prepare an appropriate piece to perform.) While the music is playing have a child or assistant light the 13 candles.

Open the service by saying, "Jesus was sometimes known as the 'Light of the World,' perhaps because he helped people to understand that even during dark and gloomy times love and hope are alive. In our service today we will hear once again the events of the last week of Jesus' life. With each sad event we will extinguish one candle, and our room will become a little darker. The candle in the center is the Jesus candle [or Christ candle]. When we come to the part of the story where Jesus is crucified, that person (#13) will pick up the candle and silently walk out of the room. We shall sit in silence for a moment, and as we begin to sing, he or she will return to replace the candle. This is to remind us that the hope and love that Jesus brought into the world through his teachings have not been extinguished."

The children then will come forward one at a time to read or tell their portion of the story and extinguish one candle. You can help by silently indicating which candle is to be extinguished, alternating from right to left, working from the outside toward the center. When the Jesus candle has been returned and the song has ended, sit quietly for a moment with the single candle burning, then close the service with these words:

As we leave this friendly place
Love give light to every face.
May the kindness which we learn
Light our hearts 'til we return.
　　　　　　　—Vincent Silliman

If Your Time Is Limited

• Prepare the worship center in advance.
• Sing a song your group already knows, which needs no rehearsal.
• Make preparations today and conduct the Tenebrae as the children's chapel service for all the religious educaton groups next week.

If You Have More Time

• Make palm crosses, following the instructions at the end of this session plan. Order from your florist or church-goods store one palm frond. (Each frond has many parts, enough for your entire group.) Separate the individual leaf parts and give one to each child. Help them to fold the leaf to make a cross, as shown in the diagram below. Say something like, "The palm cross is an excellent symbol to remind us of the events of the last week of Jesus' life. It takes us on a journey in our memories from his entry into Jerusalem to his death on the cross."

Making a Palm Cross

1. Cut a leaf into two equal lengths.
2. Fold one length in half. Fold the other length in thirds.
3. Insert the shorter piece inside the longer to form a cross.
4. Using a fiber pulled from another palm leaf, wrap the cross as shown below. Tie the fiber in the back. (String or thread may also be used to wrap the cross.)

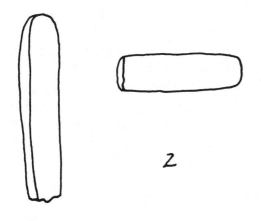

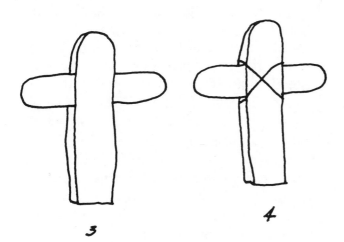

The Crucifixion of Jesus

ONE SUNDAY three years after Jesus began his public ministry, when he was thirty-three years old, he and his disciples went to Jerusalem. On the way into the city it was obvious that the people had heard about him, for they greeted him with great joy. As he rode into the city on a colt, the people spread their cloaks on the road, and others spread leafy branches that they had cut in the fields. Everyone was shouting "Hosanna! Blessed is the one who comes in the name of the Lord! Blessed is the coming kingdom of our ancestor David! Hosanna in the highest!"

The way Jesus was greeted made those in power very nervous. They were afraid the people would try to put Jesus in charge instead of them. For the next two days, the priests, scribes, and elders questioned Jesus, trying to make him say something that would get him in trouble. But they were unable to trick him.

By Tuesday the priests and scribes were looking for a way to arrest Jesus in secret so they could kill him. One of Jesus' disciples, Judas Iscariot, didn't approve of some of the things Jesus did, so he went to the chief priests to betray Jesus. The priests promised Judas money.

The celebration of Passover began on Thursday night. Jesus and his disciples were eating their Passover meal when Jesus said, "Truly I tell you, one of you will betray me, one who is eating with me."

The disciples all anwered, "Surely not!"

That night they went to pray in the Garden of Gethsemane. He said to three of his disciples, "I am deeply grieved, even to death; remain here, and keep awake." But while Jesus prayed, they fell asleep.

Jesus woke them just before those who were to arrest him arrived. Judas had said, "The one I will kiss is the man; arrest him and lead him away under guard." So Judas went up to Jesus, said "Rabbi!" and kissed him. Immediately Jesus was arrested and taken away.

On Friday morning the priests, elders, and scribes decided to turn Jesus over to the Roman governor, Pilate. Pilate knew the priests were jealous of Jesus, so he offered Jesus' release. But the crowd was shouting for Jesus to be crucified. They wanted the murderer Barabbas released instead. Pilate had Jesus whipped, and then handed him over to be crucified.

After putting a crown of thorns on Jesus' head, and mocking him, the crowd led Jesus, carrying his cross, to Golgotha to be crucified. By nine o'clock in the morning they had put him on the cross and divided his clothes among themselves. His enemies all came by to mock.

At noon a darkness came over the whole land until three in the afternooon. At three, Jesus cried, "My God, my God, why have you forsaken me?" Then Jesus breathed his last.

Were these his last words? Not "Into thy ---I commend my soul?

160 •

SESSION 33

MARY MAGDALENE

Sources: Luke 8:1-3; Matthew 27:55-28:9; John 20:1-18

Theme: Changing Attitudes Toward Women

Goals for Participants

- to understand the story of Mary Magdalene, particularly the events immediately after the crucifixion
- to learn of Jesus' attitudes toward women, unusual for his time
- to consider changes in attitudes toward women from biblical times to today
- to reinforce their understanding that women today play many roles.

Background

Only four episodes from the life of Mary Magdalene are recorded in the New Testament. Having been healed of seven demons, she follows Jesus. She witnesses the crucifixion. She discovers the open tomb. And she receives and bears the news of the risen Jesus. All four of these episodes are referred to in the children's story.

Additionally, however, many traditions have been associated with Magdalene, most generally that she was a reformed prostitute, a sinful and sexual woman whose conversion was based on her love of Jesus. She is often pictured with red hair and in the frescoes of Giotto, the 14th-century Italian artist, is easily identified by her long, wavy, flaming tresses. No basis for these depictions is found in the gospel accounts of Magdalene, but they continue to persist in the minds of many. Indeed, Mary Magdalene is perhaps the most misunderstood character in the New Testament.

The gospels disagree on the details of the stories—who it was that the women encountered at the tomb (Matthew: an angel; Mark: a young man; Luke: two men); whether Mary Magdalene alone received the news of the resurrection directly from Jesus (John), or whether the group of women met him as they fled from the open tomb (Matthew). In the children's story, we have combined the four gospel accounts to give a more complete picture of Magdalene as a woman involved in Jesus' ministry. *Gospel Parallels*, or some other resource that places the gospel narratives side by side, would be helpful in comparing the different versions. In the four episodes described, it is important to note the varied activities or roles Mary Magdalene engages in: a "patient" healed of demons; a follower of Jesus; a witness and mourner at the crucifixion; a preparer of spices and oils to anoint Jesus' body; a witness to the open tomb; and a recipient of the news of Jesus' resurrection. In each case she is accompanied by other women, but it is her name that the gospel accounts highlight. The fact that all four gospels record her involvement in the last days of Jesus' life confirms her personal importance in Jesus' ministry, as well as the importance of women in general.

Women in biblical times have been expected to mourn and to prepare a body for burial, but not to leave their homes and follow an itinerant preacher (providing for his ministry from their own means). The fact that the writer of John makes Mary Magdalene the key witness to the resurrection points up the changing attitudes toward women effected in Jesus' brief lifetime. Not only is Mary Magdalene the first to see the risen Jesus, but she also bears the news of the resurrection to Simon Peter, upon whom Jesus has promised to build his church. Placing her between Jesus and Peter at the most crucial point in the gospel story, the author of John, writing at the end of the first century C.E.,

Session 33 • 161

seems to be emphasizing the importance of women to the early Christian movement: "The discipleship and leadership of the Johannine community is inclusive of women and men. Although the women mentioned in the Fourth Gospel are examples of discipleship for women as well as men, it is nevertheless astonishing that the evangelist gives women such a prominent place in the narrative. S/he begins and ends Jesus' public ministry with a story about a woman. . . . Mary of Magdala is not only the first to witness the empty tomb but also first to receive an appearance of the resurrected Lord. . . . That such a preeminence of women in the Johannine community and its apostolic tradition caused consternation among other Christians is expressed in 4:27f where the disciples are 'shocked' that Jesus converses and reveals himself to a woman. The evangelist emphasizes, however, that the male disciples knew better than to openly question and challenge Jesus' egalitarian praxis" (Fiorenza, *In Memory of Her*, p. 326).

Children in the mid-elementary years probably have little awareness of the changes in societal attitudes toward women. What they will be aware of is the wide range of roles today's women carry out, as exemplified by their own mothers and female relatives. By adding details from their own experience, teachers can help children see how much change has already taken place, and how we can expect change to occur in the future.

Societal changes take place over long stretches of time, but during the last century changes in the roles of women have been dramatic in many parts of the world. It is important for children to acknowledge these changes and explore their own feelings toward continuing change. The activities in this session have been designed to encourage this self-exploration.

In this session we have referred to the "risen Jesus" and the "spirit of Jesus." The concept of resurrection is very difficult for children (and for many adults, too). Leaders may choose to reintroduce the term, but it would be best to do so in the simplest form, "the state of having risen from the dead," leaving layers of theological understanding to develop as the children grow older. See the definition provided in the previous session. Once again, leaders are urged to allow the narrative of the story to speak for itself, with a minimum of interpretation.

Materials

- Pencils, colored markers or crayons, and scissors
- Newsprint, markers, and tape, or chalkboard and chalk
- Paper for nametags
- Pins or tape
- 3" x 5" cards
- Drawing paper

Preparation

- Think through your own answers to the motivating and discussion questions.

Session Plan

Gathering   Varies

As the children arrive, explain that today's story will be about Mary of Magdala, or Mary Magdalene. She is called by that name to distinguish her from all the other women associated with Jesus who were also named Mary. Since there were no last names in biblical times, a person's hometown was often used to identify her or him. (Another common reference was "son of" or "daughter of.")

Invite the children to make nametags for themselves, indicating the city in which they live: "Joe of Westlake" or "Cindy of Newton." Make a nametag for yourself, and encourage the children to refer to one another by these names during today's session.

Motivating Questions   10 min.

Tell the children, "Long ago a woman was considered part of a man's property; she belonged to her father or her husband. Women were not allowed to own property or have any legal rights. They weren't even allowed to raise their own children if their husbands thought they shouldn't."

Ask the children, "Are women treated differently today from the way they were treated years ago? Do you think people today treat women the same way they treat men?

"Perhaps you have noticed that throughout the program, we have had very few stories about women. Why do you think that is?"

Allow the children to respond, then continue by saying, "The stories of women were often not recorded in biblical times. We don't know much about most of the women who are mentioned. Today's story is pieced together from several places in Christian scripture where Mary Magdalene is mentioned, but as with most women in Hebrew and Christian scriptures, we have only a very sketchy picture of her. Christian scripture does tell us that Jesus treated women better than most of the men in his time did. He was often criticized, even by his disciples, for his willingness to talk to and teach women as well as men. Mary Magdalene was one of these women."

Definitions

anoint   to prepare a body with oils for burial
cast out to force away
demons   evil spirits
disciples followers of Jesus

Read the Story   5 min.

Discussion   15 min.

Lead a discussion of the story guided by the following questions.
1. What would you say to someone who told you they have seen the spirit of someone who had died? Do you think Jesus' followers saw the spirit of Jesus? Why?
2. How would you have felt if you had been a woman during Jesus' time? Would you have enjoyed being a man's property? (Encourage boys as well as girls to respond.)
3. What things can women do now that they were not allowed to do in Jesus' time? (List the children's responses on newsprint or chalkboard.)
4. How do you think women's roles have changed since the days of your grandparents or parents? Do women have rights today that they didn't have years ago? (For example, in the United States, women have gained the right to vote, to hold property, and to testify in court.)

Act Out the Story   20 min.

Before acting out the story, have the children consider the feelings of the characters involved. Read aloud once again the end of today's story where the women visit the tomb. Ask the children to listen carefully. Help them prepare for the reenactment by listing on newsprint or a chalkboard the characters of the story:
- Mary Magdalene
- Mary, the mother of Jesus
- Salome
- the young man at the tomb
- the other followers of Jesus
- the risen Jesus

Next to each name write all the feelings that the children associate with that character. If they have difficulty, help them by saying, "How did Mary Magdalene feel when [she saw the tomb was empty, the followers of Jesus did not believe her, etc.]?"

Once you have completed the lists of feelings and talked about the characters, ask the children to act out the portion of the story that tells about the empty tomb and the appearance of Jesus' spirit. Encourage them to try to express the feelings that they have discussed. It is important to play the story more than once, perhaps several times, in order to allow different interpretations and different feelings to surface. When you have finished your replaying, you might ask the children, "Who in the story is most like you? Why?"

Get the Picture?   20 min.

Tell each participant to pick up a 3" x 5" card and a sheet of drawing paper. Ask each one to think of a special woman in his or her life—mother, grandmother, aunt, friend, sister, teacher, etc. Then say, "I'd like you to think of as many things as you can that that person does, and the roles she fills. For example, say the woman cooks, then she plays the role of a cook, or say she drives kids around a lot, so she is a chauffeur, or she helps people get well, so she's a doctor. Make a list on the card of all the roles you can think of. Then take your sheet of drawing paper and mark it into eight sections. In each section write one of the roles you have on your list."

When the children have filled in their sheets,

continue: "Turn your paper over. On the other side, draw a full-page portrait of the special woman you have chosen. Try to use most of the paper."

Again pause for the children to do this. While they are working, collect all their cards. When the drawings are complete, say, "Now turn your paper over again, and cut it apart on the lines that divide the different roles. Lay the pieces out in front of you, role side up. When everyone has done that, we'll be ready to play a game."

To play the game, make a stack of the children's note cards. Read one role from the top card, checking it off as you read it. If, for example, you read "cook," all the children who have "cook" in front of them can turn that piece over. Read an item from the next card, and so on. As the children turn over their pieces they can reassemble their drawings—like putting together a puzzle. Play until one child's picture is complete, then allow that child to read the roles. Each time a child completes a picture, he or she takes over the role cards. Play until all pictures are complete.

End the game with a reminder of the many roles these women play, and how different that is from women in biblical days.

Closing   5 min.

Gather the children together, light a candle or chalice, and say, "Jesus was a great teacher. One of the most important things that he taught was that each person is of value. He included women among his followers, even though others thought it was strange. He walked and talked with the poor, the lame, the tax collectors, and the outcasts. As Unitarian Universalists, we know that we must work together to keep Jesus' ideas of equality alive. Listen to these words from a song we know:

Jesus lives on in our own hearts
When love shines in all we do;
Acts of justice, truth, compassion
Keep his love forever new.
Alleluia.

(The words are the second verse of "Alleluia" from *Holidays and Holy Days*. If you sang the song last week, it would be appropriate to sing it here. Since the tune is very easy to learn, you might read the verse and then have the children join in on the "Alleluias.")

If Your Time Is Limited

• Omit "Get the Picture?" or do part of the activity. For example, you could make the picture while talking about women's roles.

If You Have More Time

• Sing "Amen," chorus and verses 6, 11, and 12.

Mary Magdalene

MARY WAS FROM MAGDALA, on the Sea of Galilee, so she was called Mary Magdalene. When Jesus first met her, Mary Magdalene was ill because there were seven demons in her. But Jesus cast out the demons. Mary Magdalene was then well again; and she became one of Jesus' most loyal followers.

Some of Jesus' disciples criticized him for letting Mary Magdalene and other women follow him, for it was against the custom of the day. These disciples thought that it didn't "look right" and that people might not listen to Jesus' teachings because of it. But Jesus didn't let the customs of his day decide how he would treat women.

Jesus spent three years traveling the countryside with his followers, teaching people the way to live a good life. The people liked Jesus' message very much, and this made the men in power very nervous. They decided he must be crucified. When Jesus was crucified Mary Magdalene waited by the cross with Jesus' mother, Mary, until he died. Jesus died on a Friday, and he was laid in a tomb to wait until the Sabbath was over, because no work could be done on the Sabbath, not even for a burial.

Mary Magdalene and Mary, the mother of Jesus, saw where the body was laid. Very early on the first day of the week, when the sun had risen, Mary Magdalene, Mary the mother of Jesus, and Salome brought spices to the tomb, so that they might anoint Jesus' body for permanent burial.

They had been saying to one another, "Who will roll away the stone for us from the entrance to the tomb?" When they looked up, they saw that the stone, which was very large, had already been rolled back. As they entered the tomb, they saw a young man, dressed in a white robe, sitting on the right side; and they were alarmed. But he said to them, "Do not be alarmed; you are looking for Jesus of Nazareth, who was crucified. He has been raised; he is not here. Look, there is the place they laid him. But go, tell his disciples and Peter that he is going ahead of you to Galilee; there you will see him, just as he told you." So they went and fled the tomb, for terror and amazement had seized them; and they said nothing to anyone, for they were afraid.

Later, Jesus appeared first to Mary Magdalene. She went and told those who had been with him, while they were mourning and weeping. But when they heard that Jesus was alive and had been seen by Mary Magdalene, they would not believe it.

THE GOOD SAMARITAN

Source: Luke 10:25-37

Theme: Helping Others

Goals for Participants

- to understand the meaning of the commandment "love your neighbor"
- to become familiar with the story of the Good Samaritan
- to identify some of our neighbors today.

Background

Though Jesus told many parables, his most famous one is found only in Luke. Parables are like metaphors; they use common, ordinary experience to point toward transcendent meanings. Pheme Perkins, in *Hearing the Parables of Jesus*, says a parable "might be described as a poetry that seeks to establish God's rule [kingdom] in our lives" (p. 2). Parables often do so by use of reversals, surprises, and the unexpected.

For example, those who listened to Jesus' parables would have been startled to learn that the example of "a loving neighbor" was a Samaritan. The Samaritans were a schismatic Jewish group in the north who were considered to be ritually unclean and therefore to be shunned. In John 4:9 the Samaritan woman says to Jesus, "How is it that you, a Jew, ask a drink of me, a woman of Samaria? For Jews have no dealings with Samaritans."

The Samaritans may have been descendants of intermarriage between colonists brought in to populate this area after the Exile and the remaining Jews, or they may have been descendants of Jews who returned after the Exile. Although they considered themselves Jews, there were differences in their beliefs and practices,

and they built their own temple on Mount Gerizim.

At any rate, it would have surprising enough for the story to have a Jew caring for a Samaritan as an example of "love your enemy," but to have the Samaritan providing loving care of a Jew was even more startling. The questioner was so taken aback by the ending of the story that he could not bring himself to say "the Samaritan" in answer to the question, "Who proved a neighbor?" He could only say, "The one who showed mercy." The story shows in a dramatic way that a neighbor is anyone who shows mercy to another, or anyone who is in need of help.

The Levite was an assistant in the temple, and both he and the priest would have been considered ritually unclean if they had touched a dead body, which the victim may have seemed to be. The Samaritan traveler and the injured man were probably merchants, who might have commonly carried oil and wine with them. The trip from Jerusalem to Jericho (not the Jericho of the Hebrew Bible) is 17 miles and entails a drop of 3,400 feet.

It is important for children to understand that the Samaritan was a hated enemy, and for them to have the opportunity to discuss times when it might be dangerous for them to try to help another. But the wisdom in the story is not so much in the details as in the opening of one's heart to include all people as one's neighbor, even those who are considered enemies or "unclean."

Materials

- 12" x 18" drawing paper, one for each child
- Colored markers, crayons, and colored pencils
- List of all stories and themes of the *Timeless Themes* curriculum, photocopied for each child

- Snacks and drinks
- Paper plates, cups, and napkins
- Copies of Song 38, "Song of the Good Samaritan"

Preparation

- Think through your own answers to the motivating and discussion questions.
- Think of some groups who are "in disfavor" at the time you are leading this program, as the Samaritans were in biblical times. Make a sample Group Drawing to estimate how much room to allot for each child's drawing and the time to do it.

Session Plan

Gathering   Varies

As the children arrive, give them a copy of the stories that they have heard this year. Ask them to choose their favorite story; take a sheet of drawing paper and begin to draw a small picture about the story, leaving enough room on the paper for small drawings by all of the other children in the group. Show them your sample drawing. Explain that they can use one medium or two or three, and be sure to put their names on the back of their paper.

Motivating Questions   5-10 min.

When all the children have arrived, ask them to leave their drawings and gather around a table or on a rug. Engage them in a discussion of the following.

Have you ever received help from someone you thought wouldn't help you? Have you ever had help from someone you thought you wouldn't want help from? Were you surprised when that person helped you? Why?

Then say, "Stories about a person helping another have always been popular. They cause us to realize that people really do care about one another. They remind us of how good people can be.

"At the time of today's story from Christian scripture, there were three groups of people living under Roman rule in Israel: the Gentiles, who were the people living in Israel before the Jews; the Jews, who had been there since the Exodus from Egypt; and the Samaritans, who were the people left in the northern part of Israel after it was conquered by the Assyrians. The Samaritans claimed to be descendants of Abraham and to have their own Law of Moses, which is the first five books of the Hebrew Scripture. The Samaritans also did not recognize Jerusalem as the center of Judaism. These differences between the Jews and Samaritans caused much hatred over the years, hatred that frequently developed into violence.

"Today's well-known story is about a Samaritan who helped another person. Today, whenever a stranger helps a person in distress, he or she is called a 'good Samaritan.'"

Read the Story   3 min.

Discussion   10 min.

Lead a discussion of the story guided by the following questions.
1. What did Jesus mean when he said "Go and do likewise" at the end of the story?
2. What does it mean to be a "good Samaritan"? Have you done things that would cause people to call you a "good Samaritan"? Can you give us an example?
3. Are there people today who are in need of help? Who are they? How can we help them?
4. Are there times when we should not try to help someone in distress by ourselves? What else could we do?
5. According to Jesus, who is a "neighbor"?
6. Jesus often used stories like this to teach people what he believed. Why are stories a good way to teach people?

Act Out the Story   15 min.

With the children, identify a group of people who are "in disfavor" at the present time in our culture or in your community, as the Samaritans were "in disfavor" during biblical times. Then invite the children to reenact the story as it might happen today, with the person in need being a member of that group.

End this activity by listening to "The Song of the Good Samaritan" on the cassette tape and then singing along with it as you play it a second time.

Group Pictures of Favorite Bible Stories   20 min.

Gather around your work tables and tell the children that they can now finish the picture they started during Gathering time. Say that in a few minutes you will ask them to pass their paper to the person on their right, who will draw a small picture of her or his favorite story on the paper. Explain that this process will continue around the group until everyone gets her or his own paper back, with drawings on it by everyone in the group!

Depending on the number of children and the time available, tell the children the number of minutes they have for each drawing. Urge them to make small, simple drawings, so there will be room for everyone's picture and they will be finished in the allotted time. Say that if they have more than one favorite story, they can draw different pictures on the papers circulating.

When all the pictures are finished, ask all to hold up their pictures to show, and then ask for a few volunteers to tell the group what they drew and why they liked that story.

Celebrating the Experience   15 min.

Ask the children to help you set out refreshments, then gather together on the rug or around the table and sing together your most-liked Bible songs as you partake of drinks and goodies.

Closing   2 min.

Light or ask a child to light the chalice or candle. Say, "This year we have heard many stories from the Hebrew Bible and from the New Testament of the Christian Bible. These stories were written a long time ago by people who wondered and worried about many of the same things that we wonder and worry about today. The meanings you gain from them are yours to explore. So be it." Close by singing the the first verse of "Amen."

If Your Time Is Limited

- In place of the group picture, ask each participant to draw her or his own picture depicting a favorite Bible story. When the drawings are completed, post them on the wall.
- Omit the drawing activity, and move directly to the Celebration.
- Invite the children to talk about their favorite times with *Timeless Themes* as they partake of the refreshments. Follow with the songfest.
- End with the Closing described above.

The Good Samaritan

ONE DAY, after Jesus had said that we must love our neighbors as ourselves, he was asked, "And who is my neighbor?" Jesus, who loved to tell stories, surprised his followers by telling this story about their supposed enemy, the Samaritans.

"A man was going down from Jerusalem to Jericho and fell into the hands of robbers, who stripped him, beat him, and went away, leaving him half dead. Now by chance a priest was going down that road; and when he saw him, he passed by on the other side. So likewise a leading member of the temple, when he came to the place and saw him, passed by on the other side. But a Samaritan while traveling came near him; and when he saw the beaten and robbed man, he was moved with pity. The Samaritan went to him and bandaged his wounds, having poured oil and wine on them. Then the Samaritan put the man on the Samaritan's own animal, brought him to an inn, and took care of him. The next day he took out two denarii and gave them to the innkeeper, saying, 'Take care of him and when I come back, I will repay you whatever more you spend.'"

Then Jesus asked his listeners, "Which of these three, do you think, was a neighbor to the man who fell into the hands of the robbers?"

His followers answered, "The one who showed him mercy."

Jesus said, "Go and do likewise."

PUPPET PATTERN

COAT PATTERN AND INSTRUCTIONS

Using the drawings below as a guide, make a pattern for a coat from a double sheet of newspaper. Fold your fabric in quarters and lay the pattern on it. With a marker, outline the parts of the pattern which do not fall on folds. Remove the pattern and carefully turn over the fabric. Mark the other side in a similar manner. Then open the coat, leaving a fold at the shoulder and neckline. Cut through both layers of fabric. Test to see if the neck hole is large enough, and enlarge it if necessary. Cut down the center front if you wish to make an open-style coat.

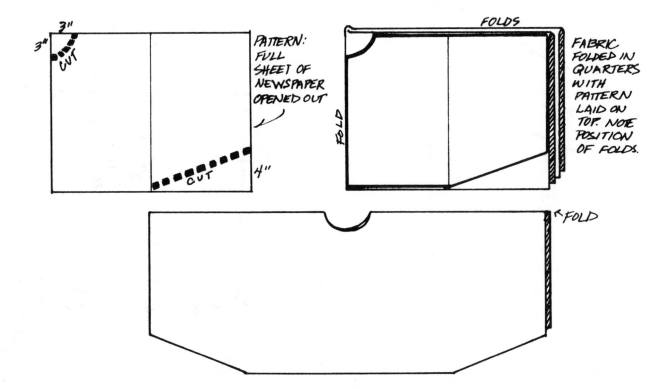

Unitarian Universalist Association

SPONGE-STAMP PATTERNS

FLIES

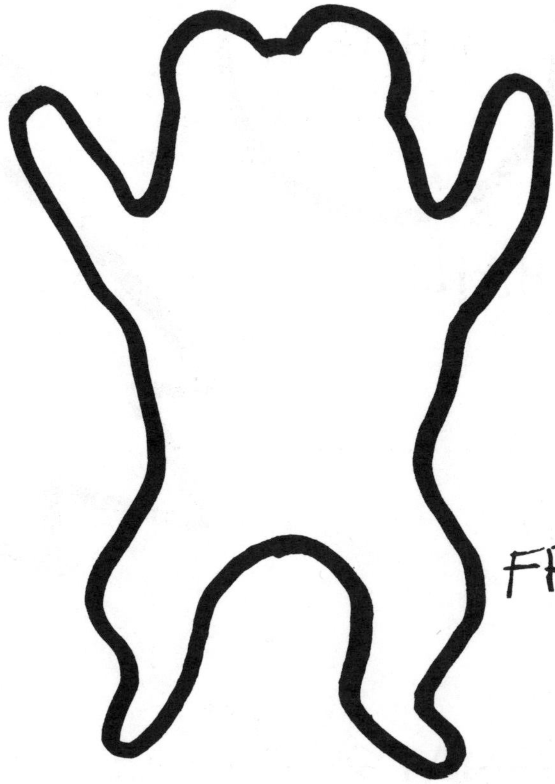

FROGS

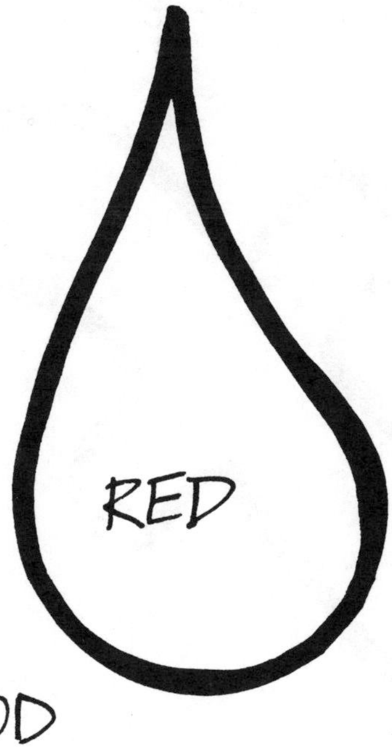

CATTLE DISEASE

RED

BLOOD

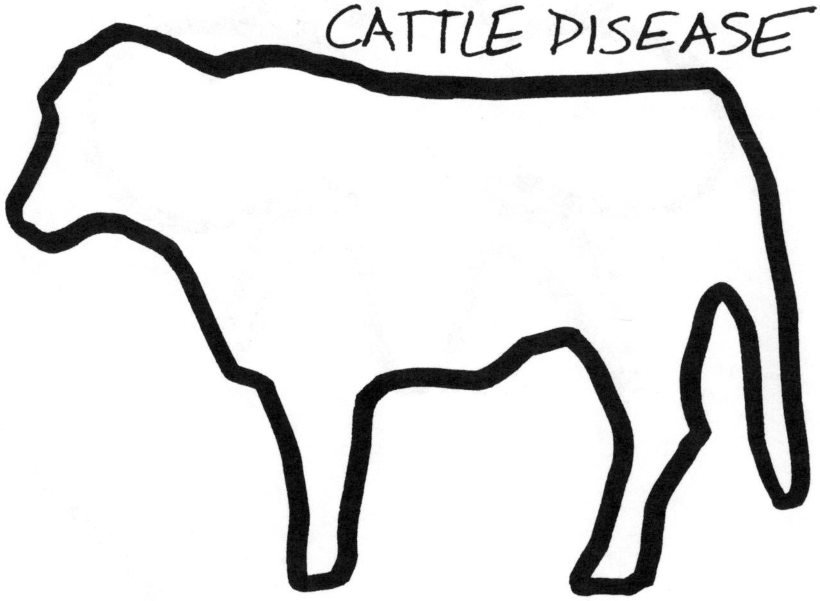

WHITE

HAIL

LOCUST

GNATS

DEATH OF FIRSTBORN

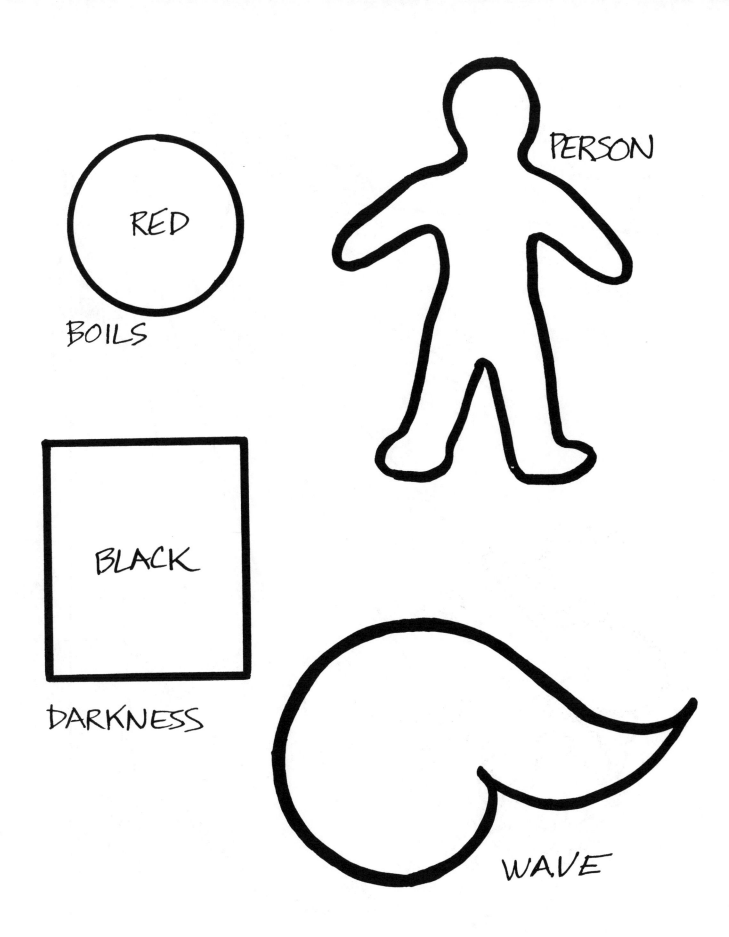

RED

BOILS

PERSON

BLACK

DARKNESS

WAVE

PICTURE OF PHARAOH

LET MY PEOPLE GO!

SOLOMON'S PROVERBS

From the New English Bible (slightly adapted for gender).
Photocopy and cut apart on dotted lines.

Bread gained by deceit is sweet, but afterward the mouth will be full of gravel. (20:17)

A glad heart makes a cheerful countenance, but by sorrow of heart the spirit is broken. (15:13)

The miser is in a hurry to get rich and does not know that loss is sure to come. (28:22)

Better is a dinner of vegetables where love is than a fatted ox and hatred with it. (15:17)

A gossip reveals secrets; therefore do not associate with a babbler. (20:19)

Pride goes before destruction, and a haughty spirit before a fall. (16:18)

If you have found honey, eat only enough for you, or else, having too much, you will vomit it. (25:16)

A soft answer turns away wrath, but a harsh word stirs up anger. (15:1)

Do not love sleep, or else you will come to poverty; open your eyes, and you will have plenty of bread. (20:13)

Truthful lips endure forever, but a lying tongue lasts only a moment. (12:19)

A good name is to be chosen rather than great riches, and favor is better than silver or gold. (22:1)

Argue your case with your neighbor directly, and do not disclose another's secret. (25:9)

To watch over mouth and tongue is to keep out of trouble. (21:23)

Do not boast about tomorrow, for you do not know what a day may bring. (27:1)

Whoever walks with the wise becomes wise, but the companion of fools suffers harm. (13:20)

Let another praise you, and not your own mouth—a stranger, and not your own lips. (27:2)

Wealth hastily gotten will dwindle, but those who gather little by little increase it. (13:11)

Just as water reflects the face, so one human heart reflects another. (27:19)

Grandchildren are the crown of the aged, and the glory of children is their parents. (17:6)

DOVE PATTERN

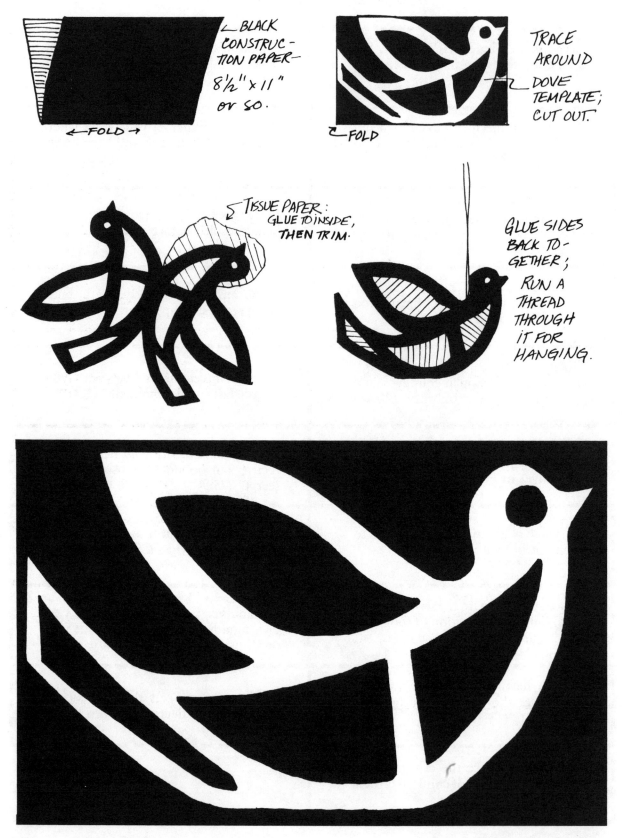

BLACK CONSTRUCTION PAPER— 8½" × 11" or so.

←FOLD→

TRACE AROUND DOVE TEMPLATE; CUT OUT.

FOLD

TISSUE PAPER: GLUE TO INSIDE, THEN TRIM.

GLUE SIDES BACK TOGETHER; RUN A THREAD THROUGH IT FOR HANGING.

TENEBRAE LIST

Photocopy and cut apart on dotted lines.

1. On Sunday Jesus entered Jerusalem for the last time. He and his disciples were welcomed with cries of "Hosanna!"

2. Jesus was questioned by the scribes, priests, and elders. They tried to trick him into saying something that would get him into trouble.

3. Judas went to the chief priests to betray Jesus. The priests offered him money.

4. Jesus and his disciples gathered to eat the Passover meal. This was to be his last supper.

5. Jesus said to those at the table, "One of you will betray me."

6. Jesus went to a place called Gethsemane to pray. His friends who were keeping watch fell asleep.

7. Judas came to Gethsemane and betrayed Jesus with a kiss.

8. Jesus was arrested and taken to the courtyard of the high priest.

9. Jesus was put on trial. When asked, "Are you King of the Jews?" he answered, "You say so," and made no further reply.

10. Because it was the festival of Passover, the Roman governor, Pilate, offered to release Jesus. The crowd shouted to have another man, Barabbas, released.

11. When Pilate asked again about Jesus, they shouted, "Crucify him!"

12. Soldiers led Jesus out to Golgotha and put him on a cross. They placed a crown of thorns on his head and mocked him.

13. It was nine o'clock on Friday morning when they crucified Jesus. At noon a darkness came over the whole land. At three o'clock Jesus breathed his last.

CREST NAMETAG

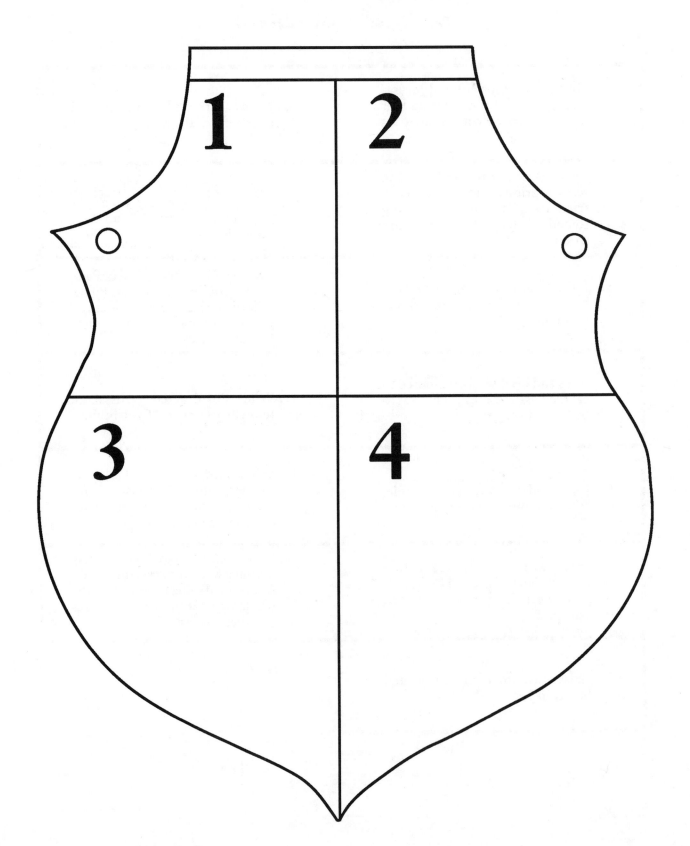

MAKING NOAH'S ARK

Noah was told to make his ark with three decks, a roof, and a door in one side. He was to put pitch on it to keep the water out. It was made out of gopher wood.

Find the other people who are working on the ark. Work with them to make an ark something like the one God told Noah to make. Gather together four boxes—a small one, a medium one, a large one, and a very large one.

1. Make a door in the side of the very large box so that the people and the animals can enter. Make two cuts only so that the door can open and close.
2. Turn the large box upside down and cut two doors in it. Add windows if you wish. Place this box in the center of the very large box.
3. Turn the medium-sized box upside down also. Cut doors in it and windows if you wish. Place it on top of the large box, in the center.
4. Place the smallest box on the top of the medium box, in the center. Fold the cardboard top of the large box in half, and place it on top of the small box to make a roof.
5. Take a pencil and draw around the bottom of the large, medium, and small boxes. Lift each box up and put glue where your lines are. Then glue the boxes into place. Put glue where the roof touches the top box and attach it.
6. Paint the whole ark with brown paint, making it look as much like wood as you can. As it dries, you can use a black marker to show where you think the pitch might have been put to make it waterproof.

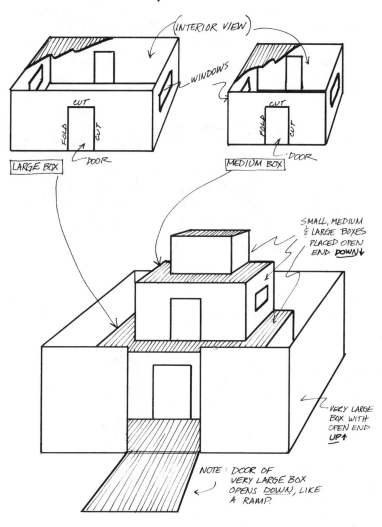

COMPLETING THE ARK

A Rainbow

Either

1. Draw a rainbow on mural paper, curving it to look like the bow of a bow and arrow.
2. Color it with markers: red on top, then orange, yellow, green, blue, and purple.
3. Cut out the rainbow and attach it to the wall.

Or

1. Make a rainbow by attaching colored strips of crepe paper to the wall in the following order: red on top, followed by orange, yellow, green, blue, and purple.
2. Curve the colored strips as a rainbow curves, placing tape at the top, on each end, and wherever else needed to hold it in place.

Noah's Family

Includes Noah; Mrs. Noah; sons—Shem, Ham, and Japheth; Shem's wife; Ham's wife; and Japheth's wife.

1. Take a popsicle stick. Decide which family member you are making and use pens to draw a face on the top part.
2. Choose a piece of cloth and make a tunic. Glue it onto your figure.
3. Choose another piece of cloth and make an outer robe or cloak; glue it into place.
4. If your figure is a woman, choose another piece of cloth and make a headdress. Glue it on. Cut a piece of string and hold the headdress in place with it.
5. Cut another piece of string and tie around the waist for a belt.

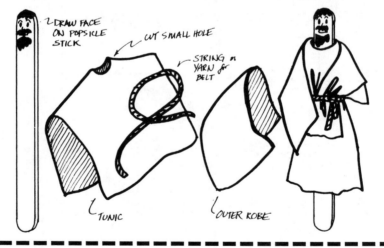

The Animals

1. Decide which animal you wish to make.
2. Decide about how big your animal should be. Take a look at the ark so you can be sure the animal will fit inside.
3. Mold the clay in the shape of the animal you have chosen.
4. Make a second one just like the first.

THE TEN COMMANDMENTS

א   NO OTHER GODS

ב   NO CARVED IMAGES

ג   RESPECT GOD'S NAME

ד   KEEP THE SABBATH HOLY

ה   HONOR YOUR PARENTS

ו   DO NOT MURDER

ז   NO ADULTERY

ח   DO NOT STEAL

ט   NO FALSE EVIDENCE

י   DO NOT COVET

THE TEACHINGS OF JESUS

1. "You have heard that it was said, 'An eye for an eye and a tooth for a tooth.' But I say to you, Do not resist the evildoer. But if any one strikes you on the right cheek, turn the other also."

   Turn the Other Cheek

2. "You have heard that it was said, 'You shall love your neighbor and hate your enemy.' But I say to you, Love your enemies and pray for those who persecute you."

   Love Your Enemies

3. "Do not judge, so that you may not be judged. Why do you see the speck in your brother's eye, but do not notice the log in your own eye?"

   Judge Not

4. "In everything do to others as you would have them do to you; for this is the law and the prophets."

   The Golden Rule

5. "'You shall love the Lord your God with all your heart, and with all your soul, and with all your mind.' This is the greatest and first commandment. And a second is like it: 'You shall love your neighbor as yourself.' On these two commandments hang all the law and the prophets."

   Love God and Love Your Neighbor as Yourself